Contemporary Issues in Organized Crime

edited by

Jay Albanese

© **CRIMINAL JUSTICE PRESS**

**a division of
Willow Tree Press, Inc.
Monsey, New York
1995**

Contents

❑

PEDAGOGICAL TOOLS

Discussion questions and answers for each chapter are available for instructors who wish to use this book as a teaching tool. Interested parties should contact the publisher for information.

ABOUT THE AUTHORS

Jay S. Albanese is professor and Director of the Graduate Program in Criminal Justice Administration at Niagara University. He holds a B.A. degree from Niagara University, and M.A. and Ph.D. degrees from the School of Criminal Justice at Rutgers University. He was the first Ph.D. graduate in Criminal Justice from Rutgers. Dr. Albanese is the author of seven books on issues of crime and justice, including *Organized Crime in America*, *Dealing with Delinquency*, and *White Collar Crime in America*. He was recipient of the Teaching Excellence Award from the Sears Foundation in 1990. He is past president of the Northeastern Association of Criminal Justice Sciences, and is President of the Academy of Criminal Justice Sciences for 1995-96.

Margaret E. Beare's career combines academic teaching with research and policy development. She completed her undergraduate studies in Canada at the University of Guelph, studied criminology in England at Cambridge University, and obtained her Ph.D. in sociology in the U.S. at Columbia University. She served two years as Director of Police Policy and Research within the Department of the Solicitor General Canada, and is presently a visiting associate professor in the Sociology Department at Queen's University in Kingston, Ontario. Her previous research includes two volumes on legalized gaming and police powers, an assessment of the RICO Statute, and a report titled *Tracing of Illicit Funds: Money Laundering in Canada*. She is currently writing a book on *Organized Crime in Canada*.

James D. Calder, Ph.D is an associate professor of Criminal Justice in the Division of Social and Policy Sciences at the University of Texas at San Antonio. Recently, he authored *The Origins and Development of Federal Crime Control Policy: Herbert Hoover's Initiatives*. Other relevant articles include, "Al Capone and the Internal Revenue Service: State-sanctioned Criminology of Organized Crime" (in *Crime, Law and Social Change*), and "Presidents and Crime Control: Kennedy, Johnson and Nixon and the Influences of Ideology" (in *Presidential Studies Quarterly*). Currently, he is writing a book on intelligence and espionage scholarship, and he is conducting research on social and psychological dynamics of Mafia family life.

Larry K. Gaines currently serves as the Chair of the Police Studies Department at Eastern Kentucky University. He also serves as the Executive Director of the Kentucky Association of Chiefs of Police. He received his doctorate from Sam Houston State University. His research interests include police personnel issues, drug problems and enforcement, and police operations. He has published extensively in these areas.

Matti Joutsen is the Director of the European Institute for Crime Prevention and Control, affiliated with the United Nations and located in Helsinki, Finland. He has been a consultant to many European nations on crime and criminal justice problems, and has published numerous monographs and edited volumes on these subjects.

Robert M. Lombardo is a 25-year veteran of the Chicago Police Department. He has served as the Commanding Officer of the Chicago Police Department Asset Forfeiture Unit, and as the Administrative Assistant to the First Deputy Superintendent of Police. He recently received a Ph.D. from the University of Illinois, Chicago, where he has studied the continued existence of racket subcultures in American society. He is also a graduate of the Federal Bureau of Investigation National Academy, and has served as a board member of the International Association for the Study of Organized Crime. He is an adjunct instructor at the University of Illinois, and has lectured extensively on organized crime and forfeiture investigations in the U.S. and abroad.

Arthur J. Lurigio, a social psychologist, is currently an associate professor of Criminal Justice at Loyola University, Research Associate at Northwestern University, and Director of Research for the Cook County, Illinois Adult Probation Department. He received his doctorate from Loyola University of Chicago in 1984. His research interests include drugs and crime, community crime prevention, criminal victimization and victim services, intermediate punishments, monetary sanctions, decision making in sentencing, crime and mental disorders, and AIDS in the criminal justice system. He is co-editor of several books, including *Victims of Crime: Problems, Programs, and Policies, AIDS and Community Corrections: The Development of Effective Policies, Smart Sentencing: The Emergence of Intermediate Sanctions,* and *Gangs and Community Corrections.*

Richter H. Moore, Jr., a professor of Criminal Justice and Political Science at Appalachian State University, received his Ph.D. from the University of Kentucky. He has published numerous criminal justice, private security, and law-related articles. He has served as President of the Academy of Criminal Justice Sciences, the Southern and North Carolina Criminal Justice Associations, and held many other offices in professional organizations. He was a founding member and served on the Board of Directors of the International Association for the Study of Organized Crime. He has received the ACJS and Southern Criminal Justice Association Founders Awards. Currently he is involved in research on the future of organized crime, the private security industry, and technology in criminal justice. He is now co-authoring a book on comparative criminal justice.

Gary Potter is a professor in the Police Studies Department at Eastern Kentucky University. He received his doctorate from Pennsylvania State University. He has authored a number of books and articles dealing with drugs, organized crime, and white collar crime. His most recent research centers around criminal organizations in rural settings.

Donald J. Rebovich has been Director of Research for the American Prosecutors Research Institute (APRI) in Alexandria, Virginia since 1990. In that role, he has been responsible for the direction of a number of national research programs dedicated to the study of the prosecution of environmental crime, organized crime, domestic violence, and drug-related offenses. His book *Dangerous Ground: The World of Hazardous Waste Crime* (1992) represents the first empirical effort to provide insight into critical characteristics of hazardous waste offenses, offenders, and mechanisms used to effectively control these crimes. Before coming to APRI, he served for 10 years with the Office of the New Jersey Attorney General, and was responsible for research and evaluation of environmental and drug crime enforcement initiatives. He received his B.S. degree in Criminal Justice and Psychology from Trenton State College, and received his M.A. and Ph.D. degrees in Criminal Justice from Rutgers University.

David C. Whelan is an assistant professor of Justice and Law Administration at Western Connecticut State University. He received his Ph.D. in Criminal Justice from City University of New York-John Jay College.

His decade of urban law enforcement experience included organized crime investigation. His recent publications are in the area of police personnel issues and sports gambling. His current research interests include Native-American casino gambling as it relates to organized crime and law enforcement.

❑

ACKNOWLEDGEMENTS: Several people deserve thanks for their support of this book's development. Rich Allinson, publisher at Willow Tree Press, thought the idea for this book had merit, and he warrants praise for seeing the project through. The copy editor, Leslie Bachman, helped to improve the manuscript's uniformity and style. Finally, thanks are due to my children, and friends at the Academy of Criminal Justice Sciences, whose constant distractions make all my projects extend longer than they should, but who also make things much more fun along the way.

Introduction

Organized crime is one of the most fascinating forms of criminal behavior. Its long history, many forms, diverse activities, and new manifestations continue to draw both public and scholarly interest. This book adds to existing knowledge about organized crime by focusing on contemporary activities that, thus far, have been little known or little understood. Organized crime evolves with changing opportunities, and this book explains how these opportunities arise and how they are most effectively met.

Four contemporary issues that comprise the forefront of concern about organized crime are examined in this book: its connection to legitimate business; how groups become organized; the effectiveness of different law enforcement approaches; and new criminal opportunities. Several chapters are devoted to each issue.

ORGANIZED CRIME AND LEGITIMATE BUSINESS

For many years, organized crime has been characterized as an urban, monolithic conspiracy dominated by Italian-Americans. Investigations in recent years, however, have established that this portrayal of organized crime is both limited and inaccurate. In fact, organized crime has been found to be most often a local problem that operates in much the same way as legitimate business. Organized crime groups emerge and respond to supply and demand for products and services. They react to changes in regulatory measures and enforcement strategies. They seize upon opportunities for profit-making, in much the same way that legitimate business reacts to changes in the marketplace by developing new products and services. Illustrations of the relationship between organized crime and legitimate business are the subject of the first section of this book. These chapters show how casino gambling, college sports and certain characteristics of other legitimate businesses make them susceptible to infiltration by organized crime.

Chapter 1 offers insight into the often-claimed link between casino gambling and organized crime. Casino gambling has been the hottest economic development issue of the 1990s, and organized crime has a long history in the casino business, which is detailed in this article. Changes in the regulatory and licensing structure for both casinos and their vendors in Nevada and Atlantic City are examined. It is shown that these changes have made it more difficult for organized crime interests to infiltrate the legitimate gaming industry. Chapter 2 provides a fascinating account of the four major basketball point-shaving scandals of the last 40 years. An explicit link is drawn among the players, organized crime interests, and gambling public that demonstrates how and why these scandals occurred. Chapter 3 tests a model that tries to predict the circumstances under which organized crime becomes involved with legitimate business, as well as the provision of illicit goods and services. It uses a sample of 167 organized crime cases from around the U.S. to develop a prediction tool that can serve as a screening device in organized crime investigations.

HOW CRIME BECOMES ORGANIZED

The most highly developed and longest-standing organized crime group, the U.S. Mafia or Cosa Nostra, has been under attack by American law enforcement officials for more than a decade. Hundreds of alleged Mafia figures have been convicted and given long prison sentences over this period. This has resulted in a significant change in the leadership of American Mafia groups, as well as a weakening of their influence compared to other organized crime groups. The issue that remains is how and why criminal groups emerge to take their place, or seize their territory. Simply put, why is organized crime persistent, despite many successful prosecutions in recent years?

The answer is provided, in part, in Section 1, where the entrepreneurial nature of organized crime is explained. The precise method by which individuals organize and associate with criminal groups is discussed in the second section of this book. Case studies of organized crime in a rural setting, in Chicago, and among women associated with Mafia groups all illustrate how organized criminal activity is developed with or without connections to established criminal organizations.

The second section of the book provides case studies that illustrate how crime becomes organized under varying conditions. Chapter 4 contributes a unique look at organized crime in a rural county. Using public documents and ethnographic methods, an insider's perspective is provided into the workings of criminal networks in Kentucky. Marijuana growing, liquor distribution, prostitution and cocaine transportation are among the activities detailed in this study. Also, the nature, structure and common features of the criminal enterprises involved are compared.

Chapter 5 provides a counterpoint to Chapter 3's look at rural organized crime. Here, the focus is Chicago. Using informant information and public documents, the authors describe the evolution of organized crime in the Chicago area. Specifically, it is shown that organized crime "street crews" remain a significant aspect of organized crime there, due to "roving neighborhoods" where the local subculture has transcended geographic boundaries. Chapter 6 provides an insightful look into the rarely re-searched issue of women and organized crime. The author reviewed all published biographical accounts of Italian-American organized crime to assess the role of women. Interestingly, it was found that so-called Mafia women are often not the passive functionaries that they are usually portrayed to be in fiction. Instead, the author provides evidence to show that many women play complex and consequential roles in both the lives of the men involved in Mafia activities, and also in the organized crime activity itself.

THE LAW ENFORCEMENT RESPONSE

The investigation and prosecution of organized crime has long been problematic. The extended nature of activities, the size and complexity of some groups, and the limits of the criminal law itself were barriers to successful prosecutions for many years. More recently, new laws and investigative techniques have been developed to improve the effectiveness of the criminal justice response to organized crime. Two specific strategies are discussed in this section: the utilization of racketeering laws and the prevention of money laundering.

Chapter 7 evaluates local racketeering laws as an enforcement tool. The history of the federal RICO (Racketeer Influenced and Corrupt Orga-nizations) statute, and legal challenges to it, are presented. The chapter assesses state efforts to duplicate RICO for state-level crimes. A survey of 150 prosecutor's offices around the U.S. is used to provide information regarding the implementation of racketeering laws at the local level. Interviews also were conducted with a number of prosecutors' to deter-mine the reasons for their use or disuse of racketeering laws in organized crime cases. Chapter 8 offers an interesting analysis of money laundering in the U.S., Canada and elsewhere. The nature and method of money laundering is detailed, and its history and the problems engendered by the disposing of bulk cash are explained. Lingering issues raised by new legislation and continuing problems of law enforcement coordination are enumerated.

NEW CRIMINAL OPPORTUNITIES

It has been held by many that organized crime was imported into the U.S. from Italy and elsewhere. This is not entirely true. Most U.S. organized crime, as illustrated in Sections 1 and 2, is uniquely American in origin. Nevertheless, there is concern about organized crime activities among new immigrant groups, as well as the impact of organized crime on the stability of governments in other countries. The final section of this book examines these issues of national and international consequence.

Chapter 9 describes how fuel tax scams work in practice. It shows the interaction between traditional and Russian immigrant organized crime groups in conspiring to carry out these schemes. Continuing problems with new laws and the criminal justice response are detailed, providing insight for more effective responses in the future. Chapter 10 examines recent events in central and eastern Europe, and their implications for the growth of organized crime. The shift to a market economy, the political climate, and crime conditions before these changes are shown to influence the opportunities for organized crime activity. Implications of current trends for the future are explained.

Each chapter in this book offers engaging and unique perspectives on new and changing manifestations of organized crime. The maxim that "organized crime is more than the Mafia" is demonstrated in every chapter. Sports gambling, casinos, organized crime in rural settings, city street crews, the role of women, money laundering, local racketeering laws, motor fuel tax scams, and changes in eastern Europe have all been mentioned in public debate and private conversation, but few have been addressed adequately with information and expert interpretation as they are here. Only through an improved understanding of how these activities and groups emerge, operate, and infiltrate business will more productive responses be forthcoming from the criminal justice community and from the public in general.

Jay Albanese

Casino Gambling and Organized Crime: More Than Reshuffling the Deck

Jay Albanese

Abstract: *Casino gambling operations have a long history of attracting organized crime involvement because of the possibility of "skimming" large amounts of money from the proceeds. However, the lessons learned in Las Vegas, Atlantic City and elsewhere indicate that organized crime involvement can be readily discovered and minimized when: casino applicants, vendors and their personnel are screened carefully; the games themselves are monitored; and close surveillance is undertaken of opportunities for skimming and labor union infiltration. Only where regulations are substandard, or insufficient emphasis is placed on screening, monitoring, and enforcement, can organized crime operate with impunity.*

Casino gambling as a business to revive local economies has been rediscovered. At last count, casinos have been either approved or are under discussion in a majority of U.S. states, and the number continues to grow. The era of legalized gambling as a mechanism to raise money through tourist spending, without raising taxes on local residents, arrived in full force during the 1990s.

The question is whether the deleterious effects of such enterprises outweigh the economic rewards. This chapter examines one of the most prominent questions raised in the debate regarding casino gambling: to what extent have organized crime elements been involved in casino gambling in the past, and to what extent can the casino-organized crime link be avoided in the future?

THE PAST

Today, both regulatory officials and casinos managers in Las Vegas claim that organized crime plays no significant role in casino gambling there. If this is true (a topic to be addressed later), it certainly was not always the case. And the specter of organized crime continues to play an important role in government and voter decisions about casino gambling (Dombrink and Thompson, 1990).

Casino licensing officials in Las Vegas, Atlantic City and elsewhere now conduct exhaustive investigations of all casino applicants. At times these investigations can border on witch-hunts, but the motivation is clear: the demand for casino licenses is very high, a large number of legitimate corporations and individuals are involved in the business (and even more desire to be), and a single organized crime scandal hurts the entire industry.

In the past, the bad reputation of Las Vegas was highlighted by two distinct events. First, in 1950 the Kefauver Committee, headed by U.S. Senator Estes Kefauver, held televised hearings announcing that a national Mafia controlled much of organized crime in the U.S., and that gambling profits supported most of its illegal activity (U.S. Senate Special Committee to Investigate Organized Crime in Interstate Commerce, 1951; Kefauver, 1951). Although subsequent investigations found the conclusions of the Kefauver Committee to be overblown and based on no investigation whatsoever, it had the effect of placing the Mafia in the public consciousness as an issue of national concern (Moore, 1974; Bell, 1953; Woodiwiss, 1988).

Second, the bad reputation of casino gambling in Las Vegas was promoted by a 1963 book by journalists Ed Reid and Ovid Demaris titled *The Green Felt Jungle.* The book described organized crime in Nevada casinos in graphic detail, and each of Las Vegas's 11 existing casinos appeared to be affected. Some historical background on the genesis of casino gambling in Nevada offers clues about its role as the "test case" for legal gaming in North America.

The Nevada Experience with Organized Crime

Nevada legalized all forms of gambling in 1931 for the same reason it has since been legalized elsewhere. It was seen as a way to generate revenue without raising taxes on the resident population. Under worse conditions than today's difficult economic times, Nevada legalized gambling during the Great Depression. There were no North American precedents to rely upon, and little regulation of gambling was imposed. Most of the early investors in legal gambling were career gamblers, and most gambling occurred in pool halls (Demaris, 1987). As Zendzian has observed, Las Vegas was not infiltrated by mobsters, "but rather mobsters controlled casino operations from the start" (1993:125).

Organized crime involvement in the Las Vegas casino industry has been traced back to Meyer Lansky and Benjamin "Bugsy" Siegel in 1941. They and their criminal associates usually used "front men" to own a casino on paper, while they exercised actual hidden control. Much of the money used to buy and operate the casino appears to have been taken from pension funds, most notably the Teamster's, and primarily from Chicago (Cook, 1980). Meyer Lansky, living in Miami, had the accounting role of keeping track of everyone's interests in the casinos, whether they be in Chicago or elsewhere (Lacey, 1991; Skolnick, 1978). Using this method of operation, Siegel had Lansky finance the first Nevada hotel-casino, The Flamingo, named after Siegel's girlfriend (Jennings, 1992).

The method by which organized crime has made much of its money in Las Vegas casinos is "skimming." Before the daily take from slot machines and table games is calculated, part of it "disappears," making the casino look on paper as somewhat less financially successful than it really is. According to former U.S. Federal Bureau of Investigation (FBI) agent William Roemer, the money skimmed from Las Vegas casinos was the primary source of income for the Chicago "Outfit" for more than two decades (Roemer, 1991). Organized crime groups from New York, New Jersey, Cleveland, Kansas City and Milwaukee also have been linked to the financing and skimming of profits from some Las Vegas casinos from the 1940s through the 1980s (Reid and Demaris, 1963; Turner, 1984; Abadinsky, 1994).

The involvement of organized crime in Las Vegas casinos did not occur unnoticed. In fact, both the media and Nevada gaming officials reported in 1946 that Las Vegas was "being infiltrated by hoodlums" (Zendzian, 1993:20). The following year Bugsy Siegel was shot for skimming additional money without permission in a killing apparently approved by Meyer Lansky and Lucky Luciano (Zendzian, 1993; Monaco and Bascom, 1991; Eisenberg et al., 1979).

These events served to enhance public receptivity to the Kefauver Committee hearings in 1950. The hearings were televised and held in cities around the U.S. U.S. Senator Estes Kefauver also linked the bootlegging industry to the genesis of contemporary organized crime, and linked the term "Mafia" and "national conspiracy" to the more city-specific "gangs" and "hoodlums" that characterized terminology about organized crime up to that time. Even though the Kefauver Committee produced no new evidence, and did not result in any trials or criminal convictions, it served to raise public consciousness about organized crime and to establish its existence as a multi-city network, rather than as a phenomenon confined to specific gangs in specific cities.

A New Era of Regulation and Its Impact

The Kefauver Committee ushered in a new era of scrutiny for Las Vegas. In 1955, the *Las Vegas Sun* published an exposé of hidden ownership of the Thunderbird Hotel and Casino, built in 1948. By 1959, new legislation was passed in Nevada creating the State Gaming Commission and the Gambling Control Board, which together exercised broad legal authority to regulate casino gambling. These agencies also exercised their authority to remove stockholders and to refuse casino licenses to those found to be linked to organized crime. This occurred in the cases of the new Dunes and Frontier hotel-casinos (Zendzian, 1993).

Prior to these new controls, Nevada had been "caught up with the gaming whirlwind," and *reacted* to problems, rather than *anticipating* them (Zendzian, 1993:32). The Nevada Corporate Gaming Act of 1967 specifically made publicly held corporations (i.e., those that sell stock) the preferred avenue for casino investment. This sparked the entrance of large, established corporate interests into the casino business. It also brought the U.S. Securities and Exchange Commission (SEC) into the regulatory process through the SEC's responsibility to regulate all publicly held corporations.

The new regulatory framework in Nevada that developed through legislation in the 1950s and '60s appears to have had an impact on organized crime in the casino industry. It led the National Gambling Commission in 1976 to conclude that organized crime had become a "negligible factor" in Nevada casinos. The change to corporate ownership and control and the moderate crime rate in Nevada were used as evidence to support this conclusion.

The Stardust Case

Since the 1960s, there have been occasional cases of casino skimming, and severe penalties have been exacted. An example is the Stardust Casino. A significant figure in Chicago's hidden control of Las Vegas casinos was Frank "Lefty" Rosenthal, who ran a sports book operation but organized a profit-skimming scam at the Stardust. Rosenthal obtained a position as a senior executive at the Stardust, and used his position to set up a separate counting room for slot-machine money that was equipped with false scales for weighing the money. This resulted in skimming up to $40,000 per week in coins and another $40,000 in $100 notes. A similar scam was developed for drop boxes at gaming tables.

The FBI eventually discovered this skimming operation in 1976 through wiretapped conversations in Kansas City among organized crime figures discussing how to set up a similar scam at the Tropicana (Demaris, 1987). An excerpt from those taped conversations is illustrative:

CARL THOMAS (inside man): When you go back in the counting room, you go in the back and there's a mirror, see, and you hide from the glass, plus you're blocking the camera off—

JOSEPH "CAESAR" AGOSTO (a Tropicana hotel manager): You cover the plunger, see. I have control of the camera. There's no problem with the camera.

CARL "TUFFY" DeLUNA (alleged *caporegime* of the Kansas City organized crime group): Is it in your office?

AGOSTO: Yeah, I can shut the camera off.

NICK CIVELLA (alleged boss of the Kansas City group): How many keys are there for the lock?

THOMAS: There's two locks on the box. One key's supposed to stay in the cage, one key stays with the comptroller upstairs. When the count team comes in the morning, they come get this key...Now, what I've done for the last—I don't know how many umpteen years—when they make those keys, you have a key made that you keep in the palm of your hand and you go back that night. See, the cashier's with us. You follow me? You grab the cashier's keys, go in the vault, open the boxes, and snatch the money.

I can remember one night in Circus Circus [a casino] we had an obligation to meet. There were two guys from the state outside [the vault] and I was in there on my fucking back, snatching money and they weren't as far from me as that refrigerator. Putting money in my pockets. I think if you do things out in the open, you stare the guy right in the face, the guy won't think you're doing nothing.

CIVELLA: Sometimes the most obvious is the best way [Demaris, 1987:322].

The Stardust had its gaming license suspended, and a temporary management group was installed by the Gaming Control Board (Zendzian, 1993). Rosenthal was forced out of the Stardust by the Gaming Control Commission in 1978 (Roemer, 1991). Another raid on the Stardust in 1983 uncovered a new skimming operation, resulting in the indictment of four executives for tax fraud. In 1985, the Stardust was sold to a privately held company.

Common Elements of Casino Scams

The Stardust offers a good illustration of casino scams. Although there are many fewer cases of organized crime involvement since the advent of new regulatory controls and the emergence of a serious commitment to enforcement, there are common elements to all casino scams.

In virtually every case of this type there has been cooptation of casino management and/or workers at some level. As the Stardust case makes clear, individuals on the inside must agree to cooperate to make the scam work. There are simply too many controls on the money made at casino tables and machines to make a scheme work without help from casino workers. This led Atlantic City, and other areas, to closely monitor or license those working in casinos. As Zendzian has suggested, the Nevada gaming industry may still be experiencing a "weeding-out effect" that began with the new era of regulation begun in the 1950s and 1960s (1993:126).

Another attraction of the Las Vegas casinos, besides the money earned, has been the fact that they are frequented by celebrities. The glamour of associating with well-known singers and actors was important to the organized crime figures, who otherwise were largely uneducated street toughs from poor neighborhoods. This combination of ego involvement; a high cash-yield business; and questionable casino backers, operators, and controls resulted in some notorious cases over the years. Improved controls on casino ownership have produced a marked decline in organized crime involvement in the industry. In fact, most scandals in recent years involve organized crime in ancillary businesses, such as labor unions, rather than involvement in the casinos themselves.

THE PRESENT

The events of the past undoubtedly help to shape the present, something especially true in Nevada and Atlantic City. The current casino licensing system in Nevada was introduced by the governor during the early 1960s, due to a fear that then U.S. Attorney General Robert Kennedy would introduce legislation to prohibit state-sponsored gambling altogether (Spanier, 1992). The new licensing rules were effective in screening new casino applicants, but they were not effective in rooting out existing organized crime elements.

Moving from Individual to Corporate Ownership of Casinos

Organized crime in Nevada may have been a casualty of its own success. Perhaps the most significant factor in the removal of organized crime figures from the ownership (hidden or otherwise) of casinos was the shift from individual to corporate ownership. This shift occurred largely due to the popularity of Nevada as a tourist destination. The capital needed to build a casino with restaurants, entertainment areas, and an attached hotel of hundreds of rooms is beyond the means of virtually all individuals (and organized crime groups), resulting in corporate acquisitions of casino properties. Again, due to the size of investment required, only large, publicly held corporations can often qualify. As a result, small-time operators and smaller corporations, more easily infiltrated or controlled by organized crime, found themselves excluded from the market.

Combined with this fact is the realization that publicly held corporations must pay close attention to the stock market, their balance sheet and their public image. Together, these considerations serve as a bulwark against attempts to corrupt or unduly influence the corporations, a process also frustrated by their immense size and capital. Therefore, the growth of casinos in Nevada from nightclubs to multi-million-dollar hotel-entertainment complexes has done much to squeeze out traditional organized crime elements. As a former FBI agent has said, "Today, the situation in Las Vegas is entirely different than it was just several years ago. I feel quite strongly that the mess is pretty well cleaned up" (Roemer, 1991:135).

Ironically, the primary arguments heard in the casino gambling debate are often not borne out when public opinion is actually surveyed. In a 1979 survey by the Institute for Social Research, it was found that casino gambling had nowhere near the criminal, economic or moral dimensions often ascribed to the public.

> In sum, casino gambling is regarded mainly as a recreational activity by most people. There are probably a lot of people who would partici- pate if the availability problem were solved by legalizing casinos nearer to them. Financial reasons for casino gambling (or not) seem to be second in importance. Moral reasons against gambling were mentioned by surprisingly few people [Kallick et al., 1979:246].

The chief industry in Nevada is tourism, with 26 million out-of-town visitors each year. There are currently more than 300 casinos in Las Vegas, with 40 hotel-casinos commanding gaming revenues of over $20 million each in 1990 (Von Brook, Siegel and Foster, 1990).

The Atlantic City Experience

Atlantic City became the second major tourist destination to establish casino gambling. A referendum that would have permitted casino gam- bling throughout New Jersey was voted down in 1974, but an Atlantic City-only referendum passed in 1976. The first casino opened in May 1978.

Unlike Nevada, Atlantic City placed extensive controls on casino gam- bling from the start. This occurred for two reasons. First, the city had learned from the Nevada experience that regulation and enforcement are necessary to keep the industry honest. Second, New Jersey had a long history of problems with organized crime. New Jersey Governor Brendan Byrne's comments in 1977, when he signed the Casino Control bill, are telling: "Organized crime is not welcome in Atlantic City! And we warn them again: keep your filthy hands out of Atlantic City and keep the hell out of our state!" These comments imply, of course, that organized crime was already present in New Jersey, which it was (see Dorman, 1972).

Ironically, the genesis of organized crime in Atlantic City has similar roots to Las Vegas. In the late 1800s, there was illegal gambling and 24 brothels in Atlantic City (Demaris, 1987). Atlantic City was booming by the early 1900s, largely due to Prohibition, and its associated speakeasies, gambling, and prostitution. It was a popular summer resort for celebrities, politicians and gangsters, including Al Capone and Lucky Luciano (Demaris, 1987; Eisenberg et al., 1979), although it was never a year-round destination until the advent of casino gambling in 1978. Consider this description of Atlantic City in 1925:

> By 1925 Atlantic City was bursting at the seams. It had 1,000 hotels and rooming houses that could accommodate 400,000 visitors, 99 daily trains in the summer and 65 in the winter, and three airports. It had the world's longest boardwalk, stretching seven miles, with five piers, and [a] fabulous beach...The city had 21 theaters, three country clubs, four newspapers, the Miss America Pageant, and an Easter Parade as famous as Fifth Avenue's [DeMaris, 1987:28-29].

The downfall of Atlantic City as a thriving center of activity was linked to a changing national economy and to political corruption. The Great Depression and the repeal of Prohibition dealt a severe blow to the area, as they had in Nevada. By the late 1930s, Atlantic City's real estate base was two-thirds of what it was in the 1920s. By the time the national economy turned around during the 1950s, combined with the advent of low-cost air travel in the 1960s, Americans looked further from home for their vacations. Miami, Las Vegas, the Caribbean and even Europe became popular destinations, leaving Atlantic City tourists largely poor and elderly (DeMaris, 1987).

Atlantic City has a long history of corruption in local government, dating back to the early 1900s when the city was run by Louis Kuehnle. He ran for governor in 1910 and lost to Woodrow Wilson, who discovered Kuehnle received more votes in Atlantic County than there were voters. This marked a 30-year cycle of corruption in the area. After Kuehnle was sent to prison in 1911 after 30 years of running Atlantic County, Enoch "Nucky" Johnson landed in prison in 1941 for income tax evasion. It was alleged that his income from vice operations totaled more than $500,000 per year. Johnson was succeeded by Frank "Hap" Farley, who lost his seat in the State Senate in 1971 after he was implicated in conversations among mobsters as interceding in their behalf (DeMaris, 1987). In a taped conversation between Angelo DeCarlo and Frank Ruggieri, two alleged organized crime figures, Ruggieri claimed that Farley promised to intercede for him, despite Ruggieri's bookmaking conviction and the fact that he was barred from the racetrack.

What historian Mark Haller found to be the case in many neighborhoods during the early 1900s has been true in Atlantic City throughout its history: "...it was not so much that gambling syndicates influenced local political organization; rather, gambling syndicates *were* [emphasis added] local political organizations" (Haller, 1979:88; Fabian, 1990:142). It is clear from this long history of local corruption in Atlantic City—which was associated with organized crime figures and with illegal alcohol, prostitution, and gambling—that strong regulatory and enforcement measures were needed to insure honesty in casino gambling.

Casino Gambling and Success in Atlantic City

Economically, casino gambling in Atlantic City has been a successful source of revenue by any measure. According to the 1976 Casino Act, 2% of gross profits was earmarked for city, county and state non-gaming development. In their first 10 years of existence (1978-88), casinos contributed $1.3 billion from their gross profits (plus $55 million in interest). This is a significant total, considering there are only 12 Atlantic City casinos.

The stringent requirements placed on casino-hotels undoubtedly contributed to this success. All casino applicants in Atlantic City must undergo a prolonged and detailed background check that is paid for by the applicant. These strict licensing requirements have been upheld in court challenges (O'Brien and Flaherty, 1985). In order to eliminate small-time operators, all casinos had to have a minimum 500-room hotel attached. In addition, the games themselves were strictly regulated. Requirements were established regarding surveillance of games, obtaining credit, junkets, and even prohibiting dealers from dealing cards with their hands (only a "shoe" was permitted). Poker was prohibited where players handle the cards. Also, vendors and ancillary services are regulated (see Gutierrez, 1979; Hicks, 1981).

Ancillary services include tobacco, cleaning, construction, food, catering, flowers, furniture, equipment, entertainment, laundry, liquor, garbage and security services that do more than $10,000 worth of business with any one casino, or $150,000 with the casino industry in general. In Atlantic City, and now in Nevada, these ancillary services must be licensed (and have their backgrounds checked). Vendors provide the same services but do business with casinos in less than the amounts above. These businesses must only register with the casino control authorities; there are simply too many of them to license. A study of ancillary services and vendors in Atlantic City found, as in Nevada, that "the weakest of all casino controls is...where vending registration rather than licensing occurs" (Zendzian, 1990:10; State of New Jersey Commission of Investigation, 1977, 1991). A proper balance must be reached in this situation between the costs of compliance (by government, and by the casino industry and its vendors) and the costs of possible infiltration of organized crime into the casino industry.

Atlantic City's strong regulatory structure has resulted in surprisingly few substantiated allegations of organized crime involvement in casinos there. One exception is that made by the Senate Permanent Subcommittee on Investigation, which reported that Local 54 of the Hotel and Employees International Union was under the "substantial influence" of organized crime. It was said that Local 54 was controlled by Frank Gerace, who was in direct contact with Nickodemo Scarfo, alleged head of the Bruno organized crime family in Philadelphia and in Atlantic City. Together with a New Jersey State Commission of Investigation report that linked the Scarfo group to promoting and managing boxing there, the Casino Control Commission forced Frank Gerace to resign as President of Local 54 (Demaris, 1987; Zendzian, 1993). This example demonstrates that gaming-control officials do not have to wait for a criminal conviction to oust those found to have ties to organized crime. Bonafide allegations of misconduct, or improper associations, are sufficient. In the long run, this helps the credibility of the casino industry in promoting honesty and integrity the of the games themselves.

THE FUTURE

Interestingly, the image of organized crime in Las Vegas may have actually increased its attraction as a tourism destination, according to a recent chairman of the Gaming Commission there. "When people gamble—particularly in American society, where everyone has been raised to believe in thrift and hard work—they want to feel an edge of excitement, of transgression, of living on the edge" (Spanier, 1992:214-215). In fact, organized crime has been driven to the fringes of casino gambling, due to the firm control of the industry exercised by large, publicly held corporations. This has led to a change in the image promoted by the casino industry.

Disney World in Reverse

Beginning in the 1970s with Circus Circus, many casinos started developing into casino-hotel-entertainment complexes. By appealing to the family-oriented middle class, Circus Circus has become one of the most successful casino complexes in history. It grossed nearly $1 billion in 1993 (Bennett Bows Out, 1994). The opening in recent years of "kid-friendly" resorts, such as the MGM Grand, Luxor, and Treasure Island complexes, continues the trend (Graham, 1994). In fact, it can be argued that Las Vegas has become Disney World in reverse. Rather than an amusement park for kids, which has successfully added attractions to make it interesting for adults (as Disney World has), Las Vegas is transforming adult casino entertainment into a diversity of activities attractive to the entire family. The long-term success of casino gambling probably lies in attracting successive generations to the same location for a wide array of activities.

Market Saturation and Illegal Gambling

There is support in some sectors for limiting legal gaming to the areas already approved. Certainly, there exists a saturation point beyond which legalized gambling cannot continue to make money. A simple economic principle is that any one community can support only a certain number of supermarkets, nightclubs, banks or legal gaming opportunities. Also, the more that casinos are patronized by local residents versus tourists, the less beneficial is their economic effect on the community (Passell, 1994).

On the other hand, there is the well-documented existence of illegal gambling. Although it has not been shown that legal gambling eliminates illegal gambling in the same area, surveys have found that 80% of police and two-thirds of citizens agreed that "profits from illegal gambling are used to finance other illegal activities such as loan-sharking and drug distribution" (Fowler et al., 1978:36). Interestingly, a study of gambling law enforcement in 16 U.S. cities of 250,000 population found that

> in about half of the cities visited, police did not believe that illegal gambling operations were directly controlled or run by regional, multi-service syndicates; and in some of the other cities, police said that some bookmakers and, even more often, numbers operators were

independent of such large-scale criminal organizations [Fowler et al., 1978:37].

The important finding of this study is that "in about half the cities in this country the police do not see a direct link between organized crime and gambling" (Fowler et al., 1978:37).

In the same way that Prohibition served to organize criminals into partnerships and networks that survived its repeal, it is not surprising that other profitable vices, such as illegal gambling and drug use, are often run by these same criminal groups. Of course, illegal gambling is not run exclusively by organized crime groups. There are a number of studies which show the tenuous control exercised by the mob over illegal gambling in many cities (for a review, see Rosecrance, 1988). The liquor industry, however, has moved from an illegal business in the purview of the police to a business now regulated by agencies funded through a tax on the product itself (see Albanese, 1989). Likewise, legal casino gambling has moved in many jurisdictions from a police concern funded by the public to a regulatory concern funded by the casinos themselves. Table 1 summarizes this comparison between legal and illegal casinos and their implications for regulation, organized crime and where the profits go.

It can be seen from Table 1 that properly regulated and monitored casino gambling can reduce the burden on local taxpayers as the sole source of funding in the battle against organized crime. The profits from casinos, which are generated largely through tourist spending, can be used to support law enforcement efforts to suppress illegal gambling, organized crime and dishonesty in the operation of legal games.

The Need for Vigilance

It has been found that "there has been no significant evidence of racketeering operations associated with casino activities in Atlantic City" thus far (Zendzian, 1993:133). Nevertheless, vigilance is necessary in the casino industry for three primary reasons:

(1) The long history of organized crime involvement in illegal gambling provides these groups with preexisting interest and expertise in running (and stealing from) gaming operations.

(2) Casinos must be regulated closely due to the speed at which they accumulate cash. Unlike other cash businesses, where a business must wait for a product or service (e.g., a drink, food, laundry, entertainment) to be used or exhausted before that customer can

be solicited again, casino games move much more quickly. Multiple bets and pay-outs occur in seconds, permitting a large number of business-customer transactions in a very short period, resulting in large cash accumulations.

Table 1: The Regulation of Illegal vs. Legal Casino Gambling

	Illegal Casinos	Legal Casinos
Regulation of Casino Games	Police investigate illegal games (funded by taxpayers)	Regulatory agency monitors casinos (funded by the casino industry)
Organized Crime Threat	Operation and management of illegal betting operations with associated loansharking and extortion problems in debt collection and paying for "protection"	Screening and monitoring of applicants and operators of casinos, employees, hotel/casino servicing agencies, and unions for organized crime links and prevention of skimming
Profits	Used to fund other organized crime group activities (e.g., loansharking, narcotics)	Casinos taxed by government to pay for regulation of the industry and other government services

(3) Ancillary services, vendors and particularly labor unions must be monitored closely, as these are the most vulnerable remaining avenues for organized crime infiltration now that casinos are run primarily by large publicly held corporations. The immense size and wealth of these corporations, and their corresponding interest in stock prices, shareholders, public image, and the SEC, reduce their susceptibility to organized crime infiltration.

The long history of organized crime involvement with illegal gambling is well-documented, as is the speed with which casinos can generate income. Indictments in 1994 linked members of the Gambino and Genovese crime families in New York to the Marcello family in New Orleans in a scheme to skim profits from video poker games in Louisiana (Davis, 1994; Marcus, 1994). This illustrates continuing interest in skimming as a method of making money for organized crime groups. The link between organized crime and labor unions has been established in a number of cases, most notably, the Scarfo case cited earlier, as well as in the New York City construction industry (New York State Organized Crime Task Force, 1990). The need for continued vigilance is apparent (see Beare, 1989), although not always heeded. One measure of commitment to the strict enforcement of gaming regulations is the resources allocated to the task. In Atlantic City, for example, there are approximately ten gaming control investigators for every casino. In Mississippi, the situation is reversed. There are nearly ten casinos for each investigator.

CONCLUSION

The future of casino gambling can be expected to mirror its past, with the singular added benefit of the lessons learned in Las Vegas, Atlantic City and elsewhere. Hence, the result is more than a mere reshuffling of the deck. In places where casino applicants, vendors and their personnel are screened carefully; where the games themselves are monitored; and where close surveillance of opportunities for skimming and labor union infiltration occurs, attempts at organized crime involvement can be readily discovered and dealt with. Only where regulations are substandard, or insufficient emphasis is placed on screening, monitoring, and enforcement, can organized crime exist untouched. Organized crime survives only where we have allowed it to endure.

REFERENCES

Abadinsky, H. (1994). *Organized Crime* (4th ed). Chicago, IL: Nelson-Hall.

Albanese, J. (1989). *Organized Crime in America* (2nd ed.). Cincinnati, OH: Anderson.

Beare, M. E. (1989). "Current Law Enforcement Issues in Canadian Gambling." In: C.S. Campbell and J. Lowman, eds., *Gambling in Canada: Golden Goose or Trojan Horse?* Burnaby, BC, CAN: Simon Fraser University School of Criminology.

Bell, D. (1953). "Crime As an American Way of Life." *Antioch Review* 13(June):131-154.

"Bennett Bows Out" (1994). *USA Today*, July 11, p.1B.

Cook, J. and J. Carmichael (1980). "The Invisible Enterprise." *Forbes* 126:7-11.

Davis, R. (1994). "Feds: 3-State Bust Hunts Mob." *USA Today*, June 1, p.3.

Demaris, O. (1987). *The Boardwalk Jungle*. New York, NY: Bantam.

Dombrink, J. and W.N. Thompson (1990). *The Last Resort: Success and Failure in Campaigns for Casinos*. Reno, NV: University of Nevada Press.

Dorman, M. (1972). *Payoff: The Role of Organized Crime in American Politics*. New York, NY: David McKay.

Eisenberg, D., U. Dan and E. Landau (1979). *Meyer Lansky: Mogul of the Mob*. New York, NY: Paddington Press.

Fabian, A. (1990). *Card Sharps, Dream Books, & Bucket Shops: Gambling in 19th Century America*. Ithaca, NY: Cornell University Press.

Fowler, F.J., T.W. Mangione and F.E. Pratter (1978). *Gambling Law Enforcement in Major American Cities*. Washington, DC: U.S. Government Printing Office.

Graham, J. (1994). "The Odds of Having Family Fun in Las Vegas." *USA Today*, February 24, p.5D.

Gutierrez, J.M. (1979). "Casino Act: Gambling's Past and the Casino Act's Future." *Rutgers Camden Law Journal* 10(Winter):269-321.

Haller, M.H. (1979). "The Changing Structure of American Gambling in the Twentieth Century." *Journal of Social Issues* 35:87-114.

Hicks, A.J. (1980-81). "No Longer the Only Game in Town: A Comparison of the Nevada and New Jersey Regulatory Systems of Gaming Control." *Southwestern University Law Review* 12:583-626.

Jennings, D. (1992). *We Only Kill Each Other*. New York, NY: Pocket Books.

Kallick, M., D. Suits, T. Dielman and J. Hybels (1979). *A Survey of American Gambling Attitudes and Behavior*. Ann Arbor, MI: Institute for Social Research.

Kefauver, E. (1951). *Crime in America*. Garden City, NY: Doubleday.

Lacey, R. (1991). *Little Man: Meyer Lansky and the Gangster Life*. Boston, MA: Little, Brown.

Marcus, F. (1994). "Video Poker in Louisiana is Mob Target, Inquiry Says." *New York Times*, June 4, p.3.

Monaco, R. and L. Bascom (1991). *Rubouts: Mob Murders in America*. New York, NY: Avon.

Moore, W.H. (1974). *The Kefauver Committee and the Politics of Crime, 1950-1952*. Columbia, MO: University of Missouri Press.

New York State Organized Crime Task Force (1990). *Corruption and Racketeering in the New York City Construction Industry.* New York, NY: New York University Press.

O'Brien, T.R. and M.J. Flaherty (1985). "Regulation of the Atlantic City Casino Industry and Attempts to Control Its Infiltration by Organized Crime." *Rutgers Law Journal* 16(Spring-Summer):721-758.

Passell, P. (1994). "The False Promise of Development by Casino." *New York Times,* June 12, p.F5.

Reid, E. and O. Demaris (1963). *The Green Felt Jungle.* New York, NY: Trident Press.

Roemer, W. (1991). *Man Against the Mob.* New York, NY: Ballantine.

Rosecrance, J. (1988). *Gambling Without Guilt: The Legitimation of an American Pastime.* Belmont, CA: Brooks/Cole.

Skolnick, J.H. (1978). *House of Cards: Legalization and Control of Casino Gambling.* Boston, MA: Little, Brown.

Spanier, D. (1992). *Welcome to the Pleasuredome: Inside Las Vegas.* Reno, NV: University of Nevada Press.

State of New Jersey Commission of Investigation (1977). *Incursion by Organized Crime into Certain Legitimate Business Activities in Atlantic City.* Washington, DC: National Institute of Justice.

——(1991). *Video Gambling.* Washington, DC: National Institute of Justice.

Turner, W. (1984). "U.S. and Nevada Agents Crack Down on Casinos." *New York Times,* January 28, p.1.

U.S. Commission on the Review of the National Policy Toward Gambling (1976). *Gambling in America.* Washington, DC: U.S. Government Printing Office.

U.S. Senate Special Committee to Investigate Organized Crime in Interstate Commerce (1951). *Third Interim Report, 81st Congress.* Washington, DC: U.S. Government Printing Office.

Von Brook, P., M.A. Siegel and C.D. Foster, eds. *Gambling: Crime or Recreation?* Wylie, TX: Information Plus.

Woodiwiss, M. (1988). *Crime Crusades and Corruption: Prohibitions in the United States, 1990-1987.* Totowa, NJ: Barnes & Noble Books.

Zendzian, C.A. (1990). *In the Shadows: The Vulnerability of Casino Ancillary Services to Racketeering.* Doctoral dissertation, Graduate School, City University of New York.

—— (1993). *Who Pays?: Casino Gambling, Hidden Interests, and Organized Crime.* Albany, NY: Harrow and Heston.

Organized Crime and Sports Gambling: Point-Shaving in College Basketball

David C. Whelan

Abstract: *Case studies of four major point-fixing scandals suggest that the mechanics of college basketball lend themselves to such fixed games. These include the small number of players on a team (five versus 11 for many other sports), and the ability of a single player to influence the outcome of a contest. Traditional organized crime, or, at least, organized criminal networks, have been instrumental in point-shaving scandals.*

No other form of intercollegiate competition has suffered so many game-rigging scandals as basketball. Between 1951 and 1985, the integrity of college athletics in the U.S. was shaken on four separate occasions by disclosures that student-athletes had participated in basketball point-shaving schemes orchestrated by organized crime figures. The full importance of these conspiracies lies in the overlapping contexts in which they have taken place. This chapter addresses the mechanics of point-shaving, and the direct role of traditional organized crime and organized criminal networks in the fixes themselves.

FIXING SPORTS CONTESTS

On December 6, 1993, Andrew Garguilo, Nicholas Cammareri, and Theresa Geritano were arrested and charged under New York State's Organized Crime Control Act for allegedly taking in at least $86 million a year in illegal wagers on professional and college sports. "Superbookie" Garguilo, the alleged head of the illegal sports gambling operation, is, according to authorities, a "made" member of the Genovese crime family. His operation is believed to have handled wagers funnelled from approximately 300 bookmakers in the New York metropolitan area and in other states. The operation is presumed to have taken bets on, among other sports, college basketball.

When bets are being taken on college basketball games, and organized crime is involved, the possibility of scandal and point-shaving cannot be far behind. History has repeated itself four times in four decades.

The fixing of sports contests did not, of course, originate with the college basketball scandals of the past 40 years. The earliest example of bribes offered to athletes in exchange for a reduced level of performance stems from the time of ancient Greek Olympics (Kiernan and Daley, 1965). In nineteenth-century America, there were many instances of gamblers influencing sports outcomes, and, in fact, so prevalent were such cases of corruption that a new term, "hippodroming," was coined to designate them (Beezley, 1985).

The most famous example of a sports-rigging scheme in the U.S. during this century involved a professional baseball team, the Chicago White Sox (hereafter referred to as the Chicago Black Sox), which "threw" the 1919 World Series in exchange for payment provided by a New York gambling ring with ties to organized crime (Berry and Wong, 1986). Nevertheless, despite the cases that have afflicted other sports at other moments in time, it is modern collegiate basketball that has suffered the most harm as a result of point-shaving disclosures. Straw (1986:261) states that "of all sports shaken by hints of fixes and rigged outcomes, none has been so badly bruised as college basketball."

It is a contention of this author that the mechanics of college basketball lend themselves to point-shaving fixes, in that the technical features of the game mesh with the idea of point-shaving. But it is the summaries of the four major cases of point fixing that will be examined in this article. These will provide further information in support of the influential role of organized crime and organized criminal networks in point-shaving schemes.

MECHANICS OF POINT-SHAVING

Point-shaving conspiracies revolve around the "point spread" offered by sports bookmakers to their customers. The "spread" is defined by Abt et al. (1985:261) as "a handicap in the form of points added by oddsmakers to the score of teams, in games of predictable outcomes that are the object of betting." Two teams—Team A and Team B—are slated to compete in a game. There is the general perception that Team A, based upon its past performance and existing resources, will probably defeat Team B. In order to bring the two into closer alignment, an oddsmaker, often an employee of a legal Nevada sportsbook, will assign additional points to Team B. Those wishing to wager on Team A must "give" points; let us say, for the purposes of illustration, seven points. If Team A wins by more than seven points, its backers win their bets; if Team A loses *or* wins by less than seven points, those having bets on Team B will collect. According to Strine and Isaacs (1978), although the point spread originated in the late 1920s, its use was not widespread until after World War II, when interest in betting on football and basketball games increased and the point spread became standard practice. At the same time, the sports section of newspapers and television broadcasts of sporting events assisted in popularizing the point spread: both media began to carry the "latest line," thereby making point-spread information immediately available to readers and viewers.

One common misconception is that the point spread is supposed to reflect accurately the relative chances of two teams involved in a game—using the hypothetical example, that Team A is "objectively" seven points better than Team B. As *Boston Globe* editor Vincent Doria told the U.S. Presidential Commission on Organized Crime (1985:358), while "the spread *may* be a rough gauge of comparative ability, that is not its underlying purpose. The accurate line is simply trying to get as many people to bet on each side of the line. The job of the bookmaker is to put out a line that will draw equal play."

Most bookmakers do not make their own line. Instead, they use a line calculated by legal sports bookmakers in Nevada as their frame of reference. The bookmaker may adjust the line to fit local market conditions, but his or her job, again, is to draw roughly equivalent volumes of action on either side of the line. Given the comparatively slim profit margin common to sports bookmaking, if the amounts wagered on a particular game are lopsided, then the bookie has a stake—a "position"—in that game. Normally, bookmakers would prefer not to have a position. Hence, when too much money is bet on one team in a given game, the bookmaker may try to "lay off" part of the action, reducing exposure to that team's winning by placing bets on that team with other sports bookies.

The aforementioned Andrew Garguilo was accused of dealing in these types of bets from other bookmakers. They protect the bookmaker against large losses on a game in which most of the bets are on one particular team. Investigators in the Garguilo case believe that he took a 10% fee for accepting the laid-off bets. Kuehn (1977) states that "depending upon market conditions, other bookmakers may, or may not, accept these 'lay off' wagers." It is quite possible, then, that a sports book will lose money as a result of an imbalance in the betting on either side of the point-spread line.

HOW POINT-SHAVING WORKS

Point-shaving involves the use of bribes by a gambler, or, more often, a group of gamblers, to participants in a game for which a point-spread line has been prepared and bookies are accepting wagers on either side of that line. Normally, the bribes come in the form of money. Sometimes they include "goods" (ranging from consumer appliances to narcotics) and, albeit rarely, are accompanied by threats to reluctant players. Most games require that several individuals on a particular team be bribed in this manner. If the gambler can find enough player recruits, he can direct them to lower their performance standards in a way that influences the game's final outcome. The players need not decrease their collective performance to a level at which their team loses; they may be asked merely to reduce the team's margin of victory below that of the spread. On other occasions, when the bribed team is an underdog that is likely to lose in any event, the players will be asked to simply increase the favorite team's margin of victory above the spread. The fact that a fixed team need not lose the game serves two ends: it makes participation in the scheme more palatable to the players; and it masks the existence of the fix in the eyes of the general public and of bookmakers accepting bets on the game.

Once the required arrangements with the players have been made, the point-shaving group faces a second task. It must wager a large sum of money with (generally) an illegal sports bookmaker on the premise that the fixed team will not "cover" the spread. Large bets, however, frequently set bookies to wondering about the possible existence of a point-shaving fix, and, on the basis of such doubts, they may refuse the "fixer's" bets (Sasuly, 1982). Straw (1986) believes that to prevent such refusals, the fixer may reduce the size of his bets by dividing his action among several bookies.

These deceptions are necessitated by factors other than placating the bookies' suspicions prior to a fixed game. After the rigged contest is over, a bookie may have noticed that the performance of certain players was inexplicably poor, that there was something unusual about the game. These post-game doubts may have negative consequences for the fixers on three fronts. First, since the fixers are often street-level organized crime "wiseguys," a well-connected bookie might call upon other organized crime muscle to assist in resolving a disputed bet. Second, through indirect channels, the fixers may send out word to a team's coach, an athletic council or law enforcement officials to keep an eye on either the fixer and/or the suspected player(s). Finally, setting up a point-shaving scheme entails a great deal of advanced effort. To justify this overhead, fixers will not normally stop at one betting coup; they will want to continue the conspiracy in future games. Thus, fixers may use techniques, such as spreading money to several different bookmakers, to allay any suspicions they may have after a game is over and to keep them "open" to bets on other games involving the same bribed team.

CASE EXAMPLES

CCNY/Kentucky Scandal of 1951

Several years prior to the point-shaving disclosures of 1951, individuals inside and outside of college basketball periodically mentioned that a major fixing scandal might be in the offing. Beezley (1985) cites a 1944 example of Kansas University coach Phog Allen warning officials from the then National Association of Intercollegiate Basketball that something was seriously amiss in the games being played in New York City's Madison Square Garden. Allen was chastised at that time for his "deplorable lack of faith in American youth and meager confidence in the integrity of coaches" (Beezley, 1985:82). Simultaneously, according to Rosen (1978), Midwest bookmaker Charles McNeil approached a major college basketball conference to complain that a conference referee was on the take. He, too, was met with scorn and rejection. Berry and Wong (1986) note that a year later, in 1945, the first of the postwar collegiate basketball cases came to light when five Brooklyn College players admitted that they had accepted bribes to lose a game.

At the time, this case of "dumping" games, as opposed to point-shaving, was thought to be an isolated incident. The five Brooklyn College players were expelled, and it was widely believed that whatever had been wrong with college basketball was no longer present.

It was a sports editor from the now-defunct *New York Journal-American*, Max Kase, who began to develop the information that would eventually lead to the revelation of point-shaving in the early 1950s. Kase had heard his colleagues in the press corps voice their suspicions about a number of "inexplicable" upsets in games played at Madison Square Garden. On his own initiative, Kase consulted with a cooperative New York bookmaker who confirmed these doubts by alluding to wild swings in betting patterns on the suspect games (Straw, 1986). Armed with this information, Kase went directly to Manhattan District Attorney Frank Hogan, who, unlike association and conference officials, took the implicit charge of point-shaving seriously.

In 1950, concrete evidence of point-shaving schemes at work was given to Hogan by Manhattan College star Junious Kellogg. Kellogg told the district attorney that he had been offered a bribe to shave points by a former Manhattan College player named Henry Poppe, who, as it turned out, was a confederate of organized crime figure Salvatore Sollazzo. Kellogg had refused to go along with the plot, but two of his teammates had accepted syndicate money (McCallum, 1978). Through Kellogg's cooperation, and a close retrospective look at some 100 questionable games, Hogan caught a Sollazzo intermediary in the act of offering a bribe, and the entire scheme began to unravel.

The case against the Manhattan College players was only the beginning. Hogan widened his investigation to games involving other New York teams, including New York University, Long Island University and, most surprisingly, the City College of New York (CCNY)—one of the premier teams of the day (Sasuly, 1982). But Hogan's net was not confined to New York teams. Following up on initial leads provided by Eddie Gard, a Long Island University player, Hogan's staff discovered that schools like Bradley University, Toledo University and national power University of Kentucky were also involved. While cases were eventually developed against a total of 33 players from six schools, additional schools and scores of other players were named in Hogan's indictments. The problem of point-shaving, then, was not limited to New York teams playing in Madison Square Garden, but was a national phenomenon— fixed games were played in 22 other cities in 17 states—that had tainted the scores of at least 49 games in 1947-48 and in 1950-51 (Straw, 1986).

Among the chief fixers was New York-based gambler Salvatore Sollazzo, whose main line of business was illegal gold sales and who, through his own gambling activities, was in serious debt to local bookies. According to Rosen (1978), Sollazzo and his cohorts were not "made" members of the Mafia, but were professional criminals associated with mob boss Frank Costello. Hobson (1951) states that the same status was accorded to

Sollazzo by Judge Saul Streit, who would sentence him to a prison term of eight to 16 years as the mastermind behind the plot. At the time, the press reported that hundreds of thousands of dollars had been made on the fixed games by Sollazzo and his henchmen. In fact, as Rosen (1978) states, Sollazzo realized very little from his bribes and entered jail penniless.

While charges would ultimately be brought against players from several teams, it was the news that two national champion teams had shaved points that lent Hogan's investigation widespread publicity. The CCNY team of 1950 was the first and only team in history to win both the National Invitational Tournament (NIT) and the National Collegiate Athletic Association (NCAA) title in the same year. Tournament structure today would not allow this to happen again. The University of Kentucky had preceded CCNY as national champions in both 1948 and 1949, and three players from that team—All-Americans Alex Groza, Ralph Beard and Dale Barnstable—admitted that they began to accept bribes shortly after anchoring the U.S. Olympic basketball team of 1948 (McCallum, 1978). Between 1945 and 1949, the Kentucky team had compiled a record of 130 victories in 140 games, making them the last squad to evoke public doubt. Such is the nature of point-shaving that the talent-rich Kentucky team could win consistently by a margin of victory less than the point spread.

One game in particular, Kentucky's performance against Loyola University of Chicago in the opening round of the 1949 NIT, had raised eyebrows. In line with its superior talent, Kentucky had been made a 10-point favorite in the contest. The final score found Loyola winning by a margin of 11 points. In return for receiving some $2,000 from Sollazzo, team members Groza, Beard, and Barnstable had tried to keep the game close but still win and, in the process, encountered a stunning upset (Straw, 1986). Kentucky was not the only team with All-American players on the take: Bradley University's star guard, Gene Melchiorre, had received as much as $4,000 from Sollazzo's Chicago associates to shave points in games played in Peoria (Hobson, 1951). Not only was point-shaving national in scope, it was aimed at the very top of the nation's collegiate basketball hierarchy, at the best teams and the best players in the U.S.

The 1951 scandal had major repercussions for the named players, their teams and college basketball as a whole. Some 21 players would plead guilty to charges of sports bribery; four players were convicted as game-fixers and received sentences ranging from six months to three years. The Kentucky squad was barred by the NCAA from post-season play, while the entire basketball program at Long Island University was jettisoned (McCallum, 1978). Many college basketball coaches followed the NCAA's post-scandal recommendation that they not play games in public arenas, especially Madison Square Garden, but instead reduce the size of big-time college basketball by playing in smaller, college gym venues. According to Beezley (1985), the public's confidence in college basketball was shaken to the point that attendance at all intercollegiate basketball games dropped sharply during the 1952-53 season.

The 1961 Scandal

A decade after the CCNY/Kentucky revelations, public faith that college basketball was legitimate had been largely restored. However, one individual who continued to harbor doubts that the 1951 scandal was the last word in point-shaving was New York City District Attorney Frank Hogan. Using contacts developed years earlier, Hogan had been following the activities of two mob gamblers, Aaron Wagman and his chief accomplice, Joseph Hacken. Hogan's initial investigation centered on two New York metropolitan teams, Seton Hall University and St. John's University, with investigators trailing players from those schools to clandestine meetings with Wagman and Hacken (Cohane, 1962). Ultimately, based on undercover activity, the two were arrested.

The scope of this point-shaving scheme was found to be even larger than that of its predecessor. Beezley (1985) states that 50 players from 27 different schools were charged with receiving a total of $45,000 to shave points in 44 games between 1956 and 1961. New York-area teams included New York University and Columbia University, while other axles were discovered in North Carolina (University of North Carolina [UNC] and North Carolina State [NCS]) and in Philadelphia (St. Joseph's and LaSalle). The final list included players from schools outside these ambits, including Mississippi State, Tennessee, Colorado and Connecticut.

Just as diverse was the amount of money paid to individual players by the fixers. In an investigation paralleling Hogan's, Raleigh County (NC) Solicitor Lester V. Chalmers sought indictments against the fixers, including Wagman, Hacken and Joseph Green, describing them as "members of the biggest gambling network in the country" (Beezley, 1985). It has been suggested by others that this network may have been extremely loose-knit, involving two or three fixing alliances that sold fixed games to bigger gamblers who would realize large profits on individual games. The major group revolved around Wagman, Hacken and a former Columbia University basketball star, Jack Molinas, who had become an attorney after being expelled from professional basketball for wagering on his own team (Beezley, 1985). Joseph Green headed another group, concentrating his efforts in the New York area, while Robert Kraw headed a third fixing faction. There were times when the factions were at cross-purposes. In a game between NCS and LaSalle, Kraw's group had successfully bribed three NCS players to shave points, while two LaSalle stars had received money from Wagman to do the same. The game, in fact, was fixed both ways. Beezley (1985) adds that when Wagman got word that the NCS players were on Kraw's payroll, he succeeded in getting two of them to turn to his side, thereby undercutting Kraw.

Compared to the 1951 scandal, the central fixers in the 1961 wave of point-shaving schemes were full-time criminals with deep ties to organized crime. Had they not been caught, these individuals would have been hugely successful in their endeavors from a monetary standpoint. It is also apparent, however, that this was not a unified conspiracy where, for example, Wagman, Green and Kraw were taking orders from a central source, casting some doubt over organized crime's control function in the collective fixes. Molinas, identified as the "master fixer" of the whole conspiracy, had ties to traditional organized crime. After serving a prison term for his involvement in the basketball scandals, Molinas moved to Los Angeles and financed his gambling ventures with other illegal activities, including pornographic movies. Cunningham (1977) states that federal investigators remarked "it's not a question of whether Jack had any mob connections. The only question is which mob and which connection."

Grand juries in New York and North Carolina focused on the fixers rather than the players, most of whom soon confessed to their roles in the schemes and were allowed to avoid indictment in exchange for testimony. Many players were blacklisted from professional basketball and wrongfully implicated in the gambling scandal. The tragedy of the 1961 scandal followed some players for a lifetime.

Boston College Scandal of 1981

College basketball remained comparatively free of fixing scandals for nearly two decades following the 1961 investigation, other than a 1965 case involving two players from Seattle University charged with outright "dumping" (Straw, 1986).

Evidence of a third point-shaving conspiracy arose during the course of a U.S. Federal Bureau of Investigation (FBI) interrogation of Henry Hill. Hill was a drug trafficker, overall hustler and member of an organized crime "crew" that had robbed some $5.8 million in merchandise from the Lufthansa Airlines cargo terminal at Kennedy Airport in 1978. In his organized crime capacity, Hill was apparently under the control of Paul Vario, a *capo* in the Lucchese crime family of New York. Under seven separate indictments, Hill decided to cooperate with the FBI and entered the Federal Witness Protection Program.

In testimony that would be transcribed and incorporated into the government's case against chief fixer Jimmy Burke (United States v. Burke [1983], 700 F. 2d 70, 2d Cir.), the Boston College (BC) scandal was seen to be a very limited case, involving only three BC players—Rick Kuhn, Jim Sweeney and Ernie Cobb—and nine games that took place in BC's 1978-79 season (Looney, 1985).

While the third major point-shaving scandal in the post-World War II era was not national in scope, it was the most fully documented owing to aggressive prosecution of its principals and featuring the most direct linkage to traditional organized crime.

The scheme began to unfold during the summer of 1978, when Rick Kuhn first engaged in a leisurely conversation with his neighbor, Tony Perla, in Swissville, PA. Perla began to question Kuhn about BC's prospects for the coming season, telling the BC center that he was a fan who occasionally wagered money and could use some inside information about the team's status. Kuhn supplied this information, and Perla contacted his brother, Rocco, a professional gambler, who in turn spoke with Paul Mazzei, a low-level member of the Lucchese family. Together, the Perlas and Mazzei cooked up a point-shaving scheme and presented it to Kuhn. Kuhn indicated interest in being a part of the plot, and was given cocaine and merchandise by Mazzei throughout the summer.

The Perlas and Mazzei began to have second thoughts about attempting to operate the scheme independently as the beginning of the BC season neared. Mazzei contacted Henry Hill, who had spent time in jail with Jimmy Burke, a well-known mob associate of Paul Vario. The Pennsylvania connection needed a person who had "status" for two reasons: as an associate of the Lucchese family, connection to mob muscle would prevent retaliation by disgruntled bookmakers; and, as known gamblers in bookmaking circles, this crew had the money and contacts necessary to lay large bets without evoking suspicion. In November 1978, with the blessing of the Lucchese family, Hill met with Rick Kuhn and the other BC players, agreeing that a December 6, 1978 game against Providence College would serve as a "trial" of scheme viability. Kuhn received drugs and money from Hill, and attempted to recruit the team's star players, Sweeney and Cobb. But they apparently refused to go along, and Kuhn could only enlist the cooperation of the less-talented starters and bench players. Worse, Kuhn himself had been replaced as BC's starting center. The test did not go well. BC won the game by a margin wider than the point spread. The crew lost thousands of dollars, and Burke directed Hill to go to Boston to inform Kuhn of the violence he would encounter if there were any more complications.

Four of the next five BC games were successful from the fixer's standpoint. The fifth game, against St. John's, was a "push" in which the gamblers neither won nor lost money. Having received an average of $2,000 a game for the previous four fixes, Kuhn was informed that the next scheduled contest, a nationally televised game against Holy Cross, would involve critical monetary bets. The point spread had Holy Cross as a seven-point favorite, meaning that BC would have to lose by eight or more points for the scheme to succeed; they lost by two. The gamblers wound up losing $50,000, Rick Kuhn lost the $10,000 he was to have received for his part, and the group apparently quit the field.

In the final accounting, the BC point-shaving scheme was unsuccessful; the Burke crew and, presumably, the Lucchese crime family members who were in on the fix, evidently suffered a net loss. According to testimony before the U.S. President's Commission on Organized Crime (1985), Burke's crew never retaliated against Kuhn, despite threats to do so, and the entire affair would not have come to light were it not for Hill's role as an FBI informant. Burke, Mazzei and the Perlas were all convicted for their parts in the scheme. The sentencing judge described the Perlas as "small-time gamblers with big-time ideas," but their direct ties to traditional organized crime were beyond question (Berry and Wong, 1986). Rick Kuhn became the first player in a point-shaving scheme to receive a non-suspended jail sentence—a full ten years in a federal prison (Berry and Wong, 1986).

Tulane Scandal of 1985

The fourth major point-shaving scheme to hit college basketball came to light during a dinner conversation between attorney Edward Kohnke and two of his brothers at a New Orleans restaurant in mid-March, 1985. Kohnke was a Tulane University basketball enthusiast, so he was naturally taken aback when his brother mentioned that rumors were circulating around campus that a recent Tulane game had been fixed (Serrill, 1985). After he attempted to verify the rumor, Kohnke contacted the office of New Orleans District Attorney Harry Connick.

Again, like the BC case, the Tulane scandal was an extremely limited instance of corruption. It reportedly involved five players (four starters and one reserve guard) who had conspired with a local network of gamblers and drug dealers to shave points on two games. Unlike the principal teams of the 1951 scandal, Tulane sported a mediocre (15-13) record, and four of the players allegedly involved (Clyde Eads, Jon Johnson, David Dominique and Bobby Thompson) were merely average in their abilities. The fifth player, was, however, the team's star, John Williams. Williams was the team's leading scorer, rebounder and shot blocker, and in the previous season had been chosen as the conference Player of the Year. He had allegedly accepted a total of $5,300 to participate in the point-shaving scheme.

The point-shaving scheme began when player Eads became friendly with an alleged campus drug connection, Gary Kranz. In time, Eads allegedly exchanged athletic gear for drugs, and introduced Johnson, Dominique, Thompson, and Williams into a cocaine circle that reportedly included Kranz and fraternity brothers Mark Olensky and David Rothenburg. In addition to his drug activities, Kranz also allegedly ran a campus bookmaking operation. Olensky, whose father had something to do with a gambling newspaper, was an able assistant. Thompson's father was a former bookmaker, and Thompson reportedly connected the Kranz group with New Orleans gambler Roland Ruiz, who helped distribute the wagered money. On the day of the first game to be rigged (a match between Tulane and Southern Mississippi), Kranz allegedly approached Eads and asked for his participation in a point-shaving scheme. Eads allegedly enlisted the other four players, and a total of $7,000 was bet on the game. Tulane won by a margin less than the point spread, and some $3,500 was distributed to the five players.

Kranz and his alleged associates attempted to work a point-shaving scheme two weeks later in a game against Virginia Tech, but by this time Eads and Johnson wanted to quit the conspiracy. Urged on by Kranz, and feeling loyalty toward the other players, they allegedly agreed to throw a different game and bypass the Virginia Tech matchup. When that time came, Kranz's group allegedly gathered $34,000 to bet that Tulane would not cover the spread in a game against Memphis State. To place a wager of this size without arousing suspicion, Olensky and Rothenberg reportedly flew to Las Vegas, where they wagered about half of the money with ten different sports books. An additional $10,000 was allegedly bet with illegal bookmakers in Birmingham, AL, and $6,000 was placed in New Orleans betting circles. The scheme worked, with Tulane losing by more than its assigned underdog spread of seven points. Approximately $13,500 was allegedly given to the five players. Shortly thereafter, rumors came to Kohnke's notice and the entire plot came crashing down as Eads and Johnson became witnesses for the district attorney.

As for the alleged fixers themselves, they had no direct connection with traditional organized crime. Kranz, Olensky and Rothenberg were recent graduates of Tulane living at their fraternity house and allegedly operating a small cocaine business. While there was no fixed evidence that New Orleans bookmaker Ruiz had ties to the Marcello organized crime family, the possibility of association cannot be dismissed. It was allegedly Bobby Thompson who approached Ruiz and told him that a game could be fixed for $6,000, with Thompson himself acting as intermediary for the cash. Ruiz, with a police record featuring convictions for bookmaking and counterfeiting, reportedly paid Thompson the $6,000, unaware that the game had already been fixed by Kranz et al. with Thompson reportedly pocketing the bulk of the bribe (Looney, 1985). Through Thompson's actions, in direct contrast to the three other point-shaving scandals, professional criminals and organized criminal networks were both duped by a player, and, briefly, benefitted from the schemes.

Three of the Tulane players—Dominique, Thompson and Williams—were charged under Louisiana's Bribery of Sports Participants law. Rothenberg and Olensky were named in similar indictments, as was Kranz, who was also charged with conspiracy to distribute narcotics. Ultimately, as a consequence of prosecutorial error, all three of the Tulane players were set free when a mistrial was declared. The Tulane basketball program was abolished and has since been reinstated by university president Eamon Kelly.

CONCLUSIONS

It can be argued that the mechanics of college basketball lend themselves to point-shaving fixes. There are several technical features of the game of basketball that make it a prime candidate for such schemes. These include the small number of players on a team (five versus 11 for many other sports), and the ability of a single player to influence the outcome of a contest. The more important element is that traditional organized crime, or, at least, organized criminal networks—no matter how loose-knit they are—have been instrumental in point-shaving scandals. This raises suspicion about the association between organized crime and sports gambling, and there is no question that such a relationship exists.

Walker (1994) states that gambling has long been the primary source of revenue for organized crime; it has underpinned corruption. Law enforcement officials, at local, state and federal levels, have always believed that there is a relationship between traditional organized crime and gambling. The Kefauver Commission in 1950, the McClellan Committee in 1962, and the President's Commissions in 1967 and 1986 essentially agreed that illegal gambling, most of which is sports wagering, provides organized crime with resources for other ventures. Boyd (1977) says that "from a gross dollar volume standpoint, sports wagering is the king of bookmaking." Abadinsky (1990) agrees that most illegal wagering today involves sports betting. These are statements that may not be easily substantiated, except for estimations. There is also no clear evidence to suggest that illegal gamblers associated with traditional organized crime or organized criminal networks would reinvest their monies in other areas of criminal activity where simple economics and risk of discovery might not be compatible.

Many authors and informers have referred to gambling and bookmaking in their discussion of organized criminal activity. In his seminal work on the mob, Peterson (1983) links organized crime figures like Frank Costello, Thomas Lucchese and Vito Genovese with gambling rackets. Hoffman and Headley (1992), in their expose on contract killer Tony "Greek" Frankos, connect numerous bookmaking establishments with Carmine Tramunti, longtime boss of New York's Lucchese family, and with the entire Gambino crime family. In his revelation of deep-cover operations, Pistone and Woodley (1987) note that the largest part of Frank Balistrieri's bookmaking operation was sports gambling. Balistrieri was the ruling organized crime boss of Milwaukee, the transactions of which extended to Cleveland and Detroit. Pistone and Woodley (1987) also indicated that a major portion of the income of New York's Bonanno crime family came from the bookmaking business.

While traditional organized crime figures and associates may have been marginal to the central action in a few point-shaving cases, roles have been ancillary, if not initiating. Clearly, organized crime figures or organized criminal networks were involved, but did not resort to exploiting their connections to coerce others into compliance.

College basketball in the nineties is thriving; it is an enormous business. Despite the warnings of history, major college basketball is back in the big-city arenas for conference and NCAA tournaments. Wagering on college basketball games is a widespread and persistent activity in the U.S., and organized crime has an active role in this trade. Couple the vulnerability of college basketball players with motivated organized criminals, and there exists an atmosphere for future point-shaving scandals. It would be foolhardy to take the small number of proven point-shaving cases as grounds for complacency; policy measures should be adopted to reduce the potential for this type of illegal activity.

REFERENCES

Abadinsky, H. (1990). *Organized Crime* (3d ed). Chicago, IL: Nelson-Hall.

Abt, V., J.F. Smith and E.M. Christiansen (1985). *The Business of Risk: Commercial Gambling in Mainstream America.* Lawrence, KS: University of Kansas.

Beezley, W.H. (1985). "The 1961 Scandal at North Carolina State and the End of the Dixie Classic." In: D. Chu, J.O. Seagrave and J. Becker eds., *Sport and Higher Education.* Champaign, IL: Human Kinetics Press.

Berry, R.C. and G.M. Wong (1986). *Law and Business of the Sports Industry: Common Issues in Amateur and Professional Sports,* Vol. II. Dover, MA: Auburn House.

Boyd, K.T. (1977). *Gambling Technology.* Washington, DC: U.S. Government Printing Office.

Cohane, T. (1962). "Behind the Basketball Scandal." *Look,* February 13, pp.84-86.

Cunningham, B. with M. Pearl (1977). *Mr. District Attorney.* New York, NY: Mason/Charter.

Hobson, H. (1951). "How to Stop Basketball Scandals." *Colliers,* December 29, pp.27-ff.

Hoffman, W. and L. Headley (1992). *Contract Killer.* New York, NY: Thunder's Mouth Press.

Kiernan, J. and A. Daley (1965). *The Story of the Olympic Games, 776 B.C. to 1964.* New York, NY: J.B. Lippincott.

Kuehn, L.L. (1977). "Syndicated Crime in America." In: E.S. Sagarin and F. Nontanino eds., *Deviants: Voluntary Actors in a Hostile World*. Chicago, IL: Scott, Foresman and Co.

Looney, D.S. (1985). "Big Trouble at Tulane." *Sports Illustrated*, April 8, pp.36-39.

McCallum, J.D. (1978). *College Basketball, U.S.A.: Since 1892*. New York, NY: Stein and Day.

Peterson, V.W. (1983). *The Mob: 200 Years of Organized Crime in New York*. Ottawa, IL: Green Hill.

Pistone, J.D. with R. Woodley (1987). *Donnie Brasco: My Undercover Life in the Mafia*. New York, NY: New American Library.

Rosen, C.D. (1978). *Scandals of '51: How the Gamblers Almost Killed College Basketball*. New York, NY: Holt, Rinehart and Winston.

Sasuly, R. (1982). *Bookies and Bettors: Two Hundred Years of Gambling*. New York, NY: Holt, Rinehart & Winston.

Serrill, M.S. (1985). "The Fix Is On." *Time*, April 15, p.89.

Straw, P. (1986). "Point Spreads and Journalistic Ethics." In: R.E. Lapchick ed., *Fractured Focus: Sports as a Reflection of Society*. Lexington, MA: D.C. Heath.

Strine, G. and N.D. Isaacs (1978). *Covering the Spread: How to Bet Pro Football*. New York, NY: Random House.

U.S. President's Commission on Law Enforcement and Administration of Justice, Task Force on Organized Crime (1967). *Task Force Report: Organized Crime*. Washington, DC: U.S. Government Printing Office.

U.S. President's Commission on Organized Crime (1985). *Organized Crime and Gambling*. Washington, DC: U.S. Government Printing Office.

Walker, S. (1994). *Sense and Nonsense About Crime and Drugs: A Policy Guide* (3d ed). Belmont, CA: Wadsworth.

A scam often involves a quiet change in ownership or management of a business, where a large bank deposit is used to establish a credit rating. Then large orders are placed. Once the goods are received, they are quickly liquidated, management disappears, and the company is forced into bankruptcy by its competitors (De Franco, 1973).

It has been argued that the savings and loan scandal of the 1980s is an example of such a scam. The deregulation of the banking industry during this period provided for more lenient borrowing and lending provisions. This led to speculative, high-risk and fraudulent transactions. As Pontell and Calavita (1993) note, "some of the transactions were legitimate, if foolhardy, attempts to raise capital; others were outright scams involving insiders, borrowers, Wall Street brokers, and developers" (Pontell and Calavita, 1993:34). The U.S. General Accounting Office investigated 26 of the most costly bank failures in the savings and loan crisis. They found that the bank was the victim of fraud and abuse *in every case*. In one case, a majority stockholder used $2 million of institutional funds to buy a beach house, and spent an additional $500,000 for household expenses (U.S. Comptroller General, 1989).

Irresponsible and illegal behavior on such a large scale has been called "collective embezzlement" (Calavita and Pontell, 1991:100). This suggests siphoning off (or "looting") institutional funds for personal gain, with at least the implied endorsement of the management. This method of bankrupting a legitimate business historically has been associated with force and extortionate threats. The case of the savings and loans industry in the 1980s illustrates that this is not always the case. It is not necessary that thieves come from outside the institution, nor is it necessary that they threaten the institution's managers. Simply put, it is possible "to make an offer they can't refuse" by merely creating an environment where lax regulatory controls make stealing not only profitable, but an accepted business practice.

If we reserve the term "organized crime" for continuing conspiracies that include the corruption of government officials, "then much of the savings and loan scandal involved organized crime" Pontell and Calavita, 1993:39). Pontell and Calavita's interviews with regulatory agencies, agents of the U.S. Federal Bureau of Investigation, and Secret Service investigators uncovered a "recurring theme" of conspiratorial arrangements between "insiders"—savings and loan officials—and "outsiders"—accountants, lawyers, real estate agents, and developers (Calavita and Pontell, 1993:530). A comparison of these fraudulent arrangements in the savings and loan industry with more traditional organized crime infiltration of legitimate business—through no-show jobs at construction sites, or pay-offs for "protection"—show them to be more similar than different. For example, Charles Keating made large political contributions as head of Lincoln Savings and Loan that resulted in five U.S. Senators intervening on his behalf in a regulatory matter. This caused a delay which ultimately cost taxpayers an additional $2 billion, when the bank failed (Mayer, 1990). How this differs from corruption of government officials by members of traditional organized crime groups is not a matter of kind or, in many cases, even a matter of degree. As the U.S. National Advisory Committee on Criminal Justice Standards and Goals (1976) has recognized, "the perpetrators of organized crime may include corrupt business executives, members of the professions, public officials, or members of any other occupation group, in addition to the conventional racketeer element."

The Pizza Connection

The so-called "Pizza Connection" case involved an elaborate drug-smuggling operation that began in Turkey and ended with distribution of heroin through pizza parlors in the U.S. It culminated in a case that ended in one of the longest and most complex trials in U.S. history, covering 18 months and 22 defendants.

The use of pizza parlors as a front for illegal activity was the end of an international drug conspiracy between organized crime groups in Sicily and New York. Tons of morphine were smuggled from Turkey to Sicily, where they were processed into heroin. Then, the heroin was smuggled through U.S. airports and distributed through pizza parlors in the Northeast and Midwest. Finally, illegal profits in excess of $40 million were funnelled back to Sicily in a money-laundering scheme that involved banks in the Bahamas, Bermuda, New York and Switzerland.

Eighteen defendants ultimately were convicted, most notably Gaetano Badalamenti, a former leader of the Sicilian Mafia, and Salvatore Catalano, a New York City bakery owner with ties to organized crime. The pizza connection case was perhaps one of the most sophisticated drug importation and distribution conspiracies ever to be exposed. It clearly illustrates how linkage is established between legitimate businesses (i.e., pizza parlors and banks) and their knowing misuse to engage in illegal acts (i.e., distribute heroin and accept and transfer large sums of cash in small

small denominations with no questions asked). (For interesting summaries of the Pizza Connection case, see Blumenthal, *Last Days of the Sicilians: The FBI Assault on the Pizza Connection* [New York: Times Books, 1988]; Alexander, *The Pizza Connection: Lawyers, Money, Drugs, Mafia* [New York: Weidenfeld and Nicolson, 1988]; and Baer and Duffy, "Inside America's Biggest Drug Bust," *U.S. News and World Report*, 104 [April 11, 1988], pp.18-29.)

A typology of infiltration of legitimate business is shown in Table 2.

Table 2: Typology of Infiltration of Legitimate Business

Type of Infiltration	Nature of Activity	Harm
Scam	Using a legitimate business primarily as a "front" for illegal activity (e.g., pizza parlors to launder drug money).	* To government in tax evasion. * To other businesses in non-competitive practices. * Use of coercion and/or co-optation.
Corruption	"Bleeding" a legitimate business of its profits through illegal means (e.g., no-show jobs, creative bookkeeping).	* Legitimate profits siphoned. * Business can be bankrupted. * Use of coercion and/or co-optation.

Business-Type Activities of Organized Crime

An important study of business activities engaged in by organized crime was conducted by Edelhertz and Overcast (1990). They analyzed 167 indictments and civil complaints occurring over a two-year period in a purposive sample taken from state and federal investigators and prosecutors of organized crime. The business-type activities they examined formed a continuum from strictly legal businesses, to legal businesses that were conduits for illegal activity, to illegal businesses that were a vehicle for legal activity, and to entirely illegal businesses.

Edelhertz and Overcast (1990) found "no consensus" regarding any preferred method by which organized crime either establishes new businesses or infiltrates existing ones. They found patterns to depend on local concerns regarding market, competition and opportunity. Indeed, as they conclude, "there is no reason to think that organized criminal groups act differently than other businessmen when they acquire an interest in a business" (Edelhertz and Overcast, 1990:114). These groups follow accepted business procedures and respond to the demands of the marketplace.

Scams involving the use of a legitimate business as a front for illegal activity can range from the wholesale meat industry to the savings and loan industry. In both cases, offenders (be they organized crime figures or "legitimate" businesspersons) misuse a lawfully existing business for purposes of exploiting its assets for personal gain.

The data gathered by Edelhertz and Overcast (1990) are reanalyzed here to assess a method designed to predict infiltration of business by organized crime. The analysis is presented later in this chapter.

CORRUPTION OF A LEGITIMATE BUSINESS

In many cases of infiltration, the purpose is not to steal from the business until it is bankrupt. Instead, it makes more sense to misuse the business so as to provide a steady source of illegal income without endangering its survival, i.e., using the golden goose without killing it. This was clearly the objective in the savings and loan scandal, although the extent of the abuse was so great, the banks failed. There exist several fascinating case studies of organized crime infiltration of legitimate business, however, where conspiracies work as intended: exploiting a business in illegal ways without bankrupting it.

The New York City Construction Industry

A massive investigation of corruption and racketeering in the New York City construction industry was carried out by the New York State Organized Crime Task Force (1990). The task force report found that control of construction unions was the "base of power and influence in the industry" by organized crime, together with direct interests in contracting and construction supply companies. This hidden interest in construction companies was accomplished by using "nominees" who "fronted" for the company on public records for purposes of certificates of incorporation, accounting, licensing and permits (New York State Organized Crime Task

Force, 1990). For example, the report found that Anthony Salerno, later convicted as the "boss" of the Genovese crime family in New York City, controlled Certified, one of the two major concrete suppliers in Manhattan. Paul Castellano, boss of the Gambino crime family until his murder in 1985, controlled Scara-Mix Concrete Company, which was owned by his son.

In other cases, it was discovered that known organized crime figures were openly listed as owners, managers or principals of construction companies. Salvatore Gravano, counselor to John Gotti, was president of the JJS Construction Company. John Gotti, Jr., is president of the Sampson Trucking Company, and John Gotti, convicted boss of the Gambino crime family (and convicted for the murder of Paul Castellano) held the position of salesman for the ARC Plumbing Company. Even though these individuals were sometimes found to have very little to do with the business that employed them, such an "on-the-books" profession "provides a legitimate position in the community and a reportable source of income" (New York State Organized Crime Task Force, 1990:85).

The ability of organized crime interests to infiltrate the construction industry in New York City was promoted by several factors. Unlike most industries, the employment of a construction worker lies in the hands of the union, rather than the employer. The unions have been all too easy for racketeers to control and exploit because there historically has been no oversight of union affairs, despite a number of criminal prosecutions. Dissidents within the unions have had little success because the unions have effective control over layoffs, blacklisting, and physical intimidation (New York State Organized Crime Task Force, 1990). Added to union control is the construction marketplace itself, where there are a large number of contractors and subcontractors, with many small firms among them, all locked in intense competition. This makes legitimate businesses vulnerable to extortion. Racketeers can coerce payoffs by threatening loss of labor, loss of supplies, delays or property damage. Likewise, businesses can be easily corrupted when given competitive advantages by powerful racketeering elements, such as "sweetheart" contracts (to avoid some union requirements) and cartels that allocate contracts among favored firms.

The Business of Garbage Collection

Reuter et al. (1983) conducted a case study of the garbage (solid waste) collection business in New York City and also in an unnamed northeastern state. In both cases, they found the market to be dominated by small partnerships or family corporations. Reuter et al. (1983) found that the garbage collection business "has a longstanding reputation for anti-competitive practices and racketeer involvement" (pp.10-13). The investigators discovered there are "mutual benefits derived by entrepreneurs and criminals in the operation of cartel arrangements," where independent businesses are organized into a "cartel" that prevents open and fair competition in the marketplace (Reuter et al., 1983:13). As a result, the role of the infiltrating racketeers centers around disputes about "customer allocation agreements" in dividing up the garbage collection market. Corruption characterizes the role of organized crime in this instance, more than does extortion. Indeed, as Reuter et al. observe, "policies which assume that the racketeers are parasites on unwilling hosts, and that the legitimate entrepreneurs would welcome a clean-up of the industry, are doomed to failure" (p.13).

Rebovich's (1992) study of 71 cases of hazardous waste crime in four states found "little evidence," based on his case analysis and interviews with law enforcement officials, that syndicate (traditional organized) crime has established strong control of the hazardous waste transport and disposal industry. Nevertheless, those cases connected to organized crime were found to be "among the most flagrant offenders," with many firms dumping hazardous waste illegally at the highest levels and for the longest periods (Rebovich, 1992:103-104).

Predicting the Infiltration of Legitimate Business by Organized Crime

If the conditions that give rise to the infiltration of organized crime into legitimate businesses could be predicted, lawful businesses, law enforcement agencies and the general public could realize major benefits. Police resources would not be wasted on fruitless investigations, regulatory personnel could be allocated more rationally according to which industries are predicted to be especially vulnerable, and the long-range interests of the community would be better served through a concentration on truly serious organized misbehavior.

The good news is that criminological prediction models have proved to be fairly simple. Therefore, they are easily adopted in practice. A number of states and the federal government are using probation, parole, and sentencing guidelines that are based on prediction models. These models utilize the experience of past probation or parole candidates, or those awaiting sentences, and compare it with similar current cases to help make an informed judgment.

A prediction model merely summarizes the experience of the past to use as a guide in making decisions that affect the future. Given the case studies discussed earlier of the infiltration of legitimate business by organized crime, there appear to be common elements that can be isolated.

Albini (1971) found that an important factor in both business and personal relationships involving organized crime was "patronage." Obviously, in certain markets there are individuals who hold positions of power and influence ("patrons"), who can help others ("clients") requiring their assistance. A patron-client relationship forms as a natural consequence of these conditions. For example, in certain businesses it may be difficult to obtain a license or loan, or to attract customers. If a financially or politically influential patron can assist in overcoming these problems, a patron-client relationship is formed. Now, the client owes his patron money or favors, which may result in a wide variety of illicit activities such as loansharking, political "favors" or extortion. This relationship can become extended throughout a business or market when the client later acts as a patron for someone with less power and influence. The result, according to Albini (1971), is the emergence of "powerful syndicate figures who serve as patrons to their functionaries [and who] may also serve as clients to others more powerful than they" (p.265). It is reasonable to hypothesize, therefore, that poorly trained owners or managers, who are ill equipped to deal with business problems, are more likely to become targets (potential clients) for organized crime infiltration than are professional, well-trained, and well-equipped operators.

Borrowing from general organization theory, Smith (1980) hypothesized that organized crime develops in the same manner as does legitimate business. That is, it responds to the "task environment" of a market, consisting of customers, suppliers, regulators and competitors. Like legitimate business, organized crime attempts to survive and make a profit while dealing with the pressures of its task environment (Smith, 1980).

Applying the Model in Practice

Extrapolating from Smith's and Albini's explanations, it would appear that certain types of business conditions (i.e., configurations of customers, suppliers, regulators, competitors and patron-client relationships) would be more conducive to organized crime infiltration than others. An application of the principles of Smith's theory of enterprise to Reuter et al.'s investigation of the garbage collection industry in New York City found corresponding conditions: it was easy for individuals to enter the market (little regulation); the industry was populated by numerous "small, frequently family-based, enterprises" with little difference in service among vendors (open competition in a market of nonprofessional managers); there was inelastic demand for the service (customers always available); and many firms were identified with "minimal capital and no reserve equipment" (supply for illicit patrons). In fact, when one examines the circumstances of infiltration in the New York City construction industry, or even the massive savings and loan scandal, there appear to be common factors in each case.

Table 3 summarizes the prediction model. The first four predictors are taken from Smith's use of organization theory, the fifth from Albini's notion of patron-client relationships, while the sixth (prior history) is taken from previous research in criminological prediction (Gottfredson et al., 1978; Simon, 1971) that has found prior record to be predictive of criminal behavior.

A PARTIAL EMPIRICAL TEST

The data collected by Edelhertz and Overcast (1990), mentioned earlier, provide an opportunity to examine both the typology and parts of the prediction model presented here. They collected 167 cases in a non-random sample of case files from 23 jurisdictions around the U.S.

Part of the data the researchers coded were the "purposes of providing legal goods and services" in the organized crime cases they examined. The reason was to assess why and how organized crime elements used legitimate businesses to advance criminal purposes. They identified 10 different purposes. Table 4 presents these purposes as they fit within the typology presented earlier.

Table 3: Predicting Organized Crime Infiltration Into Legitimate Business

Predictors	Low Risk	High Risk
Supply	Few available small, financially weak businesses	Readily available small, financially weak businesses
Customers	Elastic demand for product	Inelastic demand for product
Regulators	Difficult to enter market	Easy to enter market
Competitors	Monopoly/oligopoly controlled market	Open market with many small firms
Patronage	Entrepreneurs are professional, educated managers	Entrepreneurs are non-professionals ill-equipped to deal with business problems
Prior record	No prior history of organized crime involvement in market	Prior history of organized crime infiltration in industry

Table 4: Purposes of Providing Legal Goods and Services in Actual Organized Crime Cases

Scam	Corruption
*Front for Illegal Activities (69 cases) *Source of Illicit Profits (44) *Provide Oppor. for Illegal Activity (40) *Launder Money (12) *Sell Stolen Property (4)	*Source of Legitimate Profit (84 cases) *Protect Person from Crim. Activity (27) *Generate Money for Illegal Activity (7) *Provide Jobs (5) *Influence Public Officials (3)

Table 4 illustrates how the 10 purposes for providing legal goods and services in organized crime cases correspond to the typology. Of the 295 responses (more than one purpose could be noted for each case), 57% were characteristic of scams (where a legitimate business is used as a "front" for primarily legal activity). Infiltration of business characterized by corruption (where a legitimate business is "bled" of its profits through coercion or extortion) occurred 43% of the time. This suggests that organized crime uses legitimate businesses for one of two general types of reasons that correspond to the typology.

Table 5: Legal Business Activities in Organized Crime Cases

Business Type	Cases	Specific Businesses
Transportation/Shipping	14	Container handling, Moving services, Solid/Toxic waste disposal, transportation services, air freight, limos, tow-truck services.
Construction/Manufacturing	13	Commercial construction, manufacturing.
Labor/Union Administration	35	Employee fund admin, union admin, labor relations consulting.
Financial Services	18	Banking, mortgage lending, pension-investments mgt, financial services, insurance sales, real estate, coins (investment), securities trading/invest.
Adult Entertainment	14	Adult bookstores, adult entertainment, escort services, massage parlors.
Food and Lodging	20	Bar/tavern, fast food-pizza, hotel-motel, restaurant mgt, food products.
Parts and Supplies	15	Linen supplies, building materials, auto parts, equipment repair, mail order services.
General Services	17	Retail/wholesale sales, health spa, auto sales, photography studio, city government/law enforcement (3), legal casinos/other legal gambling (2 cases).

Edelhertz and Overcast's (1990) study identified 49 different legal business activities that occurred in the 167 cases they examined. These ranged from adult bookstores to union administration. Due to the small sample size, and a large number of legal business activities, these business activities were grouped by type into eight categories. These are presented in Table 5.

Grouping the sample into such broad categories may mask variations that exist within the 49 different types of businesses identified in the study (especially in the overly broad "general services" category), but a much larger sample of data would be necessary to examine the 49 business activities individually.

Method

After grouping the legal business activities in the sample by type (Table 5), criminal offenses charged were grouped into two categories according to the typology of organized crime presented in Table 1. Offenses were grouped because of their diversity (59 distinct crimes were charged one or more times in the sample of 167 cases). The two offense groups are presented in Table 6. These offenses were combined and grouped into two aggregate variables that became the criterion for a limited empirical test. Clearly, some overlap probably exists between these two categories of offenses, but an assessment of each offense individually would require a significantly larger data set.

A total of 22 independent variables were created, using the data collected by Edelhertz and Overcast. They collected information on more than 300 often related variables. Therefore, a number of variables were created to serve as potential indicators of organized crime infiltration of legitimate business, or the provision of illicit goods and services.

The 22 aggregate independent variables were of eight different types. They are summarized in Table 7. The independent variables are employed to investigate the extent to which organized crime infiltration and the provision of illicit goods and services can be predicted by: different types of organized crime group involvement, violence, reputation, types of business, purposes for providing legal goods and services, objectives of the business organization, market factors, and ways in which a business provides for its members. These independent variables correspond to some, but not all, of the factors hypothesized in the prediction model presented in Table 3. Information about suppliers, customers, regulators, competitors and methods of business operation have to be inferred from the data gathered, a problem common to secondary analyses of studies originally conducted for other purposes.

Table 6: Offense Groupings by Type of Organized Crime Activity

Offenses Characteristic of Provision of Illicit Goods and Services	Offenses Characteristic of Infiltration of Legitimate Business
-Drug Trafficking -Possession-drugs -Gambling-numbers -Gambling-sports -Possession-gambling records -Interstate transport-gambling devices -Fencing -Possession-stolen property -Possession-contraband -Interstate transportation-stolen property -Smuggling -Prostitution -Sexual exploitation of minor -Pornography -Interstate transportation-obscene matter -Loansharking -Possession-usurious loan records -Usury -Money laundering	-Bribery -Bid-rigging -Embezzlement -Extortion -Forgery -Fraud against government -False statements/filings -Fraud -Interstate transport-forged securities -Kickbacks -Public corruption -Racketeering -Securities fraud -Tax violations -Threat financial/economic harm -Union corruption -Threat/violence

Table 7: Independent Variables

Independent Variables Used as Potential Predictors

-Type of Organized Crime Group Involved (1 variable)
  (local syndicate v. Cosa Nostra/Labor Union)
-Violence (1)
  (aggregate variable of 7 charges from extortion to murder)
-Reputation for Violence (1)
-Type of Business
  (8 possible business categories from Table 5)
-Purposes of Providing Legal Goods and Services (4)
  (legal/illegal income, corruption/protection/jobs, front/launder)
-Objectives of the Business Organization (2)
  (allocate the market, protect the organization)
-Type of Market for the Illegal Goods and Services (2)
  (monopoly, competitive)
-Method Business Financially Supports Members (3)
  (Legal jobs, illegal jobs, money/property)

Table 8: Alternate Methods of Combining Predictors

Prediction Method	Advantages	Disadvantages
Burgess "Unit Scoring" Method	-All predictors have equal weight. Unlike other prediction methods, this is less likely to over-fit results to a particular sample.	-Ignores possible intercorrelations among predictors.
Multiple Linear Regression	-Accounts for intercorrelations among predictors. -The contribution of each predictor can be measured precisely.	-Assumes a linear relation between predictors and criterion. -Assumes regression weights are representative of any subgroups within sample.
Predictive Attribute Analysis	-Makes no assumption of linearity. -Allows for heterogeneity within the sample.	-Splitting sample on a single predictor creates risk of over-fitting predictors to sample. Validation sample needed.

The independent variables were combined using predictive attribute analysis. This prediction method involves identifying the single factor most predictive of the criterion and splitting the sample by the presence or absence of this characteristic. The two resulting subgroups are then reexamined to find the single best predictor for each subgroup, and they are divided again along this attribute. The procedure continues until no further factors can be found that are significantly associated with the criterion (MacNaughton-Smith, 1963). Predictive attribute analysis was chosen over other competing methods to combine predictors, due to the comparatively small sample size in this study and the limitations of other prediction techniques. The pros and cons of alternate statistical methods of combining predictors are presented in Table 8.

Due to the probability of distinct subgroups (of businesses and crimes) in the sample, and a small sample size, the Burgess Method and multiple regression were not employed. Predictive attribute analysis allows for a process of sorting through a number of competing independent variables to examine their significance, in hierarchical fashion, in predicting the criterion. Because each variable is examined solely in its relation to the criterion, "it may sometimes be useful to include several dichotomized forms of the same variable" to see which is the best predictor (Smith, 1971:91). Therefore, overlapping variables are desirable in predictive attribute analysis. The precise method of combining predictors may not make much difference in practice, because comparative studies of the predictive utility of various methods have found little difference in result, despite the theoretical pros and cons of each (Smith, 1972; Gottfredson et al., 1977).

The results of the predictive attribute analyses are presented in Figures 1 and 2. Figure 1 presents the results of the analysis to predict charges involving the infiltration of legitimate business. Figure 2 presents the results of the analysis to predict charges associated with the provision of illicit goods and services. Although the infiltration of business is the primary focus of this study, illicit goods and services were also included to assess the extent to which this category of organized crime can be predicted from the variables in this sample.

As Figure 1 indicates, there were four subgroups found to be predictive of charges of infiltration of business. The subgroups were: (1) businesses not related to adult entertainment (adult bookstores, escort services, massage parlors, and adult entertainment), businesses not related to labor unions (union or employee fund administration, labor relations consultation), and no charges of violence-related crimes (charges for murder, aggravated assault, attempted murder, extortion, threats of violence, firearms violations, weapons possession); (2) charges of violence-related crimes; (3) labor union-related activities, and no charges of violence; and (4) businesses related to adult entertainment, non-labor-union-related activities, and no charges for crimes associated with violence. (The stopping rule employed for the predictive attributive analysis was defined as the point at which the cases in any subgroup dropped below 20.) These subgroups are summarized in Table 9.

Figure 1: Predictive Attribute Analysis 1
Criterion: Charges Associated with Infiltration of Business

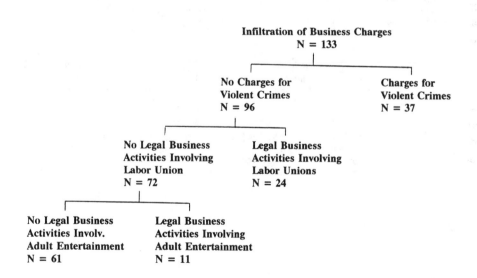

Figure 2: Predictive Attribute Analysis 2
Criterion: Charges Involving Provision of Illicit Goods and Services

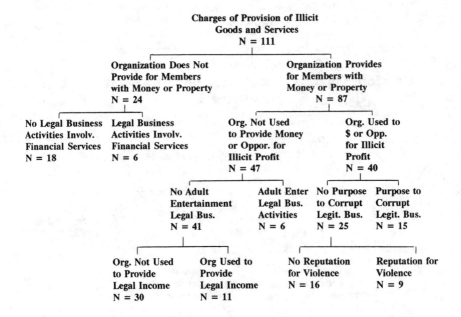

As Table 9 indicates, the first subgroup was the largest, accounting for 46% of the infiltration cases charged in this sample. The fourth subgroup (violence) accounted for 28% of the cases. Together, then, these two categories accounted for 74% of the infiltration of business cases in this sample. This means that violence-related charges alone—or lack of these charges—when associated with activities other than labor unions and adult entertainment, are the two best predictor-combinations in explaining ultimate charges involving the infiltration of legitimate business.

Validation of these results on another sample is imperative, as "shrinkage" commonly occurs upon validation, primarily because of over-fitting predictors to a particular sample (Albanese et al., 1981). Nevertheless, if these predictive categories hold up upon validation, it would suggest that violence is a good predictor in suspected cases of infiltration by itself, although violence does not appear necessary when examining non-labor union and non-adult entertainment businesses. These findings suggest several distinct subgroupings of characteristics that may be predictive of organized crime infiltration of business. Greater specifics and clarity in this effort will be forthcoming when other samples are collected, and when additional variables are coded and tested that correspond more closely with the prediction model presented in this chapter.

Table 9: Predictive Categories for Infiltration of Legitimate Business

Group	Predictor Variables	Percent of Total Charges (N=133)
1	-Business not related to adult entertainment -Business not related to labor union activity -No violent crimes alleged	46%
2	-Violent crimes alleged	28%
3	-Business related to labor union activity -No violent crimes alleged	18%
4	-Business related to adult entertainment -Business not related to labor union activity -No violent crimes alleged	8%

Table 10: Predictive Categories for Provision of Illicit Goods and Services

Group	Predictor Variables	Percent Total Charges (N=111)
1	-Purpose of business is not to provide source of legal income -Legal business not related to adult entertainment -Purpose of business is not for illegal income source -Org. does not provide for members with money or property	27%
2	-Legal business not related to financial services -Org. does not provide for members with money or property	16%
3	-No reputation for violence -Purpose of business is not to corrupt business or government -Purpose of business is to provide illegal income -Organization provides for members with money or property	15%
4	-Purpose of business is to corrupt business or government -Purpose of business is to provide illegal income -Organization provides for members with money or property	14%
5	-Purpose of business is to provide legal income source -Legal business is not related to adult entertainment -Purpose of business is not for illegal income source -Organization provides for members with money or property	10%
6	-Reputation for violence -Purpose of business is not to corrupt business or government -Purpose of business is to provide illegal income -Organization provides for members with money or property	8%
7	-Legal business is related to adult entertainment -Purpose of business is not for illegal income source -Organization provides for members with money or property	5%
8	-Legal business is related to financial services -Org. does not provide for members with money or property	5%

As Figure 2 illustrates, the subgroupings predictive of illicit goods and services were more numerous and more complex than for the infiltration of legitimate business. The total of eight categories would undoubtedly be reduced upon validation, when one acknowledges the results of other prediction studies in the behavioral sciences (see Simon, 1971:5-8, 91). The first four groups accounted for 72% of the cases, as Table 10 indicates. Clearly, the purposes of the business (in the provision of legal goods and services) appears relevant, as does the manner in which the organization provides for its members. Similar to the case for the infiltration of business, predicting the provision of illicit goods and services may require distinct constellations of variables, depending on the nature of the goods or service provided, or other unmeasured factors. Nearly every variable used in this study, including the criterion variables, were aggregate variables resulting from the secondary analysis. It is possible that a larger sample would enable a more detailed analysis of the nature, types and reasons for distinct subgroupings of predictor variables.

Of the 22 independent variables studied, it is remarkable that two were not found to be predictors in either of the analyses conducted here. First, the *type of organized crime group* involved (Cosa Nostra, local syndicate, etc.) was not a significant predictor in either analysis. This suggests that the focus on organized crime *groups* in the existing literature could be misplaced (see, for example, U.S. President's Commission on Organized Crime, 1987), and might be replaced by an emphasis on the *activities* carried out for these appear to be much better predictors of organized crime. Second, the type of market involved (monopoly versus competitive market) was not significantly related to the criterion in either analysis. This contradicts a significant body of literature on organized crime (and one of the factors in the prediction model proposed in this paper). Validation on another sample would render a more conclusive finding on the importance of this factor.

Limitations

There may exist a more disparate (or congruent) relationship between the predicted and actual predictive factors that is masked by this second-ary analysis. The eight categories in Table 5 involve diverse groupings of businesses that a larger sample would not require. Local business condi-tions were not examined in the original study, making it impossible to account for local variations in the predictor variables (supply, customers, regulators, competitors, patronage and prior record).

Importantly, the study reanalyzed here examined only business activities present in actual organized crime cases. No attempt was made to examine businesses in these locations *without organized crime problems* (or those with problems against whom cases have not yet been made). Without such information, it is impossible to assess the *comparative risk* of businesses for organized crime infiltration in any one locale.

There are other limitations of this study, most of which result from problems inherent in all prediction research. First, the model may be "overfitted" to the available empirical research. There have been comparatively few detailed, empirical investigations of organized crime infiltration into legitimate business. The studies conducted thus far may not be typical and, therefore, the model's factors may be fitted to non-representative cases or industries. Additional data are necessary to determine whether this model should be modified.

Second, a "base-rate" problem may hamper the design of a prediction model; the proportion of businesses that have problems with organized crime infiltration may be too small to develop an efficient prediction model. Simply stated, the more uncommon an event, the more difficult it is to predict accurately. The base rate for various industries can only be determined through further empirical research.

Finally, the measurement of such variables as "supply," "competitors" and the other predictors shown in the model can be difficult. Factors such as "financial condition," "types of supplier" and "competitive conditions" are nominal or, at best, ordinal measures of a business situation. Therefore, the ordering of these variables involves some creativity on the part of the investigator. Investigators must examine carefully the measurement units employed in scaling predictive factors to guard against the masking of any true predictive relationship based on inappropriate counting or measurement units. Table 11 summarizes the major limitations of the model and this research in its current form.

Possibilities

Despite the limitations noted here, there are two major reasons to believe that a prediction model may form the foundation for a more useful approach to the investigation of organized crime. First, a model with few predictive factors, as described in Table 3, may well include all the important factors. Criminological prediction models have been found, generally, to have a limited number of important predictor variables. In fact, Gottfredson and Gottfredson (1980) maintain that little predictive accuracy is gained by the inclusion of large numbers of variables in a prediction model. Therefore, a six-variable model does not necessarily oversimplify the situation.

Table 11: Some Unanswered Questions

Problems	How to Fix Them
1. Sample used here to test model is non-representative, small, and consists only of cases actually made (and does not address businesses in general *which are at risk*).	1. Need a larger, representative sample of *businesses* in several jurisdictions that includes *both* those involved and *not involved* in organized crime cases.
2. This study ignores *local conditions* that may affect the susceptibility of certain types of businesses to infiltration.	2. A future study should look at *several jurisdictions in detail*, so that the ranking of businesses can account for unique local circumstances.
3. Problems inherent in all prediction research: *base rate* of infiltrated businesses may be too small to develop efficient model, *measurement* problems in assessing (at least ordinally) the variables in the six-factor model.	3. Other prediction research has shown low predictive accuracy can still be *useful in distinguishing* *"risk" categories* (e.g., parole guidelines), and inter-coder reliability studies can reduce arbitrariness in measurement.

Second, the prediction model does not necessarily have to predict business conditions conducive to organized crime infiltration with a high degree of accuracy in order to be useful. For example, probation and parole prediction devices have found models with relatively low predictive efficiency to be useful in distinguishing "high-risk" groups of offenders from "low-risk" groups. In this way, supervision or release decisions can be based on something more rational than "unguided discretion" (Gottfred-son et al., 1978; Albanese et al., 1981). Likewise, the classification of high-risk and low-risk markets may be useful to both regulators of industry and investigators of organized crime, even if precise prediction of organized crime activity within individual businesses is not possible.

An analog to this procedure has already been attempted in case-screen-ing techniques developed for use by police. The Rochester (NY) Police Department developed a system called "Early Case Closure" where infor-mation was gathered to assess the "solvability" of robberies and burglaries. By directing their resources toward crimes with the best chance of solution (and by spending less time on cases with little chance of solution), the department was able to significantly improve its clearance rates for those crimes (Block and Bell, 1976). A similar effort was undertaken by the Stanford Research Institute and the Police Executive Research Forum. They developed a model for screening burglary cases, based on factors associated with the crime. Applying the system retrospectively, it was possible to predict whether a burglary case would be solved 85% of the time (Greenberg, 1975). In an analogous way, industry regulators and police officials can reduce the amount of time spent on dead-end investi-gations that invariably occur in proactive and regulatory enforcement, with the use of a prediction model like the one proposed here. A regulatory or police agency could use such a model as a screening device in its jurisdiction. Investigative resources could be focused on those markets identified as "high risk" for infiltration, and perhaps less time would be wasted on investigations that do not lead to prosecution.

Most often, organized crime investigations *follow* the leads of infor-mants or of hunches of investigators, rather than being truly proactive. The problem with proactive investigations is that often a great deal of time and resources are wasted in pursuing unfounded leads. As a result, many law enforcement agencies make non-serious organized crime cases involv-ing drug sales or gambling operations, and ignore organized crime linkages to legitimate businesses altogether. The prediction model proposed here would permit the screening of businesses, incorporate local conditions, reduce wasted time on investigative dead-ends, and better serve the long-range interests of the community in concentrating on the most serious forms of organized crime activity.

REFERENCES

Albanese, J. (1995). *White-Collar Crime in America.* Englewood Cliffs, NJ: Prentice-Hall.

—— B.A. Fiore, J.H. Powell, and J.R. Storti (1981). *Is Probation Working: A Guide for Managers and Methodologists.* Lanham, MD: University Press of America.

Albini, J.L. (1971). *The American Mafia: Genesis of a Legend.* New York, NY: Irvington.

Alexander, S. (1988). *The Pizza Connection: Lawyers, Money, Drugs, Mafia.* New York: Weidenfeld and Nicolson.

Baer, D. and B. Duffy (1988). "Inside America's Biggest Drug Bust." *U.S. News and World Report* 104(April 11):18-29.

Bloch, P.B. and J. Bell (1976). *Managing Investigations: The Rochester System.* Washington, DC: Police Foundation.

Blumenthal, R. (1988). *Last Days of the Sicilians: The FBI Assault on the Pizza Connection.* New York: Times Books.

Calavita, K. and H.N. Pontell (1990). "'Heads I Win, Tails You Lose': Deregulation, Crime and Crisis in the Savings and Loan Industry." *Crime & Delinquency* 36(3):309-341.

—— (1991). "Other People's Money Revisited: Collective Embezzlement in the Savings and Loan and Insurance Industries." *Social Problems* 38(1):94-112.

—— (1993). "Savings and Loan Fraud as Organized Crime: Toward a Conceptual Typology of Corporate Crime." *Criminology* 31(4):519-548.

De Franco, E.J. (1973). *Anatomy of a Scam: A Case Study of a Planned Bankruptcy by Organized Crime.* Washington, DC: U.S. Government Printing Office.

Edelhertz, H. and T.D. Overcast (1990). *Organized Crime Business-Type Activities and Their Implications for Law Enforcement.* Washington, DC: U.S. National Institute of Justice.

Gottfredson, D.M., T. Wilkins and P.B. Hoffman (1978). *Guidelines for Parole and Sentencing: A Policy Control Method.* Lexington, MA: Lexington Books.

—— and M.R. Gottfredson (1980). *Decision Making in Criminal Justice: Toward a Rational Exercise of Discretion.* Cambridge, MA: Ballinger.

Gottfredson, S.D., D.M. Gottfredson and L.T. Wilkins (1977). "A Comparison of Prediction Methods." In: D.M. Gottfredson ed. *Classification for Parole Decision Policy.* Albany, NY: Criminal Justice Research Center.

Greenberg, D. (1975). *Felony Investigation Decision Model: An Analysis of Investigative Elements of Information.* Menlo Park, CA: Stanford Research Institute.

MacNaughton-Smith, P. (1963). "The Classification of Individuals by the Possession of Attributes Associated with a Criterion." *Biometrics* 19(June):364-366.

Mayer, M. (1990). *The Greatest Ever Bank Robbery: The Collapse of the Savings and Loan Industry*. New York: Scribner's.

New York State Organized Crime Task Force (1990). *Corruption and Racketeering in the New York City Construction Industry*. New York: New York University Press.

Pontell, H.N. and K. Calavita (1993). "White-Collar Crime in the Savings and Loan Scandal." *Annals of the American Academy of Political and Social Science* 525 (Jan.):31-45.

Rebovich, D.J. (1992). *Dangerous Ground: The World of Hazardous Waste Crime*. New Brunswick, NJ: Transaction.

Reuter, P., J. Rubinstein and S. Wynn (1983). *Racketeering in Legitimate Industries: Two Case Studies*. Washington, DC: U.S. National Institute of Justice.

Simon, F.H. (1971). *Prediction Methods in Criminology*. London: Her Majesty's Stationery Office.

—— (1972). "Statistical Methods of Making Prediction Instruments." *Journal of Research in Crime and Delinquency* 9(Jan.):46-53.

Smith, D.C. (1980). "Paragons, Pariahs, and Pirates: A Spectrum-Based Theory of Enterprise." *Crime & Delinquency* 26(July):358-386.

U.S. Comptroller General (1989). *Failed Thrifts: Costly Failures Resulted from Regulatory Violations and Unsafe Practices*. Washington, DC: U.S. General Accounting Office.

U.S. National Advisory Committee on Criminal Justice Standards and Goals (1976). *Report of the Task Force on Organized Crime*. Washington, DC: U.S. Government Printing Office.

U.S. President's Commission on Organized Crime (1987). *Organized Crime Today*. Washington, DC: U.S. Government Printing Office.

Organizing Crime in "Copperhead County": An Ethnographic Look at Rural Crime Networks

by

Gary Potter

and

Larry Gaines

Abstract: *An ethnographic study describes criminal enterprises operating in rural "Copperhead County," Kentucky. Despite the differences between rural populations and urban populations, criminal enterprises in rural Appalachian counties appear to have many of the same characteristics as their urban counterparts. Criminal enterprises in Appalachia are highly adaptable, flexible and able to respond to changes in the market, in the political environment, or in law enforcement strategies with the same ease as their big city counterparts. The exigencies of the illicit market, rather than any specific organizational design or regional differences, are thus the prime explanatory factors in the organization of criminal enterprises.*

INTRODUCTION

Discussions of organized crime in America tend to focus almost exclusively on the activities of urban crime groups, with a particularly heavy emphasis on organized crime groups operating in New York and Chicago (Albanese, 1989; Albanese and Pursley, 1993). Despite the urban slant of the scholarly and popular literature on organized crime, it is abundantly clear that criminal enterprises also operate in rural areas of the U.S. Aside from the occasional reference to the "Dixie Mafia," these rural criminal enterprises have escaped serious inquiry (c.f. Abadinsky, 1986; Hunter, 1983; Schmidt, 1984).

This chapter explores criminal enterprises operating in one rural county in Kentucky, which shall be called "Copperhead County." Copper head County was selected because it has a long and documented history of involvement in criminal enterprise, and has been much in the public view recently as a result of several journalistic examinations of Kentucky's involvement in the production and distribution of illicit drugs (Caudill, 1983; Gazaway, 1969; Lee, 1981; Richardson, 1986; Tapp and Klotter, 1977). Through the use of a field research methodology, attempts have been made to document the scope of illegal entrepreneurship in the county, specifying as much as possible the nature of illicit markets, and the means of coordination and management used by criminal entrepreneurs. It is hoped that this exploration of rural organized crime will add a new dimension to the extant literature on organized crime in general, and will test some of the fundamental propositions about criminal organizations and illicit markets in a non-traditional setting.

METHODOLOGY

Data for this chapter were gathered in a relatively simple manner. First, historical, sociological, and anthropological studies of the area in which Copperhead County is located were reviewed, and historical and contemporaneous information about crime and criminal organizations were noted.[1] Then several local newspapers which cover the Copperhead County area were searched over a 12-month period for any stories dealing with illicit activities involving the goods and services traditionally associated with organized crime (i.e., drug trafficking, gambling, prostitution, organized auto theft, bootlegging). Specific criminal actions noted in the newspapers, such as indictments and convictions, were then cross-referenced against Kentucky's Uniform Citation and Uniform Arrest databases for the county. These data were then used to create a database of illicit enterprise for the 12-month period.

Following the accumulation of documentary information, a field research design was used to become acquainted with the methods and means of illicit entrepreneurship in the county. Using a participant-as-observer role in which the researchers posed as customers, observations were conducted at roadhouses, game rooms, and legitimate business establishments supporting the illicit economy of Copperhead County (Gold, 1958). In addition, informal interviews were conducted with a wide variety of local participants in illicit enterprise, particularly gamblers, bootleggers, and prostitutes, and, in two instances, drug traffickers. Standard data quality and hypothesis evaluation controls were utilized, specifically, McCall's (1969) data quality index, Glazer's (1964) constant comparative method for hypothesis evaluation, and Becker and Geer's (1960) tabular model for hypothesis evaluation.

Because the data-gathering involved the observation of illegal activities and discussions with actors involved in illicit activity, a pseudonym has been selected for the county and pseudonyms have been used for any individuals discussed in this paper.

COPPERHEAD COUNTY

Copperhead County is one of the 120 counties in Kentucky and one of the 49 counties classified as an Appalachian county (Lee, 1981). It has a long and colorful reputation for lawlessness, corruption and violence. In the mid-1800s, the county was famous for pioneering a kind of early white collar crime called "court fraud." Court fraud involved inventing crimes for the purpose of collecting fees from the state for law enforcement activities such as filing charges and complaints, conducting arraignments, and making arrests. Therefore, since no crime had been committed, the charges would summarily be dropped after the sheriff had been paid for serving the paper and making the arrests, the magistrate for the preliminary hearing, the jailer for housing the arrestee, and the witnesses for their "testifying" fees (Tapp and Klotter, 1977).

Copperhead County was also the location of Kentucky's bloodiest and longest war.[2] The Copperhead County War was a 60-year contest in which scores of people were murdered. It was a battle for political dominance in the county and for control of several local industries, most importantly, the local salt industry (Richardson, 1986). During America's decade-long flirtation with alcohol prohibition, Copperhead County was a major production site for homemade, moonshine alcohol. This alcohol supplied much of the demand in Indianapolis and Chicago in the early years of Prohibition, until organized crime syndicates developed more efficient means for importing or mass-producing high-quality liquor (Maurer, 1974; Richardson, 1986).

Copperhead County was founded in 1806, carved out of three adjoining counties. From 1806 until the end of the Civil War, saltmaking was the economic foundation of the county. In those years, about 200,000 bushels of salt were produced by 15 separate "furnaces" operating in the county. Six of the pioneer families dominated the salt trade, with the two largest producers engaging in constant and fierce competition, often slashing prices below the cost of production in an attempt to drive competitors out of business (Lee, 1981).

Copperhead County comprises 474 square miles, with a population of 16,000—down from 18,000 in 1970, 20,000 in 1960 and 23,000 in 1950. There are two cities in the county: the county seat, with a population of around 1,500; and a second city, with a population of about 800. The rest of the county is decidedly rural. While farming is a basic industry in many of the Appalachian counties, the number of farms in Copperhead County has steadily declined, dropping from 2,365 in 1954 to 1,325 in 1964, and continuing to drop to about 700 today. The fact is that Copperhead County's topography makes farming a very difficult occupation. The county is mountainous, rugged and in some places quite inaccessible. Farming must be done on a small scale. Copperhead County raises only about 5,100 head of cattle, 2,000 head of hogs and 2,800,000 pounds of burley tobacco, which are all very low numbers for Kentucky's Appalachian counties (Lee, 1981).

In the past, Copperhead County's economy has been supported by the coal industry. Most of the coal reserves are owned by out-of-state, absentee companies. Production has steadily declined over the past two decades, with production dropping from 1,154,000 tons in 1966 to a little over 500,000 tons in 1980. During that same period about half of the jobs in the coal industry also disappeared, with fewer than 300 county residents presently legally employed in the industry (Commonwealth of Kentucky, 1986; Lee, 1981).

Another absentee industry which has exploited and then partially abandoned Copperhead County is the timber industry. Eighty percent of the county's land area is in timber, but declining profits have reduced employment and output in this industry as well. Unlike some of its neighboring counties, which have been able to slightly offset the decline in coal and timber with oil and natural gas production, Copperhead County produces only about 6,000 barrels of oil a year (Commonwealth of Kentucky, 1986). There are approximately 475 manufacturing jobs in the county, primarily in plants making small electrical appliances, metal furniture, upholstered furniture, barrel staves and hardwood lumber (Commonwealth of Kentucky, 1986).

Industry in Copperhead County has been on a 40-year decline, and its residents have been left in dire economic straits. The latest available statistics indicate that 42.4% of the population live below the poverty level. The official rate of unemployment is about 25%. Per capita income as of

1983 was $6,425 and has increased in the last six years to only $7,233 (as compared to a national average of $15,481). A full 50% of the county's population live on unemployment, Social Security, disability pensions or other fixed incomes. The dropout rate for the Copperhead County high schools is 50%, compared to a national average of 28.9% (Commonwealth of Kentucky, 1986).

As of 1989 the single largest source of income in Copperhead County was crime. Everything from bootlegging liquor, growing marijuana, and transshipping cocaine, to prostitution, gambling, and food stamp fraud supports the count's citizenry. It is an economy built around vice and corruption. It is a social system resting on lawlessness.

THE ILLICIT MARKET

Criminal enterprise in Copperhead County can be classified into two major categories: wholesale production and supply, and retail sales and service. The most profitable aspect of the crime industry is in wholesale production and supply. This includes the growing and processing of high-grade marijuana crops and the transshipment of cocaine from its point of embarkation, through Kentucky, to its ultimate sales destination. The retail crime industry involves the provision of illicit goods to the residents of eastern Kentucky and to transient customers, and includes the illegal sale of liquor, drugs, prostitution, and gambling.

The Wholesale Market

While there is no systematic and reliable accounting measure available, there is widespread intersubjective agreement that the marijuana industry is the mainstay of Copperhead County's farming economy. Local law enforcement officials estimate that as many as 40% of the county's residents are employed in the marijuana industry (Kelley, 1989). The attractiveness of marijuana cultivation is easy to understand. First, and most obviously, marijuana is a highly profitable crop. According to local growers, two high-grade marijuana plants earn as much money as an entire tobacco crop for the average farmer. Second, marijuana is one of the few crops conducive to agricultural conditions in Copperhead County. The land is mountainous, rough, rocky and virtually impossible to farm. The alternative is what the locals call "hardscrabble farming," meaning small plots of vegetables, corn or tobacco which require intensive labor and care yet yield little profit. On the other hand, the climate and terrain are perfect for marijuana, a crop which can be grown in very small plots at a very high profit (Drug Enforcement Strategy Committee, 1987). The rugged terrain is not an impediment but a boon to the marijuana industry. It makes it easy to conceal marijuana plots "up the holler," intermingled with low mountain brush growth and covered by a high tree canopy, making detection far more difficult than it is in the more arable land of northern, western, and south central Kentucky. Most marijuana is planted in small plots of about 60 square feet. Such a marijuana garden, if properly tended, will yield about $60,000 worth of high-grade marijuana.[3]

The marijuana industry works very much like a truck farmers' cooperative. Buyers contract in advance with a grower for his or her crop and will simply pick up the marijuana after processing, sometimes in tractor-trailer-size loads. Alternatively, buyers will come into the county during the three harvests and visit the growers, evaluating their product and bidding for it in the same manner as the tobacco companies bid for the tobacco crop. Most marijuana in Copperhead County is destined for Florida, Indiana, Illinois, or Ohio, and state police intelligence reports indicate that it is commonly shipped to at least 15 states outside of Kentucky (Drug Enforcement Strategy Committee, 1987). A combination of an indigenous agricultural know-how, a friendly climate, a depressed economy and a bull market for the product makes marijuana cultivation a major industry in Copperhead County.

However, marijuana is not the only drug-related wholesale business in the county. In recent years the transshipment of cocaine has also become big business. As importation systems for cocaine have become more complex in their logistics in order to avoid law enforcement interference, and as the quantities of cocaine entering the U.S. have reached enormous proportions in the last five years, moving the drug has become a major cottage industry in eastern Kentucky (DeFalaise and Whittle, 1989; Drug Enforcement Strategy Committee, 1987; National Narcotics Intelligence Consumers Committee, 1985-86).

The transshipment operations take two forms. The first, and probably the most common, is to bring a load of cocaine on light aircraft into remote and temporary landing strips scattered throughout the eastern Kentucky mountains from Georgia, Florida, Alabama, Louisiana and Texas. The cocaine is then off-loaded and shipped by car or truck to its ultimate destination.

The second form of cocaine transshipment is dependent upon certain indigenous skills and knowledge found in the local population. Years ago, during Prohibition, it was common practice for local youths to run moonshine liquor to the major cities of the Midwest and the South from the Kentucky mountains. Invariably, the routes they used were small, backwater roads (many of which are hardly roads at all) which stayed clear of major highways and population centers. Those backwoods routes are still in operation. Today's cocaine runners are the descendants of the moonshine runners of a half century ago. And, surprisingly, many of them use the same combination of old logging roads, utility service roads, and "cow paths" to move their cargo from Kentucky to Chicago, Cincinnati, Indianapolis, Pittsburgh, Knoxville, and Cleveland, often avoiding major highways or cities and towns altogether. One of the ironies of this cocaine transport system is that federal money has been made available to the states for setting up interdiction points along the major interstate highways which crisscross Kentucky. While some cocaine is moved that way, most never sees a major highway. Though stopping Porsches with Florida plates and Hispanic-looking drivers may net a pound or two of cocaine every couple of weeks, huge quantities of the drug are being moved by good-old country boys far from the prying eyes of state police.

The cocaine transshipment business works simply in Copperhead County. Most of the cocaine is brought in by plane to landing strips located in four counties to the northeast of Copperhead County.[4] Local young men meet at a previously agreed upon location and pick up their loads, usually a few kilos of cocaine. They are given their destinations and their pay (in cash) and sent on their way. Transport prices vary, but, on the average, a load being taken to the Cincinnati or Knoxville areas will net $400; Pittsburgh, PA and Indianapolis, IN, $800; and Chicago or Detroit, $1,000. While no official statistics exist on how many runs are made and successfully completed, observations at one of the pickup points—a parking lot in the county seat—revealed that on a Sunday afternoon about a dozen cars take off for points north, and this is only one of several pickup points.[5] Residents of the county can recall only three cases of runners being apprehended in the last five years.

Very little of the cocaine remains in Copperhead County. A few of the runners take their pay in drugs and then sell the drugs at roadhouses or through agents working in business establishments serving the interstate, but cocaine sales in the county itself are small in both quantity and number. While the drug is readily available if one wants it, the retail cocaine trade is not a staple of the local illicit economy.

The Retail Market

The retail market for illicit goods and services in Copperhead County revolves around the basic human vices—liquor, sex and gambling—with drugs available only as an ancillary service.

Kentucky maintains a local option with regard to alcohol. As a result, a coalition of bootleggers, fundamentalists, and law enforcement officials, all of whom profit handsomely from the trade in one way or another, have managed to keep most of the state dry. All of the counties in the Copperhead area are dry. In fact, Copperhead County sits about midway in a dry belt extending from the Lexington-Richmond area in Kentucky to the Knoxville area in Tennessee. As such, liquor is a big business in the county.

The retail liquor trade takes three basic forms. First, there are the unorganized, individual entrepreneurs who simply make a weekly run to a wet city, buy a trunkload of liquor, and return to sell to their friends and neighbors—of course exacting a considerable fee for the risks they are taking. Second, and far more commonly, local residents have established illegal liquor stores in the county. These are invariably private residences or gas stations in which liquor is always available. Many of the residences have actually installed circular driveways to facilitate a drive-in trade to keep their customers moving. These establishments buy liquor in quantity every week from legal dealers in the wet areas, usually at a prearranged price that benefits both the seller and buyer. Finally, liquor is available by the drink in any of a dozen roadhouses operating in the county. Most of these roadhouses are small establishments in which there is a single room in a house set aside for drinking. It is common for these establishments to also house a very small gambling operation and two prostitutes.

There are, however, a few large roadhouses in the county which rival the nightclubs of the "wet" cities. These establishments are often converted barns, warehouses, or old farmhouses that feature a full-service bar, a live band, dancing, "strippers," a stable of prostitutes, and casino-style gambling. For example, the largest of the county's roadhouses offers four blackjack tables, a crap table, a half dozen slot machines, a half dozen poker machines, entertainment brought in from the Lexington area, a staff of six to 12 hostesses (depending on the night and the expected volume of business), and a contract arrangement with local drug dealers which enables them to fulfill requests for drugs by patrons.

Gambling occurs in three formats in the county. The most common is simply illegal machines which are omnipresent everywhere a tourist, trucker or other transient might stop. The second venue involves "game rooms," which also have pool tables, pinball games and the like. And, finally, there are the roadhouses described above. Most games in the county are low-stakes games featuring $2 and $5 dollar bets, although the volume of business is quite brisk. At the larger roadhouses there are often tables reserved in advance for high-stakes games going as high as $100 minimum bets in craps and blackjack. In addition, for a 5%-a-pot charge, the roadhouses will gladly make available a table, a dealer, refreshments and hostesses for high-stakes poker games.

Prostitution is a surprisingly common occupation for young women in this predominantly fundamentalist and conservative county. In the immediate area, these women work truck stops, restaurants, and other establishments serving the interstate; local "tanning salons," which are often fronts for prostitution in the county; and the roadhouses. The highway trade is the least sophisticated and is Copperhead County's rough equivalent of streetwalking in a major urban area. The tanning salon trade is very much like the massage parlor trade in major cities. Customers come in and pay for a tanning session during which they are assisted by an employee. During the session, a massage might be suggested or the customer might inquire about other services that are offered. Prices in these establishments range from $40 to $120, depending on the service requested. The prostitution services provided in roadhouses are quite variable. In the small "two-holers,"[6] the service is crude and the marketing strategy quite direct. Customers know why the women are present, and little attention is paid to preliminaries or ambience. In the large roadhouses, however, the prostitutes are an interesting cross between the B-girls and call girls of urban America. They are often paid a commission for the number of drinks they can get the customer to buy them. However, they are neither crude nor pushy in their approach. They will dance with customers, engage in conversation and otherwise give the impression of a "date." When the conversation turns to sexual services, it is handled discreetly and the exchange usually takes place in one of several private rooms available for such activity. The women who work in the large roadhouses are the most expensive and the most attractive of the local prostitutes.

Copperhead County "johns" come from a limited population. There are those transients who have been enticed away from the interstate in search of vice; Kentucky residents from an eight-county area, some of whom travel up to four hours to enjoy the delights of Copperhead County; and individuals engaged in illicit business themselves, such as drug wholesalers and transporters, gamblers, and the like who are doing business in the county. By Copperhead County standards, this is a sufficient customer pool to make prostitution an attractive occupation. But even so, many of the local women, particularly those who work the large roadhouses, travel to Knoxville or to Newport, KY for work on those nights that the roadhouses are not in operation or they are not needed. Interviews with local prostitutes indicated that a successful roadhouse girl can expect to make between $400 and $600 a week, while a tanning salon prostitute or one who services the interstate may make as little as $250 a week for much longer hours and a far less select clientele. Despite the fact that these are very low incomes for prostitutes as compared to their urban sisters, they are still very nice wages for poverty-wracked eastern Kentucky.

CRIMINAL ENTREPRENEURS

Our study of criminal enterprises in Copperhead County uncovered 28 separate ongoing criminal enterprises, involving 99 individuals. To be considered a criminal enterprise three criteria had to be met: (1) the individual(s) involved had to have a careerist orientation toward crime (i.e., an illicit enterprise as the primary source of income and as the primary job), (2) the involvement in illicit activity had be continual, and (3) there had to be evidence of a coordination or management role in the enterprise. These criteria exclude such actors in the illicit economy as part-time cocaine transhippers who may only be active one or two days a month, part-time prostitutes who are primarily engaged in another line of work (this would exclude the vast majority of Copperhead County prostitutes), and all individuals who support themselves through legitimate occupations and engage in illicit enterprise only as an income supplement.

The overwhelming majority of criminal enterprises involved only a small number of participants (see Table 1). Eleven of the 28 enterprises (39.29%) encompassed the activities of individual entrepreneurs. Nine of the enterprises (34.14%) were limited partnerships consisting of two to four individuals. The remaining eight enterprises were criminal networks involving between five and 11 participants. It is important to remember, however, that these numbers do not include most "employees" of these enterprises because they would not meet the basic criteria specified above.

Table 1: Number of Individuals Involved in Criminal Enterprises in Copperhead County

Number of Participants in Criminal Enterprise	Number of Criminal Enterprises	% of all Criminal Enterprises	% of all Criminal Entrepreneurs
1	11	39.29%	11.11%
2	5	17.86%	10.10%
3	2	7.14%	6.06%
4	2	7.14%	8.08%
5	2	7.14%	10.10%
6	1	3.57%	6.06%
7	0	0.00%	0.00%
8	0	0.00%	0.00%
9	3	10.71%	27.27%
10	1	3.57%	10.10%
11	1	3.57%	10.10%

Participants in Copperhead County criminal enterprises tended to be overwhelmingly male. Despite the fact that only 19.19% of the participants were female (see table 2), this seems a high proportion in view of the fact that it counts only those individuals in a management or coordination role in the enterprise. Traditional wisdom in the organized crime literature holds that organized crime is "not an equal opportunity employer," and that the participation of women is extremely rare. While no "official" count by sex has been produced by the U.S. Justice Department, a quick survey of those mentioned as organized criminals in the 1980 Pennsylvania Crime Commission report (one of the most comprehensive statewide analyses of organized crime ever done) indicates that of 357 individuals clearly identified as members of ongoing criminal enterprises, only two (0.56%) were women. Therefore, this highly impressionistic data would indicate that female participation in criminal enterprises is higher in a very rural area like Copperhead County than in traditional urban settings.

Table 2: Female Participation in Criminal Enterprises in Copperhead County

Number of Female Participants	Number of Criminal Enterprises	% of all Criminal Enterprises
0	18	64.29%
1	6	21.43%
2	2	7.14%
3	0	0.00%
4	1	3.57%
5	1	3.57%

Table 3: Relationships by Blood or Marriage among Participants in Criminal Enterprises in Copperhead County

Number of Participants in the Criminal Enterprise Related by Blood or Marriage	Number of Criminal Enterprises	% of all Criminal Enterprises
0	16	57.14%
1	1	3.57%
2	8	18.57%
3	1	3.57%
4	1	3.57%
5	0	0.00%
6	0	0.00%
7	1	3.57%

In addition to the gender makeup of criminal enterprises, it is also important to note that 31 of the 99 participants (31.31%) are related by blood or marriage (see Table 3), clearly showing the importance of familial ties to the organization of crime in rural settings. One crime network had seven individuals involved in its operation who were related to one another.

In addition to determining the characteristics of participants in the criminal enterprises, a typology was developed to indicate differences between criminal enterprises in terms of (1) numbers of participants, and (2) scope of operations. Criminal enterprises with just one participant were labeled individual entrepreneurs and then classified as operating on an intrastate or interstate level. Criminal enterprises with two to four participants were called limited partnerships, and were also classified by scope of operation. Criminal enterprises with five or more participants were called crime networks, and were similarly classified as to their scope of operation (see Table 4). All 11 individual entrepreneurships were intra-

Table 4: Types of Criminal Enterprises in Copperhead County

Type of Criminal Enterprise	Number of Criminal Enterprises	% of all Criminal Enterprises
Individual Entrepreneurs / Intrastate	11	39.29%
Individual Entrepreneurs / Interstate	0	0.00%
Limited Partnerships / Intrastate	7	25.00%
Limited Partnerships / Interstate	2	7.14%
Criminal Network / Intrastate	6	21.43%
Criminal Network / Interstate	2	7.14%

state in nature. Of the limited partnerships, seven were intrastate and two were interstate. Of the crime networks, six were intrastate and only two were interstate. These data indicate that the rural criminal organizations found in Copperhead County tend to have limited geographic and entrepreneurial scope.

Criminal enterprises were classified by number of participants and geographic scope of operation, as well as by the number of criminal activities in which they were engaged. This means that each separate type of criminal activity that was a primary income-generator for the enterprise was counted. This does not mean, however, that each crime committed was counted. Criminal enterprises are likely to commit an almost unending list of crimes. The interest resided in how many different types of illicit goods and services they delivered as part of the criminal business. The data in Table 5 show that 18 of the 28 criminal enterprises (64.29%) engaged in only one criminal activity; five (17.86%) of the enterprises engaged in two such activities; two (7.14%) of the enterprises engaged in three activities; and three (10.71%) enterprises had four major activities.

Table 5: Number of Criminal Activities Engaged in by Criminal Enterprises in Copperhead County

Number of Criminal Activities	Number of Criminal Enterprises	% of All Criminal Enterprises
1	18	64.29%
2	5	17.86%
3	2	7.14%
4	3	10.71%

It is interesting to note that there was some relationship between the type of criminal enterprise and the number of criminal activities in which it was engaged (see Table 6). For example, all of the 11 individual entrepreneurs engaged in only one principal criminal activity. Of the nine partnerships, five (55.55%) engaged in only one activity, while two (22.22%) engaged in two criminal activities and two partnerships (22.22%) were engaged in four criminal activities. With regard to crime networks, two of the eight (25%) were engaged in only one activity, while three networks were engaged in two activities (37.50%), two were involved in three activities (25%) and one was involved in four activities (12.50%).

Table 6: Number of Criminal Activities Engaged in by Various Types of Criminal Enterprises in Copperhead County

Type of Criminal Enterprise	Number of Criminal Activities			
	1	2	3	4
Individual Entrepreneurs / Intrastate	11	0	0	0
	100.0%	0.00%	0.00%	0.00%
Limited Partnerships / Intrastate	3	2	0	2
	42.86%	28.57%	0.00%	28.57%
Limited Partnerships / Interstate	2	0	0	0
	100.0%	0.00%	0.00%	0.00%
Criminal Networks / Intrastate	1	2	2	1
	16.67%	33.33%	33.33%	16.67%
Criminal Networks / Interstate	1	1	0	0
	50.00%	50.00%	0.00%	0.00%

The research then examined the nature of the criminal activities and how many enterprises were engaged in the various specific activities in the Copperhead County market (see Table 7). The data revealed that the two most common activities were marijuana trafficking (13 enterprises, 46.43%), and dealing in illegal liquor (12 enterprises, 42.86%). Much less frequently, organizations were found to be involved in auto theft (five enterprises, 17.86%), cocaine trafficking (four enterprises, 14.29%), trafficking in illegal guns and explosives (four enterprises, 14.29%), and engaging in on-site prostitution (three enterprises, 10.71%). This would seem to contradict the prevailing view of the "redneck crime groups" or the "Dixie Mafia," which engaged primarily in the stealing and recycling of automobiles and auto parts. In addition, at least one criminal enterprise was engaging in numerous criminal activities: trafficking in amphetamines, trafficking in other drugs, running an illegal lottery, operating illegal gambling machines and games, and trafficking in illegal explosives.

Table 7: Criminal Activities Engaged in by Criminal Enterprises in Copperhead County

Criminal Activities	Number of Criminal Enterprises	% of All Criminal Enterprises
Marijuana trafficking	13	46.43%
Illegal liquor sales	12	42.86%
Auto theft	5	17.86%
Cocaine trafficking	4	14.29%
Illegal gun sales	4	14.29%
On-site prostitution	3	10.71%
Amphetamine trafficking	1	3.57%
Trafficking in other drugs	1	3.57%
Running an illegal lottery	1	3.57%
Operating illegal machines	1	3.57%
Operating illegal games	1	3.57%
Illegal explosives sales	1	3.57%

Finally, the data revealed how many of the criminal enterprises operating in Copperhead County were utilizing legitimate business fronts either as means to conceal illegal activities or as money-laundering mechanisms. The results show that only four of the criminal enterprises used such legitimate fronts (14.28%) (see Table 8), although one enterprise used five legitimate businesses, and one owned and operated its illicit enterprises through eight legitimate fronts. The use of legitimate business fronts was most often connected to gambling enterprises and vehicular theft operations.

Table 8: Number of Legitimate Business Fronts Used by Criminal Enterprises in Copperhead County

Number of Legitimate Business Fronts Used	Number of Criminal Enterprises	% of All Criminal Enterprises
0	24	85.71%
1	2	7.14%
2	0	0.00%
3	0	0.00%
4	0	0.00%
5	1	3.57%
6	0	0.00%
7	0	0.00%
8	1	3.57%

CRIME NETWORKS

Eight separate crime networks were identified in Copperhead County. As indicated above, they were quite variable in the goods and services they provided and in their methods of operation. Exploring these networks in greater detail provides a better understanding of how criminal organization works in Copperhead County. The most common illicit entrepreneurs are the roadhouse operators, who provide a wide range of on-site illicit goods and services.[7]

Network #1: The "Baxter" network involves ten county residents in management and coordination positions. The network runs nine small roadhouses in Copperhead County and in four adjoining counties. The roadhouses are primarily sites for the sale and consumption of illegal liquor and for small-scale prostitution enterprises, employing more than two prostitutes at each site. The Baxter network does not handle illegal drugs directly, although they and their employees can provide ready referrals to both marijuana and cocaine dealers. The ten network members all work in the day-to-day operation of the roadhouses and employ about 36 other individuals as bouncers, bartenders, and prostitutes.

Network #2: The "Andrews" crime network is one of the two highly sophisticated Copperhead County operations. The network itself is managed by nine individuals and led by the two Andrews brothers. The Andrews network operates the major gambling, illegal liquor and prostitution racket in the county. It runs three large roadhouses, and operates gambling and prostitution enterprises under the cover of ten ostensibly legal businesses including a pool room, five truck stops, two food stores, and two tanning salons. The network is responsible for the distribution of electronic poker machines and slot machines throughout the county, in addition to operating an extensive lottery and bookmaking operation. The organization employs at least 50 individuals outside the network leadership, and is widely recognized as running the highest-class prostitutes in the county.

Network #3: The "Hawkins" network is the largest crime network in the county, and, along with the Andrews network, is the most sophisticated and successful. It is intimately tied to the local Republican Party and county officeholders including the judge, sheriff, and jailer. Although the Hawkins network lacks the business sophistication of the Andrews network, it more than makes up for this deficiency through its political ties. There are nine principal participants in the Hawkins network, three of whom are related by marriage or blood and one of whom is a member of the county's most politically powerful family. The Hawkins network will engage in whatever type of enterprise is profitable and in demand. However, it specializes in marijuana sales, illegal liquor sales and on-site prostitution. This organization operates the two largest roadhouses in the county, both on "Duck Pond Road" and both featuring extensive entertainment services. The roadhouses offer music, dancing, strippers, drinks by the glass, and have rooms set aside for prostitution. While there is gambling in both roadhouses, it is run on a contract basis. The blackjack, craps and poker games are all owned by the individual operators, who pay 10% of the total table stakes in "rent" to the network. Although cocaine is available at both roadhouses, it is not handled by network members but by independent dealers who also pay "rent" to the house. This crime network has a reputation for the extensive use of violence and for a large role in local vote-buying and political corruption. About two dozen employees work directly for the network. If the associated, nonmember participants were included the number of network employees would total about 40.

Network #4: The "Collins" network is also a very large operation, with close political connections to the county's ruling elite. This network has nine members, four of whom are related and two of whom are blood relatives of the county's leading political figures. The "Collins" network specializes in liquor, prostitution and drugs through a complicated collection of illegal enterprises. It runs three small roadhouses, and four "drive-in" liquor and drug stores. The liquor stores are actually members' homes, with circular driveways which allow for the quick and convenient purchase of liquor, marijuana, and, surprisingly, barbiturates and methaqualone. Only about ten people outside of network members work as employees for the enterprise, and the size of their businesses is quite variable. For example, one of the drive-through liquor operations had only 480 cans of beer and 10 fifths of whiskey on hand, along with a supply of Xanax, when it was visited. On the other hand, one of the roadhouses had almost 3,000 cans of beer and 147 bottles of liquor on hand, along with a supply of 2,500 Quaaludes and at least a kilo of high-grade marijuana.

Almost as well organized and pervasive as the roadhouse operators are the auto thieves. There are at least three crime networks in Copperhead County that specialize in stolen vehicles.

Network #5: The "Anderson" crime network specializes in a single type of criminal enterprise, stolen vehicles. Law enforcement officials indicate that they are the biggest car theft operation in eastern Kentucky. The central participants in the network come from three families, the Andersons, the "Dunhams" and the "Forrests." They operate out of an auto repair business and sell their vehicles through a network of dealers in Tennessee, Kentucky, and Ohio. The ten network participants conduct the enterprise themselves and have no additional employees.

Network #6: The "Tracey" network is managed by six people whose primary business is stolen cars, but who are also engaged in trafficking in marijuana and illegal guns. The network is small and works out of members' homes, employing no other participants.

Network #7: The "Chalmers" network also specializes in stolen vehicles. There are five network participants who operate under the cover of five auto dealerships in Kentucky and Tennessee. Because of the extensive business operations of this network, their nonmember employees number about 30. It is also rumored, though not documented, that the Chalmers network is a major money-laundering operation for drug traffickers in the county.

Drug networks are rare in Copperhead County. Most drug traffickers and marijuana cultivators operate as limited partnerships or as individual entrepreneurs who eventually sell their produce or buy their wholesale supplies from more elaborate criminal organizations outside the county. However, there is one major marijuana cultivating network operating in the county.

Network #8: The "Taylor" network specializes in the cultivation, processing and wholesale distribution of marijuana. The network is composed of five individuals, two of whom are brothers, who oversee the planting and care of 20 separate marijuana patches. Their annual production is about a ton of high-grade marijuana, which is sold to retailers in Florida, Michigan and Indiana. The network employs two dozen individuals, in addition to the five network members who care for and guard the marijuana plots.

ORGANIZING RURAL CRIME

From the available data, several major conclusions can be drawn about the organization of crime in Copperhead County. First, criminal organizations in the county tend not to be tightly organized, clearly defined, stable, bureaucratic organizations. Rather, criminal entrepreneurship in Copperhead County operates in the context of a loosely structured, open and informal system. Entrepreneurship is highly reactive to changes in the political and economic environment. It is true that some individuals show a long-term pattern of collaboration in illicit activities. But participation in any given criminal enterprise is determined not by a permanent organizational structure, but by circumstances subject to frequent and rapid change (i.e., the growth or decline of a market for illicit goods and services; the availability of new sources of supply and distributors; opportunities resulting from changes in law enforcement practices; and the need for special skills not available within the group). Criminal organization tends to be highly adaptive and very flexible. Criminal enterprises expand and contract to meet the uncertainties of the illicit market.[8]

Second, the data make it clear that illicit markets in Copperhead County are populated by small, fragmented and ephemeral enterprises. This makes a great deal of sense in that small size and organizational segmentation minimize exposure to the risk of successful law enforcement interventions. Because employees of criminal enterprises pose the greatest threat to the continuation of the enterprise, in that they make the best witnesses against criminal entrepreneurs, it is in the criminal organization's interest to limit the number of people who have comprehensive knowledge of the group's operations. By segmenting information so that participants know only about their own jobs, damage from a successful arrest or prosecution is controlled both vertically and horizontally in the organization (c.f., Albanese and Pursley, 1993; Hellman, 1980; Laswell and McKenna, 1972; Wisotsky, 1986). For the same reasons that criminal organizations segment their operations, they also tend to limit their geographic scope. The larger the geographic area covered, the greater the number of law enforcement agencies which can take notice of the group's operations and the more tenuous the communications process becomes (Reuter, 1983).

Finally, this study of criminal organizations in Copperhead County clearly reveals a series of exchanges between the under and upper-world which have developed into long-term corrupt relationships. The importance of establishing this corrupt relationship is not unique to rural organized crime; it has been well-documented by virtually every empirical study of organized crime (Chambliss, 1978; Gardiner, 1970; Gardiner and Lyman, 1978; Lupsha, 1987; Potter and Jenkins, 1985).

Despite the differences inherent in rural populations versus urban populations and the differences in the density of customers in a geographic area, criminal enterprises in rural Appalachian counties in Kentucky appear to have many of the same characteristics as the urban enterprises which have been subjected to such intense study. Criminal enterprises in Appalachia are highly adaptable, flexible and able to respond to changes in the market, in the political environment, or in law enforcement strategies with the same ease as their big city counterparts. It appears that the exigencies of the illicit market, rather than any specific organizational design or regional difference, are the prime explanatory factors in the organization of criminal enterprise (Albanese, 1989; Reuter, 1983).

❑

NOTES

1. In addition to the works cited previously, the following sources were consulted: Y.E. Allison (1887). "The Moonshine Men." *Southern Bivouac* 2(Feb); J.C. Campbell (1921). *The Southern Highlander and His Homeland.* New York: Russell Sage Foundation; T.D. Clark (1968). *Kentucky: Land of Contrast.* New York: Harper and Row; H.W. Coates (1923). *Stories of Kentucky Feuds.* Cincinnati, OH: W.T. Perry; J.H. Combs (1913). *The Kentucky Highlanders.* Lexington, KY: J.S. Richardson and Company; C. Crowe-Carraco (1979). *The Big Sandy* Lexington, KY: University of Kentucky; H.D. Davis and C. Smythe (1903). "The Land of the Feuds." *Munsey's Magazine* (Nov.); J. Day (1941) *Bloody Ground.* New York: Doubleday; W.H. Haney (1906). *The Mountain People of Kentucky.* Cincinnati, OH: Robert Clark Company; W.W. Harney (1873). "A Strange Land and a Peculiar People." *Lippincott's Magazine* (Oct); Kentucky Crime Commission (1988). *Drug and Violence Crime Enforcement Strategy.* Frankfort, KY: Commonwealth of Kentucky; H. Kephart (1922). *Our Southern Highlanders.* New York: Macmillan; H.M. Lewis, L. Johnson and D. Askins (eds.) (1978). *Colonialism in Modern America: The Appalachian Case.* Boone, NC: Consortium Press; E.C. Lisey (1902). "Kentucky Feuds and Their Causes." *Frank Leslie's Popular Monthly* (Jan); G. Robertson (1855). *Scrap Book on Law, Politics, Men and Times.* Lexington, KY: A.W. Elder.

2. Outside of Kentucky these events are frequently, and usually erroneously, referred to as "feuds." In fact, most of the Kentucky feuds were literally wars that extended over decades, with political control of a specific county or area the ultimate objective.

3. Marijuana, like any other crop, varies greatly in quality. "Ditchweed" crops, which are planted with low-grade local seeds, are usually not well tended, and are frequently planted in a place to allow for discovery by law enforcement agencies, register a tetrahydrocannabinol (THC) level of between 5% and 7%. The "real" marijuana crops, which are often *sensimelia* or a high-potency Kentucky hybrid and are carefully tilled, fertilized, and irrigated, test with a THC of level of 12% to 14%.

4. The terrain of Copperhead County makes it less than hospitable for landing aircraft, although several private airports in the county do manage to do a fairly brisk business in small, out of state aircraft which remain on the ground for only a few minutes.

5. Sunday is a preferred day for making the trips because of less traffic problems on the receiving end of the run in the metropolitan areas being served.

6. The term "two-holer" refers to roadhouses supporting a small gambling operation and two prostitutes.

7. These activities are reported in such local newspaper articles as the following: "Man Charged With Bootlegging" (1988). *Corbin Times-Tribune* (Nov. 30); "Local Man Charged with Bootlegging" (1988). *Corbin Times-Tribune* (Nov 11); "Raids Net Two Arrests" (1988). *Corbin Times-Tribune* (Oct 28); "Raids Net Marijuana, Arrests" (1988). *Corbin Times-Tribune* (Sept 19); "Undercover Investigations Net 11 Local Arrests" (1988). *Corbin Times-Tribune* (Dec 3); "Police Confiscate Alcohol" (1988). *Corbin Times-Tribune* (Dec 21); "Man Faces Federal Drug Charges" (1988). *Corbin Times-Tribune* (Oct 18); "Five Arrested in Marijuana Raids Tuesday" (1988). *Corbin Times-Tribune* (Sept 14); "Seven Arrested in Theft Ring" (1988). *Corbin Times-Tribune* (Oct 8); "Two Sentenced in Theft Ring" (1988). *Corbin Times-Tribune* (Oct 7); "Two Charged in Chop Shop Operation" (1988). *Corbin Times-Tribune* (Dec 1); "Two More Arrests in Police Sweep" (1988). *Corbin Times-Tribune* (Oct 14); "Undercover Operation Nets 7 Tri-County Arrests" (1988). *Corbin Times-Tribune* (Oct 13); "Local Businesses Among KSP Raids" (1988). *Corbin Times-Tribune* (Nov 19); "Local Man Charged with Bootlegging" (1988). *Corbin Times-Tribune* (Nov 26); "26 Cases of Beer Confiscated by Police" (1988). *Corbin Times-Tribune* (Sept 2); "Four Charged in Slaying of Man in Chicago Over Marijuana Purchase" (1988). *Corbin Times-Tribune* (Nov 30); "Man Guilty in Drug Charges" (1988). *Corbin Times-Tribune* (Dec 18); "Man Charged With Bootlegging" (1988). *Corbin Times-Tribune* (Dec 20); "Local Dealers Charged With Fraud" (1989). *Corbin Times-Tribune* (Jan 20); "Sheriff Candidate Among 10 Arrested in Drug, Alcohol Case" (1989). *Lexington Herald-Leader* (Feb 6); "Two Brothers Arrested in Alleged Effort to Import, Sell Drugs" (1989). *Lexington Herald-Leader* (Jan 21); "FBI Makes Drug Raid" (1989). *Corbin Times-Tribune* (Jan 21); "Raids Net 256 Marijuana Plants" (1988). *Corbin Times-Tribune* (Aug 27); "Six Face Marijuana Trafficking Charges" (1989). *Lexington Herald-Leader* (Feb 6); "Man Arrested on Bootlegging Charges" (1988). *Corbin Times-Tribune* (Dec 1); "Sheriff's Department Seizes Beer in Raids" (1988). *Corbin Times-Tribune* (Oct 20); "Weekend Raids Net 8 Arrests" (1988). *Corbin Times-Tribune* (Jan 3); "4 Are Arrested in Drug-Related Abduction" (1988). *Lexington Herald-Leader* (Nov 16); "$108,000 in Cash and Drugs Confiscated" (1988). *Mountain Eagle* (Nov 16); "Cash, Drugs Seized" (1988). *Daily News of Middlesboro* (Nov 15).

8. While this view differs considerably from the popular conception of organized crime, it is surprisingly congruent with empirical studies of organized crime in urban settings. For example, see: J. Albanese (1989). *Organized Crime in America*. Cincinnati: Anderson; J. Albini (1971). *The*

American Mafia: Genesis of a Legend. New York: Appleton-Century-Crofts;
A. Block (1979). "The Snowman Cometh: Coke in Progressive New York."
Criminology (May): 75-99; T. Bynum (1987). "Controversies in the Study of
Organized Crime." In: T. Bynum (ed.), *Organized Crime in America: Concepts
and Controversies*. Monsey, NY: Willow Tree Press; W.J. Chambliss (1978).
On The Take: From Petty Crooks to Presidents. Bloomington, IN: Indiana
University Press; J. Gardiner (1970). *The Politics of Corruption: Organized
Crime in an American City*. New York: Russell Sage Foundation; M. Haller
(1987). "Business Partnerships in the Coordination of Illegal Enterprise."
Paper presented at the annual meeting of the American Society of Crimi-
nology, Montreal, November; F.A.J. Ianni (1972). *A Family Business: Kin-
ship and Social Control in Organized Crime*. New York: Russell Sage
Foundation; G.W. Potter and P. Jenkins (1985). *The City and the Syndicate:
Organizing Crime in Philadelphia*. Lexington, MA: Ginn Press; P. Reuter
(1983). *Disorganized Crime*. Cambridge, MA: Massachusetts Institute of
Technology Press.

REFERENCES

Abadinsky, H. (1986). *Organized Crime*. Chicago, IL: Nelson-Hall.
Albanese, J.S. (1989). *Organized Crime in America* (2nd ed.) Cincinnati, OH:
   Anderson.
Albanese, J.S. and R.D. Pursley (1993). *Crime in America*. Englewood Cliffs,
   NJ: Prentice-Hall.
Becker, H.S. and B. Geer (1960). "Participant Observation: The Analysis of
   Qualitative Field Data". In: R.N. Adams and J.J. Preiss eds., *Human
   Organization Research*. Homewood, IL: Dorsey Press.
Caudill, H.M. (1983). *Theirs be the Power: The Moguls of Eastern Kentucky*.
   Urbana, IL: University of Illinois Press.
Chambliss, W.J. (1978). *On the Take: From Petty Crooks to Presidents*.
   Bloomington, IN: Indiana University Press.
Commonwealth of Kentucky (1986). *Kentucky Economic Statistics*. Frank-
   fort, KY: Author.
DeFalaise, L. and J.M. Whittle (1989). Summary of Report on Narcotics
   Trafficking for the Eastern and Western Districts of Kentucky. Unpub-
   lished report submitted to the U.S. Attorney General.
Drug Enforcement Strategy Committee (1987). *Commonwealth of Kentucky
   Statewide Drug Enforcement Strategy*. Frankfort, KY: Kentucky Justice
   Cabinet.
Gardiner, J. (1970). *The Politics of Corruption: Organized Crime in an
   American City*. New York, NY: Russell Sage Foundation.

Gardiner, J. and T.R. Lyman (1978). *Decisions for Sale: Corruption and Reform in Land-Use and Building Regulations.* New York, NY: Praeger.

Gazaway, R. (1969). *The Longest Mile.* Garden City, NY: Doubleday.

Glazer, B.G. (1964). "The Constant Comparative Method of Qualitative Analysis." *Social Problems* 12:436-445.

Gold, R.L. (1958). "Roles in Sociological Field Observations." *Social Forces* 36:217-223.

Hellman, D.A. (1980). *The Economics of Crime.* New York, NY: St. Martin's.

Hunter, J.M. (1983). "All Organized Crime Isn't Mafia: A Case Study of a Non-Traditional Criminal Organization." Paper presented at the annual meeting of the Academy of Criminal Justice Sciences, San Antonio, March.

Kelley, J. (1989)."40% in County Said to Grow Weed." *USA Today,* July 11, p.1.

Laswell, H.D. and J. McKenna (1972). *The Impact of Organized Crime on an Inner-City Community.* New York, NY: Policy Sciences Center.

Lee, L.G. (1981). *A Brief History of Kentucky and its Counties.* Berea, KY: Kentucky Imprints.

Lupsha, P.A. (1987)."Organized Crime: Rational Choice Not Ethnic Group Behavior: A Macro Perspective (More Steps Toward a Theory of Organized Crime)." Paper presented at the annual meeting of the American Society of Criminology, Montreal, November.

Maurer, D.W. (1974). *Kentucky Moonshine.* Lexington, KY: University of Kentucky Press.

McCall, G.J. (1969). "Data Quality Control in Participant Observation." In: G.J. McCall and J.L. Simmons eds., *Issues in Participant Observation.* London, UK: Addison-Wesley.

National Narcotics Intelligence Consumers Committee (1985-86). *The NNIC Report 1985-86: The Supply of Illicit Drugs to the United States from Foreign and Domestic Sources in 1985 and 1986.* Washington, DC: U.S. Government Printing Office.

Potter, G. and P. Jenkins (1985). *The City and the Syndicate: Organizing Crime in Philadelphia.* Lexington, MA: Ginn Press.

Reuter, P. (1983). *Disorganized Crime.* Cambridge, MA: Massachusetts Institute of Technology Press.

Richardson, D.C. (1986). *Mountain Rising.* Oneida, KY: Oneida Mountaineer Press.

Schmidt, W.E. (1984). "New Era, New Problems for South's Sheriffs." *New York Times,* September 10, pp.1, 15.

Tapp, H. and J.C. Klotter (1977). *Kentucky: Decades of Discord: 1865-1900.* Frankfort, KY: Kentucky Historical Society.

Wisotsky, S. (1986). *Breaking the Impasse in the War on Drugs.* New York, NY: Greenwood Press.

Joining the Chicago Outfit: Speculations About the Racket Subculture and Roving Neighborhoods

by

Robert M. Lombardo

and

Arthur J. Lurigio

Abstract: *A study highlights the importance of community contexts for the continued existence of traditional organized crime in American society. Italian-American organized crime in Chicago (i.e., the outfit) initially developed in five street crew neighborhoods, which were akin to the racket subculture areas and defended neighborhoods described in earlier studies. Recent changes in neighborhood structures brought about by emigration, urban renewal, and economic development, have occasioned the downfall of traditional Italian-American organized crime groups in some Chicago neighborhoods, but other communities have maintained the subculture and allure of the outfit and, thus, its ability to attract new members. The concept of the "roving neighborhood"—i.e., members carrying with them a shared set of values that transcends the artificial physical boundaries of the neighborhood—helps to explain the continuation of street crews even in the absence of traditional surroundings and community ties.*

Organized crime is a major social problem. Media accounts of underworld figures are commonplace, and the exploits of mobsters and gangsters have become a routine part of American culture. Their illegal enterprises have had a detrimental effect on the nation's economy and the quality of life in its urban areas for more than half a century. Over the years, congressional hearings, presidential commissions and law enforcement campaigns have highlighted organized crime as a national policy issue. Despite these counter-efforts, organized crime has endured.

This chapter focuses on traditional, Italian-American organized crime. In particular, we report findings from a study that examined "the outfit," which is the preeminent organized crime group in Chicago. The data were obtained primarily from interviews conducted in the years 1988 through 1994 with informants (N=25) who have knowledge about the outfit's activities and structure and the communities that are historically linked to the outfit. Additional data were obtained from police records of 98 street crew members.

Since the 1931 arrest of Al Capone, one of the country's most famous gangsters, an assortment of Chicago's racketeers have died or gone to prison, yet the outfit still survives. In 1983, Senator William V. Roth, Jr., told the Permanent Subcommittee on Investigations (1983) that "the criminal syndicate in Chicago is well and flourishing. It has not been eradicated nor, I regret to say, even contained" (p. 2). Notwithstanding recent prosecutorial successes against its most prominent members, the organization, which is the legacy of Al Capone, has been able to reconstitute itself for operations that will extend into the twenty-first century.

Goldstock (1987) maintained that "the incarceration of an underworld figure may disrupt an individual enterprise until new leadership is established, but the disruption, if any, is often minimal" (p. 82). The death or incarceration of an organized crime figure usually results in someone within the hierarchy moving up the ladder to take his place, while the vacancy that remains, especially if it is a lower-ranking position, is filled by a recruit. How has this been possible? How has traditional organized crime managed to attract enough new members to ensure its survival and longevity?

Although the literature on organized crime is extensive, few prior research efforts have explored the general issue of mob recruitment or have studied organized crime activities in Chicago. Moreover, no researcher since Landesco (1929) has directly addressed the significance of community contexts for the emergence and continuation of Italian-American organized crime.

LANDESCO'S LANDMARK STUDY

Sociology and racketeering both grew up in Chicago during the decades that followed World War I (Reynolds, 1992). At that time, University of

Chicago sociologists were laying the groundwork for the field of criminology. However, they virtually ignored organized crime, whose influence permeated every aspect of Chicago life. While Chicagoans and the American public alike were reading daily about Al Capone and other Prohibition-era gangsters, only John Landesco was studying the outfit.

Landesco's book, *Organized Crime in Chicago*, is probably the single most influential sociological work ever written about this subject. The study was completed in 1929 but did not receive widespread attention until it was reprinted in 1968. Its marginal status among the works of the Chicago School became the subject of some debate. According to Carey (1975), Landesco's recommendations regarding the control of organized crime, and those of Ernest Burgess, who contributed to the original edition of the book, were not embraced by the academic community or by other reformers of the period. Unlike most of the research of his contemporaries, Landesco's study had political implications and was quite critical of Chicago's business community and government.

Landesco's (1969) prescriptions included the assimilation of the immigrant community into mainstream society, the creation of a system of "boards of conciliation and arbitration" to mediate labor disputes, the removal of politics from the police department, the control of juvenile delinquency, and the separation of the city's political machine and organized crime. These suggestions made clear that the city's history, economic system, political order, and social stratification—and not its immigrant population—fostered organized crime. This finding prompted numerous questions that few people were willing to answer.

RECRUITMENT OF ORGANIZED CRIME MEMBERS

To survive, every organization must have an institutionalized process for inducting new members and inculcating in them its values and normative behaviors. With respect to organized crime, Cressey (1967) notes that some neighborhoods have all three of the "essential ingredients" of an effective recruiting process: "inspiring aspiration for membership, training for membership, and selection for membership" (p. 54). These areas were communities of local interest where ascriptive ties were based on ethnicity and kinship.

In the type of area described by Cressey (1967), adolescent males grow up believing that it is laudable to become a member of organized crime, just as young men who grow up in other areas aspire to join a certain club or to attend a prestigious university. In prime recruitment neighborhoods, young men see mob-affiliated bookies operate, they meet young mob enforcers, and they hear tales of glory recounted, that is, "who robbed what, who worked over whom, which showgirl shared which gangster's bed, who was shot by whom, and how easy the money rolls in" (Martin, 1963:61).

In his study of "Racketville," Spergel (1961) also found evidence that certain neighborhoods provide recruits for organized crime. According to Spergel, the presence of a well-organized criminal system in the community prepares young men for lifelong careers in the rackets. Ianni (1972) reported similar findings in his study of a New York crime family. He characterized this recruiting process as follows:

> In ghetto neighborhoods, kids still hang around in loosely formed gangs looking for "action" or a chance to make some money. The local "hoods" send them on little errands—buying coffee or carrying messages—and as they get older, trust them with more important tasks, such as picking up numbers or delivering number slips. Gradually some youngsters establish increasing degrees of trustworthiness with the "hoods" [Ianni, 1972:133].

Joseph Valachi, a professed member of the New York Genovese crime family who turned informant, testified before the McClellan Committee that local mobsters carefully watched young men from racket areas who sought entrance into organized crime (Cressey, 1967). As the youths participated in criminal activities such as burglary, local syndicate criminals paid special attention to their behavior when they were jailed. An adolescent who subscribed to the underworld code of being a "stand-up guy" and revealed nothing about himself or his criminal associates was a potential candidate for membership.

So-called defended neighborhoods—residential groups that seal themselves off through the efforts of delinquent gangs, restrictive covenants, sharp boundaries and forbidding reputations—also provide evidence of community areas serving as bases for recruitment into organized crime (Suttles, 1968). In these neighborhoods, the criminal value system is highly integrated into the community structure. Residents share collective moral sentiments that allow them to regard the pursuit of an underworld career as a legitimate way of life.

The types of communities that Ianni (1972), Valachi (see Cressey, 1967), and Suttles (1968) described are learning environments for the acquisition of values and skills associated with the performance of criminal roles and entrance into organized crime. A young man who lives in a racket area is automatically exposed to criminal attitudes; nonetheless, integration into organized crime also requires selection and tutelage, and only a chosen few are accorded such recognition. Although the candidates who form this pool represent a small segment of any community, their numbers have been sufficient enough over time to continually replenish the ranks of organized crime.

The current recruitment of personnel, however, has become increasingly more difficult for traditional organized crime, which is less able to attract competent, intelligent and ambitious Italian-Americans of the younger generation. Careers in organized crime offer little incentive to youngsters who are status- and security-conscious and who have grown up during periods of relative prosperity. Instead of crime, they prefer careers as lawyers, doctors and corporate executives (cf. Nelli, 1976).

Twenty-five years ago, important structural changes began taking place in large urban areas. Suburbanization, the end of machine politics and the tremendous influx of rural African-Americans into large northern cities altered the structure of urban society (Cloward and Ohlin, 1968). These changes, along with organized crime's movement toward syndicated gambling, altered the social structure of racket areas. In addition, as Raab (1990) has maintained, organized crime is on the decline because of increased federal law enforcement pressure and the dispersal of Italian-American populations away from urban neighborhoods.

O'Kane (1992) has taken a similar position on the disintegration of Italian neighborhoods and its repercussions for the mob's future. He noted that Italian organized crime figures are no longer receiving the support they once enjoyed from the broader Italian-American community. The Little Italies of our major cities are moribund communities, unable to sustain the rich cultural traditions of the past. Mainly inhabited by those abandoned in the exodus to middle-class suburbia, these neighborhoods now serve as tourist attractions for outsiders seeking restaurants, street festivals and the nostalgia of a bygone era. Minorities and young upper-middle-class professionals increasingly reside in these neighborhoods and are filling the vacuum created by the departure of Italian youths to more affluent areas.

Smith and Alba (1979) underscored the community's significance to organized crime. They noted that Bell's (1964) functionalist argument and Ianni's (1972) ethnic succession hypothesis both predict that the dominant criminal group's hold over the world of vice and crime weakens as its ghettos dissolve and its protection from police intrusion disappears. This assertion is based on the notion that in the early stages of ethnic mobility, residential segregation facilitates the illicit upward movement that allows criminal networks to flourish in urban ghettos.

Do the racket areas of the past continue to exist despite changing social and economic conditions? This research seeks to determine if neighborhood areas are still relevant, or whether other factors now explain how Italian-American organized crime groups recruit new members. Cultural deviance, anomie and various economic theories have all been utilized to explain traditional organized crime. Yet no researcher since Landesco (1929) has directly addressed the importance of community social structure for the emergence and, in particular, the continuation of this phenomenon. This study is an attempt to determine the importance of community contexts for the continued existence of traditional organized crime in American society.

STREET CREW NEIGHBORHOODS

In the Chicago metropolitan area, five communities have a history of association with organized crime. They are commonly referred to as Taylor Street, Grand Avenue, 26th Street, the North Side, and the suburb of Chicago Heights. These communities are the locations of the five original street crews of the Chicago outfit. Street crews are the organizational groupings that engage in the mob's criminal activities.

Taylor Street

Taylor Street's involvement with the Chicago outfit can be traced to the 1920s and the adolescent street-corner group known as the 42 Gang. The 42 Gang derived its name from the legend of Ali Baba and the Forty Thieves (the gang had 40 plus two members) (Brashler, 1977). The gang specialized in truck hijacking and auto theft (Landesco, 1933). When asked about the 42 Gang, respondents who had been raised in the area made statements such as the following:

> Everybody on Taylor Street knew the 42 Gang. Even the other criminals were afraid of them. There were crazy sons-a-bitches, very, very reckless guys. Once they got in a gun battle right on Taylor and May, and I had to jump down a stairwell to save my ass [Interview Respondent 24, (1994):2].

The Capone Syndicate in Chicago consisted of a number of cells, each having its own members and criminal enterprises (Murray, 1975). The 42 Gang constituted the cell that eventually became known as the Taylor Street crew. The 42 Gang played an important part in the development of the Taylor Street crew, and in the evolution of organized crime in Chicago. In spite of its history and formidable reputation, little organized crime activity now exists in the Taylor Street area. As related by a former resident of the community: "There are no wiseguys on Taylor Street anymore. You are not going to go down on Taylor Street and see gangsters anymore" (Interview Respondent 18, (1992):3).

This statement is supported by a local community organizer who believes that Taylor Street is no longer viewed as a racket area (Interview Respondent 9, (1988):1). The neighborhood has greatly changed because of the presence of the University of Illinois and the rising property values resulting from the neighborhood's proximity to Chicago's central business district. This informant felt that the place to look for organized crime activity was now in the suburbs, and that most of the original Taylor Street crew had moved west on Grand Avenue (Interview Respondent 9, (1988):1).

Grand Avenue

While organized crime activity appears to be on the decline in the Taylor Street community, it could still be found in the Grand Avenue neighborhood through the 1980s. Similar to Taylor Street, Grand Avenue had different pockets of ethnicity and social solidarity, but people living in the vicinity all shared the same residential identity.

Anthony "Big Tuna" Accardo, the long-time, senior statesman of the Chicago crime syndicate, was born in 1906 at 1353 W. Grand Avenue (Roemer, 1990). Accardo had once been a bodyguard and enforcer for Al Capone (Brashler, 1977). His involvement with Capone is commonly believed to have been the beginning of the Grand Avenue street crew. Accardo started his criminal career as a member of the Circus Cafe Gang, a group of young toughs who frequented a tavern called the Circus Cafe during the late 1920s. The Circus Gang and another near northwest side gang, the Guilfoyle Gang, were subsidiaries of the Capone Syndicate and served as counterforces to an Irish Gang on Chicago's North Side, which was led by Dion O'Banion.

Unlike Taylor Street, little has been written about the early criminal history of the Grand Avenue community, probably because much of it was originally located within the Seventeenth Ward. The Seventeenth Ward was a center of progressive political activity during the early part of the twentieth century. Although the area had its share of tenements and urban poor, the community was by no means a slum. According to an early source on social conditions in the Seventeenth Ward, even the saloons were relatively well-run and clean and served a useful purpose by providing free lunches to workers (Taylor, 1886).

Crime syndicate activities can still be seen on Grand Avenue. One respondent described the recent activity:

> You go to Covelli's at Grand and Ogden. You go there, and there are 20 bookmakers there on Friday night. They are all around. You go to that little social club down the street, Grand and May. You go in there and there is [sic] a half dozen bookmakers hanging in there. Now I don't know the jewel thieves or the safecrackers. There are 50 guys in the room [Interview Respondent 17, (1992):5].

Twenty-Sixth Street

Compared to Grand Avenue, there is even more organized crime activity today in the 26th Street neighborhood. Twenty-Sixth Street lies within the Armour Square community area of Chicago (Local Community Factbook Consortium, 1984). The 26th Street area is called the "patch." This term is increasingly being applied, by both police and pundits of the underworld, to other organized crime communities as well. For example:

> When you say the word patch, I think of 31st and Princeton, 26th Street, that area down there. But they also refer to Taylor Street as the patch. But 31st was the first. If somebody said the patch, that is where I would go. "Meet me in the patch." I would go to 26th and Princeton and park [Interview Respondent 17, (1992):10].

The 26th Street Crew is considered to be the direct descendant of the original Capone syndicate, the forerunner of today's outfit (Interview Respondent 13, (1992)). Many of the people who worked for Capone lived in the nearby 26th Street Italian neighborhood, which today is probably the strongest street crew neighborhood in metropolitan Chicago. Unlike Taylor Street and the North Side, there have been no major urban renewal efforts in this community. The homes are well-kept, and the neighborhood is racially stable. As reported by one organized crime investigator: "They are still 20 years behind" (Interview Respondent 12, (1992):12). Whereas syndicate guys from other neighborhoods have moved out, people from 26th Street have remained in the neighborhood:

They have such a base there. All of their people are right there....Yeah, that neighborhood has been like time frozen. You go back in the '60s, it is still there. They still have the social club there by Riccobene's. They still have that, and the hoods still go there. You will find the LaMantia's, the Caruso's [Interview Respondent 20, (1992):20].

North Side

Today, the North Side is an area with no organized crime activity. But the North Side was once "Honky-Tonk USA" (Lindberg, 1991). After the fall of Bugs Moran, and the infamous St. Valentine's Day Massacre, the neighborhood took on new significance. Saloons, cabarets and rialtos marked every block on Clark Street, its main thoroughfare. Clark Street was so famous that it was featured in the stage play and movie *Show Boat*. Gilbert Ravenal, the gambler in Edna Ferber's story, brought his bride to North Clark Street to live after their marriage (Smith, 1954).

By 1953, the Chicago Crime Commission reported that there were 165 "clip joints...burlesque bars, assignation houses, and gambling joints" in the Clark Street area (Smith, 1954:215). Scantily clad "26-Girls" hustled drinks from out-of-town conventioneers and local men seeking a good time. In 1953, the City Council appointed the Big Nine Committee to investigate vice and politics in Chicago. Their final report, known as the "Kohn Report," publicly revealed the connections between organized crime activities and ward politics. There is nothing presently left of the Clark Street rialto, though neighboring Rush Street contains numerous restaurants and upscale liquor establishments. The North Side, as a racket community, no longer exists. Most of the members of the original Sicilian community moved away when the neighborhood was torn down between 1941 and 1962, during the successive stages of the construction of the Cabrini-Green housing complex. As related by a former resident of the area: "After the war they tore down the whole neighborhood. First the row houses, then they knocked the neighborhood down completely for the Cabrini Green Housing Projects. So all of those people moved out" [Interview Respondent 14, (1992):2].

Chicago Heights

The development of organized crime in Chicago Heights parallels its development in Chicago. By 1908, this newly established city had a reputation for an abundance of gamblers, and many of its saloons were also supporting prostitution (Lanfranchi, 1976). That year, the city's mayor, Lee H. Hooks, was arrested with five other people on gambling charges. Crime became a recurrent theme in Chicago Heights politics. On April 8, 1915, the *Chicago Heights Star* reported that mayoral candidate Craig Hood promised to crush commercialized vice and to clean up the police department. Another mayoral candidate, John Thomas, promised in 1929 to see that commercial gambling and vice of all types did not exist in Chicago Heights while he was mayor (Lanfranchi, 1976).

During Prohibition, Chicago Heights was known for its bootlegging activities. George Golding of the Treasury Department announced in 1928 that Chicago Heights was one huge distillery, and that there was nothing in the U.S. equal to it (Lanfranchi, 1976). Conditions in Chicago Heights were so scandalous that the chief of police was murdered in his own home on December 6, 1928, because he had been subpoenaed to testify before a grand jury against two local bootleggers (Schoenberg, 1992).

Prohibition brought the influence of the Capone mob into Chicago Heights (Liebman, 1960). It also prompted an increase in violent crime as mobsters fought for control of the illegal liquor business. Reporting in February 1929 that there were 65 murders in a two-year period in Chicago Heights, the *Shanghai (China) Times* called it the most lawless community in the U.S. (*Star*, February 15, 1929).

Organized crime activity in Chicago Heights is presently in decline. The 1989 conviction of its mob boss, Albert Ceasar Tocco, was devastating to the Chicago Heights crew. According to a federal law enforcement officer who participated in the Tocco investigation, the card rooms and social clubs frequented by members of the Chicago Heights crew are gone, and it is now difficult to locate any organized crime figures in Chicago Heights (Interview Respondent 20, (1992):2). Further evidence of the decline of the Chicago Heights crew was provided by another respondent:

> I don't know if Chicago Heights exists anymore as a group because the last time I went out to the Heights, they don't [sic] have it. It's just not there anymore. The old clubs that we were aware of just aren't there. Buildings were razed. I think that the influence of it is still around, though [Interview Respondent 13, (1992):2].

THE STRUCTURE AND FUNCTION OF STREET CREWS

Gambling is the major activity of street crews today. There is evidence, however, that the various crews once specialized in certain types of crime. As stated by a member of the U.S. Attorney's Office in Chicago: "Gambling is now the mainstay of organized crime. Virtually all O.C. people are involved in some type of gambling operation" (Interview Respondent 2, (1988):2).

The Grand Avenue specialty was burglary. According to Chicago Police Department and Chicago Crime Commission records, 65% (20 of the 31 members) of the Grand Avenue crew have been arrested on more than one occasion for burglary or have been suspects in a major burglary. The 26th Street crew was noted for truck hijacking, which in Chicago was known as cartage theft. The North Side/Rush Street crew is noted for its vice operations: prostitution, pornography and liquor law violations.

Many of these criminal specializations can be related to the ecology of each area. For example, the North Side contained Clark Street, which was once Chicago's adult nightclub entertainment district. The 26th Street area contains a large number of railroad yards and associated shipping and trucking terminals, which provided opportunities for cargo theft. As related by an experienced organized crime investigator: "You had all the railroads running through 26th Street. You had the railroads. The trucking companies and the railroads were close by" (Interview Respondent 13, (1992):7).

Chicago Heights, located on the southern edge of the Chicago metropolitan area, had a reputation for automobile theft and chop-shop operations. As explained by a former Chicago police intelligence officer:

> This is what they knew, and what they knew is that they could make a ton of money from this stuff. And for some reason, the South suburbs grew better auto thieves than the North Side guys, and they just got into it. You had Indiana, you had a lot of different areas and that is what Tocco and those guys did. You had chop shops all over the place that those guys were running [Interview Respondent 20, (1992):18].

The 1990 Racketeer Influenced and Corrupt Organizations (RICO) prosecution (U.S. v. Rocco Infelise et al., 90CR00087-1) of a group of Chicago crime syndicate figures furnishes an inside look at today's street crew activities. In all, 20 members of the outfit were charged with 42 counts of racketeering. According to the indictment, a criminal organization, sometimes referred to as the Joseph Ferriola street crew, was operating in Chicago. This crew was part of a larger criminal organization commonly referred to as the Chicago outfit, or the mob. The Ferriola street crew is another name for the Taylor Street crew. Joseph Ferriola was the boss of the Taylor Street crew during much of the time of the investigation.

The indictment stated that the Ferriola Crew existed primarily for the purpose of providing income to its members in several ways, including:

> ...the operating of various illegal gambling businesses such as sports bookmaking, parlay cards and casino games; the collecting of interest, known as "juice," on usurious loans made by the enterprise; the collecting of protection money known as "street tax" from various illegitimate as well as questionably legitimate businesses; and the use of the proceeds from those activities in the enterprise and in other business ventures.

Members of the Ferriola street crew were charged with the murder of a number of people who either posed a threat to the street crew or failed to pay street tax for operating various illegal enterprises. Members of the crew were also charged with operating an illegal gambling business, and with usurious credit practices stemming from that business. In addition, various members of the crew were charged with extortion and the failure to file federal income tax returns.

The indictment also stated that the purpose of the Ferriola street crew was to recruit and retain members, and to maintain loyalty, discipline, and control over their ranks. To carry out these activities, the street crew was structured along the following hierarchy: a leader or boss, assistants to the boss, supervisors of the various income-producing activities, and agents and employees who were compensated out of the crew's earnings.

The role of the boss of each street crew was further defined in the 1992 RICO indictment (U.S. v. Sam Carlisi et al., 92-CR1064) of 11 other members of the outfit. This indictment stated that: "...the 'boss' of the crew was ultimately responsible to the head of the outfit and was required to ensure that the leadership of the outfit received a share of the proceeds from the crew's activities."

The head of the outfit in Chicago is more of an arbitrator than a director of a large corporation. Each street crew, for the most part, acts independently of the other crews, and each boss is solely responsible for the activities of his crew. The head of the outfit settles disputes among the crews and may handle relations with those outside the organization, such as corrupt public officials and organized crime groups in other cities. The street crews defer to his authority in order to avoid violence and the news media attention that is associated with it. As one federal law enforcement official explained: "These guys realize that in order to keep it going they need someone up there or else they will have the problem that they have in New York or Philly where the streets are laden with bodies" (Interview Respondent 20, (1992):11).

According to the Chicago Crime Commission (1990), each of the outfit's street crews is headed by a "capo," or captain. The members of the crews are called "soldiers," and their associates are said to be "connected." In charge of all the crews is a boss and a second in command, the underboss. The boss's advisers are usually older, successful members who serve as the mob's elder statesmen. The bosses, the elder statesmen and the street crew captains are all "made guys." Soldiers are members of the outfit, but they are not made guys.

Some disagreement can be found about the various terms that are used to describe positions within the outfit. For example, the word "soldier" is said to have "come from New York from Joe Valachi" (Interview Respondent 13, (1992):8). According to a federal investigator assigned to organized crime prosecutions in Chicago: "The outfit people that I have talked to never use the terms 'soldier' or 'capo' and those other FBI terms, and they don't use the term 'La Cosa Nostra' (Interview Respondent 20, (1992):11).

A RECONCEPTUALIZATION OF THE RACKET SUBCULTURE

Organized Crime Neighborhoods

The increasing scale and complexity of modern society has altered the social structure of urban communities. Greater social stratification and geographic mobility have essentially marked the end of ethnically defined neighborhoods. Hence, racket subcultures and street crew neighborhoods began to vanish from the American social scene as their residents became educated, found jobs and moved to the suburbs. For example, as a street crew neighborhood, the North Side is gone, and Chicago Heights is defunct. These changes support the theory that traditional organized crime is in decline because of demographic changes in racket areas and the integration of the Italian-American population into mainstream American life.

From Chicago Police Department records, Lombardo (1994) was able to identify the community of origin for half of the outfit's current membership (N=98). Within this group, he found that 59 of 98, or 60%, were born in one of the five street crew areas, and 41% were still living in one of the areas. Nativity and residency, however, varied among the neighborhoods.

Specifically, in the Grand Avenue and 26th Street crews, 85% and 89% of the members, respectively, were born in their street crew neighborhoods. Many members of the crews were also presently living in those communities. Specifically, 63% of the Grand Avenue crew and 55% of the 26th Street crew lived in those respective areas. Lombardo (1994) also reported interview findings to support these results. One of the study's informants, an experienced organized crime investigator, related that numerous organized crime figures can be seen frequenting social clubs and spending a lot of time in both neighborhoods:

> You go to the neighborhood, and everybody is standing on the corner like at the old Italian-American Social Club at 26th and Princeton. You got Angelo's Dream over there....On Shields, north of 31st Street. Those guys are wannabes, they honor these people. They all stand on the corner and go to the clubs. You see them hanging around with all the bookmakers and all the made guys, you know, the guys with the bent noses. You see the young guys, 20 to 25 years old. They are all sitting out there doing the same thing. And that holds true around Grand Avenue. You know, you go east on Grand Avenue from Halsted to, like Ogden and that area in there. There are four to five social clubs in there (only one remains today). You go there and you see all the young kids in there. [I'm] Talking, 22, 23, 25-year-old guys hanging around with all the guys that are 50 and 60 years old. Taking their cars to get washed, and running out and getting donuts and bringing them lunch [Interview Respondent 17, (1992):1].

In contrast, Lombardo's (1994) analyses of the three remaining street crews provided little evidence of nativity or residency. Only 24% of Taylor Street's crew were raised in the area, and only 8% live there today. The North Side's street crew's nativity and residency rates were both 27%, and in Chicago Heights they were both 37%.

These data indicate that community areas continue to support organized crime in Chicago. The 26th Street neighborhood, in particular, bears a number of the markings of a racket community, and serves such important functions as protecting its inhabitants from the invasion of alien minority groups and providing employment in the criminal organization. This neighborhood is in fact largely an Italian-American defended neighborhood. As explained by an experienced federal investigator:

> One of the big things in the patch is the housing and how it is set up. They are bound, everybody. They don't go east of the Ryan, don't go west of Halsted much. Geographically, you can't go south of Sox Park,

you are in the ghetto there and north is Chinatown...I am sure everyone in the patch went to the Catholic grade school down there. They knew each other from day one, and their parents knew each other from day one. They moved back to their father's apartment building when they got married, or they moved two blocks away. God forbid they moved out of that parish into the next parish, which was eight blocks away. That is what you had, and that is why they perpetuated so well down there. I am sure that if you "Yuppified" the patch, you would kill that crew. Shorty LaMantia wouldn't see his 14 compadres each day if he had to drive eighty miles [Interview Respondent 20, (1992):20-21].

The 26th Street neighborhood provides employment opportunities for members of the 26th Street crew in numerous bookmaking operations and employment with the city of Chicago. Several of the 40 members of the 26th Street Crew (22%) have held jobs with the city. These jobs are available to street crew members because 26th Street is located in Chicago's First Ward. The former Alderman of the First Ward, Fred Roti, lives in the 26th Street neighborhood. He was alderman from 1968 until 1990, when he failed to seek reelection after his arrest by the Justice Department. Roti was widely regarded as the outfit's representative in city government.

Another major finding of Lombardo (1994) is that recruitment into the Taylor Street crew has continued without its physical presence in the community. As we have suggested earlier, recruitment into the outfit is related to the social structure of community areas. Socialized in the norms of the racket subculture, individuals from the Taylor Street crew took their values about organized crime with them when they moved to other city and suburban communities. As explained by a former resident of Taylor Street, when asked about the effects of emigration: "They don't all go the same way. They all go to different spots. It's like they branch out. Follow society, suburbanization. And the patch loses its thing. But it will always be in their mind" (Interview Respondent 15, (1992):9).

The outfit has stayed alive, in part, because its members adhered to the ways of organized crime when they left street crew neighborhoods. As a former resident of the Grand and Ogden neighborhood and member of the outfit explained: "They moved from whatever neighborhood they were from. Some guys moved to Melrose Park, Elmwood Park. Some guys were from Taylor Street, they moved to Elmwood Park. Some guys were from Grand and Ogden, and they moved to Elmwood Park and they brought it there" (Interview Respondent 21, (1993):1).

Organized crime activities have appeared in suburban areas and are concentrated in places such as the Elmwood Park Social Athletic Club (SAC), which for all practical purposes is the headquarters of the Taylor Street crew. The Elmwood Park SAC has been the center of west suburban organized crime for many years. An associate of a number of organized crime members stated that: "The social club in Elmwood Park, that is where they all go. That crew, that is where they all meet in the daytime for whatever reason, whether it is to conduct business or play pinochle" (Interview Respondent 4, (1992):12).

Does this mean that a racket subculture has been reestablished in the suburb of Elmwood Park? Lombardo's (1994) residence data indicate that neither Elmwood Park nor Melrose Park have produced many recruits for organized crime. Only six (6%) of the 98 members of the outfit whose nativity and residency were identified in his analysis came from Elmwood Park or Melrose Park. Nineteen of them currently live in these two towns, 15 in Elmwood Park. All but four originally came from the Taylor Street and Grand Avenue neighborhoods. Elmwood Park and Melrose Park did not produce substantial numbers of recruits for the outfit because suburbs, by their very nature, are different from urban areas. As a federal organized crime investigator observed:

> I think that Elmwood Park got an infusion of people when people began to move. When people moved off of Taylor Street, they had to move somewhere. Some people moved to Melrose. There are still Italians there. But it is not the same kind of area. You don't have, I don't think, the population density. You had non-Italians there. In the patch, it was mostly Italians [Interview Respondent 20, (1992):29].

When questioned about the difference between city and suburban areas, a Chicago police officer and former resident of the West Side of Chicago commented:

> Certain things are tolerated in the patch that would not be tolerated in other places. The police drive by and see white kids, it's alright. That wouldn't be tolerated in the suburbs or in residential areas of the city. People in the patch feel secure when they could [sic] look out and see kids, maybe because of blacks....Look at Elmwood Park. They won't tolerate kids on the corner [Interview Respondent 5, (1988):9, 11].

When asked about differences between city and suburban areas in the circumstances that promote organized crime, a former resident of the

North Side explained that in the old neighborhood everyone was close and trusted one another. But when one moves to the suburbs:

> It gets diluted because they move into a neighborhood where people don't all think like that. Its different. You are a little more aloof out there. You go down to the neighborhood, the houses are built on top of one another, right down the street. Everybody knew everybody else, and they are all related. On one street you probably had three aunts, four brothers, a nephew and a cousin. You move to the suburbs, you buy a house on a block there, they are all strangers [Interview Respondent 14, (1992):3].

The eclipse of the urban community has resulted in a "community of limited liability" in which ascriptive ties and local community orientations still exist, but commitment is partial and varied (Hunter, 1974). The centerpiece of limited liability theory suggests that peoples' sense of community varies with their status in both the local community and the larger society, and with the demographic and social characteristics of the community. As such, their ties to the local community are often less important than their occupational status and their position within the wider society.

Although the ecological characteristics of suburban areas generally do not lend themselves to the creation of traditional racket neighborhoods, a semblance of a racket subculture still exists in some suburban communities. For example, when asked about organized crime recruitment in suburban areas, a gambler who is very familiar with the west suburban scene explained that: "In the old neighborhood, where the density and opportunity were, you could look at a bookmaker driving a big Lincoln and say, boy I would like to be a bookmaker. They don't see that much organized crime in the suburbs, but they see some of it" (Interview Respondent 3, (1988):2).

Whatever trappings of organized crime are seen in suburban areas have supported recruitment and allowed the Taylor Street crew to continue. Organized crime in suburban areas, however, takes a different form from that in the city. According to a former member of the Grand Avenue street crew, when people move to the suburbs: "They get a little bit more highfalutin'. They come out of the ghetto and move to the nice suburbs and they try not to, they wouldn't have, crap games. More or less the people hang out, cabaret, buy drinks, stuff like that" (Interview Respondent 21, (1993):4).

Besides the Elmwood Park SAC, the only other places where organized crime figures can be seen in suburban areas are in a few restaurants and bars. They are virtually anonymous in their communities. They are not seen walking the streets or standing on the corner socializing with community residents, as in patch neighborhoods. A number of crime syndicate members now live in the wealthy suburbs of Oakbrook and Barrington, yet these towns do not have reputations for organized crime. The structures of these communities are not amenable to such organized crime activity.

That members of the Taylor Street crew can be found in the Elmwood Park SAC and in a few suburban restaurants and bars is important for the perpetuation of traditional organized crime. These locations serve the same purposes as the old street crew neighborhoods; that is, they provide places for crime syndicate figures to congregate and be seen. The outfit has to be seen someplace in order to attract new members. If members of the outfit generally come from street crew neighborhoods, who is recruited by the Taylor Street crew and where do they get the idea that they want to be gangsters?

The Taylor Street crew's recruits are mostly individuals who are attracted to the outfit lifestyle. Just as people once saw real-life examples of organized crime in street crew neighborhoods, they are today seeing organized crime in the mass media. There is virtually no one in the U.S. who has not been exposed to media images of Italian-American organized crime. Gangsters have become part of American folklore. Individuals can see instances of organized crime activity on television without ever leaving their houses. People whose parents once lived in street crew neighborhoods also get information about organized crime from their families. When questioned about people's familiarity with organized crime, a former gambling investigator stated:

> It's probably something that has been handed down from generation to generation. Grandpa always told stories to the kids about Al Capone. Somebody knows somebody whose uncle probably got killed somewhere along the line, and I think there is probably still a certain amount of respect for all that [Interview Respondent 17, (1992):12].

Although information about organized crime is available to the general public, not everyone is eligible to join the outfit. A recruit still must be known (Interview Respondent 13, (1992):10). His family must have come from one of the street crew neighborhoods, or he must have proved himself trustworthy. He must still withstand the background check. Solly D'Laurentis, a convicted member of the outfit, provided an excellent example of how the Taylor Street crew now recruits members. As explained by a federal organized crime investigator:

This guy wanted to be a mobster from day one. His family grew up on Taylor Street, and he got fucked. His family moved out to Lake County, and he couldn't be a mobster because there was nobody to be a mobster with. So he gradually made connections back in the old neighborhood. Solly always had it in his mind that he was a gangster. People knew him before he was a real gangster. He always acted like a real gangster. He needed that to fit into his life. So that is how he became one [Interview Respondent 20, (1992):19].

Roving Neighborhoods

In the case of the Taylor Street crew, that recruitment is continuing without its physical presence in the Taylor Street neighborhood does not necessarily signal the end of community linkages for organized crime. Even though increasing urban differentiation has caused the decline of ethnic neighborhoods, groups of individuals can still share a common lifestyle and rules of conduct. In essence, people who seek a life in the rackets, or people who have had traditions of organized crime handed down from family and friends, constitute the community of the Taylor Street crew—no matter where they live. Hence, the street crew neighborhood of the Taylor Street crew is a "roving neighborhood."

Riemer (1950) defined the roving neighborhood as the area in which an individual travels in search of friends, recreational activities and membership in associations. Each individual conceives of the roving neighborhood in many different ways. For example, a suburban home-owner may work in a nearby city's downtown area, seek recreation in the city's nightclub district, shop at a suburban shopping mall and belong to a country club in a different town. This individual's neighborhood consists of the people he meets in each of these areas. The concept of the roving neighborhood may be used to locate the "neighborhood" of the Taylor Street crew. Today, a member of the Taylor Street crew may live in Oakbrook, attend "business" meetings at the Elmwood Park SAC, and frequent restaurants and bars on Taylor Street.

The importance of Taylor Street to the Taylor Street crew and to the outfit in general lies in the fact that Taylor Street has become the symbolic, collective representation of *the* neighborhood. This area has become an artifact of an earlier period of the racket subculture, as well as of the history of Italian immigration and settlement in Chicago. Taylor Street is now referred to as "Little Italy," a name that was unheard of in Chicago just ten years ago. Stories abound about the 42 Gang and about Al Capone as an icon of ethnic mobility, and the name Taylor Street continues to be synonymous with organized crime. A former resident of Taylor Street describes his attachment to the neighborhood in this way:

> As the saying goes, "you can take the person outta' Taylor Street but you can't take Taylor Street outta' the person." ...As soon as I see someone from the old neighborhood, we start reminiscing about life on Taylor Street. It's like we never left the place. We feel a certain bond with each other because we once lived there. It's a certain attachment we have about one [sic] another....I suppose we'll always feel this way [Interview Respondent 24, (1994):32].

Moral Sentiments

Whether centered in a street crew community or in a roving neighborhood, many Chicagoans express a definite attachment to the outfit (or its mythology), as evidenced by the following statements:

> I believe in them. I believe in them, and I respect them. They never hurt me. I am sure they hurt people. I know the police have hurt a lot more people than the outfit, and I have been around the outfit all my life. It's a part of life. It's a group of people with a belief. It's a culture. It's a way of life for many people, for a big part of society in our area. It's a way of life to many people, to many families. A lot of, lot of people [Interview Respondent 12, (1992):8].

> The outfit guys never bothered anybody except their own... If you'd cross them, they would take care of you. But as far as hurting innocent people, that just never happened. You could even say they protected the neighborhood. Nobody came on Taylor Street to do robberies or to break into houses—they'd be dead if they tried anything like that. We didn't have to lock our doors or windows; the outfit made us feel safe. And from Capone's days till now, you know, the syndicate has been known to help people out with hospital bills and whatnot....It burns me up when I see police pickin' on them and letting the real crooks go free [Interview Respondent 24, (1994):25].

Such sentiments suggest that the outfit has a community base not only in the ecological sense but also in the normative sense. For example, when street crew boss Joe "The Clown" Lombardo was tried in federal court during the early 1980s, many Grand Avenue residents testified as character witnesses in his behalf (Interview Respondent 2, (1988)).

In a separate organized crime prosecution, a group called the Committee Against Government Oppression held a fundraiser at the Carlyle Banquet Hall in Oakbrook during the latter part of 1989 that raised over $200,000 for the defense of Rocco Infelice and members of the Taylor Street crew (Interview Respondent 20, (1992):17). These same people later gathered in front of the federal building in downtown Chicago on July 2, 1992 to protest the government's methods in prosecuting the members of the Taylor Street Crew (*Chicago Tribune*, 1992). A federal organized crime investigator who witnessed the demonstration commented that:

> They had so many people come down to the federal building. Some of the guys were intrigued by it. "Who the fuck are these people?" [they said], because we didn't know who they were. There were some people who are into "mobology" who are from all different sections. We found people from the patch. We found people from Wheaton who believed that the "G" was out against Italians. Some appeared to be legit Italian-Americans who actually believed that we were into this persecution thing [Interview Respondent 20, (1992):17].

SUMMARY

Italian-American organized crime in Chicago (i.e., the outfit) developed in the five original street crew neighborhoods, which are akin to the racket subculture areas and defended neighborhoods described in earlier studies (Cressey, 1967; Ianni, 1972; Spergel, 1961; Suttles, 1972). Changes in neighborhood structures, which were brought about by emigration, urban renewal and economic development, have occasioned the downfall of the North Side and Chicago Heights as bases for mob recruitment and core operations. Nonetheless, the 26th Street crew and, to a lesser extent, the Grand Avenue street crew are still functioning in those communities. They have kept alive the subculture and allure of the outfit and, thus, its ability to attract new members.

Although Taylor Street has long disappeared as a mob neighborhood, its crew has been one of the outfit's most productive and feared branches. The concept of the roving neighborhood helps to explain, in part, the continuation of this street crew absent its initial surroundings and community ties. The Taylor Street crew maintained its solidarity because its members carried with them a shared set of values that transcended the artificial physical boundaries of the neighborhood. They were visible enough to continue recruitment through direct contact with would-be mobsters, and probably enticed men who were simply captivated by the gangster lifestyle that has become part of American folklore.

REFERENCES

Abadinsky, H. (1985). *Organized Crime*. Chicago, IL: Nelson-Hall.

Brashler, W. (1977). *The Don*. New York, NY: Harper & Row.

Carey, J.T. (1975). *Social and Public Affairs*. Beverly Hills, CA: Sage.

Cloward, R. A. and L.E. Ohlin (1968). *Delinquency and Opportunity*. New York, NY: Free Press.

Cressey, D.R. (1967). *The Functions and Structures of Criminal Syndicates*. Task Force Report on Organized Crime. Washington, DC: U.S. Government Printing Office.

Dedmon, E. (1953). *Fabulous Chicago*. New York, NY: Random House.

Goldstock, R. (1987). "Operational Issues in Organized Crime Control." In: H. Edelhertz ed., *Major Issues in Organized Crime Control*. Washington, DC: U.S. Government Printing Office.

Ianni, F.A J. (1972). *A Family Business*. New York, NY: Russell Sage Foundation.

Kobrin, S. (1967). "The Conflict of Values in Delinquency Areas." In: R. Giallombardo ed., *Juvenile Delinquency*. New York, NY: Wiley.

Landesco, J. (1929). *Organized Crime in Chicago*. Chicago: University of Chicago Press.

—— (1933). "The Life History of a Member of the '42' Gang." *Journal of Criminal Law, Criminology, and Police Science* 23:964-998.

Lanfranchi, M. (1976). "A Political History of Chicago Heights." Unpublished manuscript, Governors State University, Chicago, IL.

Liebman, C. (1960). *Some Political Effects of the Functional Differentiation of Suburbs*. Doctoral dissertation, University of Chicago, Chicago, IL.

Lindberg, R.C. (1991). *To Serve and Collect*. New York, NY: Praeger.

Local Community Factbook Consortium (1984). *Local Community Factbook for Chicago*. Chicago, IL: Author.

Lombardo, R.M. (1994). "The Organized Crime Neighborhoods of Chicago." In: R.J. Kelly, K-L. Chin and R. Shatzberg eds., *Handbook of Organized Crime in the United States*. Westport, CT: Greenwood.

Murray, G. (1975). *The Legacy of Al Capone*. New York, NY: G.T. Putnam's.

Nelli, H. (1976). *The Business of Crime*. New York, NY: Oxford Press.

O'Kane, J. (1992). *The Crooked Ladder*. New Brunswick, NJ: Transaction.

Pasley, F.D. (1930). *Al Capone*. Salem, NH: Ayer.

Raab, S. (1990). "A Battered and Ailing Mafia is Losing its Grip on America." *New York Times*, October 22, p.A1.

Reynolds, M. (1992). *U.S. Sociology and the Study of Organized Crime*. Doctoral dissertation, Fordham University, New York, NY.

Riemer, S. (1950). "Hidden Dimensions of Neighborhood Planning." *Land Economics* 26:197-201.

Roemer, W.F. (1990). *The War of the Godfathers*. New York, NY: Donald Fine.

Schmidt, John R. (1987). *The Mayor Who Cleaned Up Chicago*. DeKalb, IL: Northern Illinois University Press.

Schoenberg, R.J. (1992). *Mr. Capone*. New York, NY: William Morrow.

Smith, A.J. (1954). *Syndicate City*. Chicago, IL: Henry Regnery.

Smith, D.C. and R.D. Alba (1979). "Organized Crime and American Life." *Society* 16:32-38.

Spergel, I. (1961). *Racketville, Slumtown, and Haulburg*. Chicago, IL: University of Chicago Press.

Suttles, G.D. (1968). *The Social Order of the Slum*. Chicago, IL: University of Chicago Press.

—— (1972). *The Social Construction of Communities*. Chicago, IL: University of Chicago Press.

Taylor, G. (1886). *Social Services of the 17th ward*. Chicago, IL: Newberry Library, Chicago Commons Collection.

U.S. Congress. Permanent Subcommittee on Investigations (1983). *Organized Crime in Chicago*. Washington, DC: U.S. Government Printing Office.

Zorbaugh, H.W. (1929). *The Gold Coast and the Slum*. Chicago, IL: University of Chicago Press.

Mafia Women in Non-Fiction: What Primary and Secondary Sources Reveal

by

James D. Calder

Abstract: *A study of the non-fiction literature on organized crime examines the lifestyles of Mafia women in the U.S. In general, the evidence shows that popular, fictional impressions of Mafia wives, daughters, mothers, nieces, and sisters are incomplete and miscast. Mafia women have real lives significantly more complex and active than the lives portrayed in fiction. They should no longer be portrayed as mere passive, tangential and inconsequential functionaries in the subculture of Italian-American organized crime.*

INTRODUCTION

Italian-American women in Mario Puzo's (1969) epic, *The Godfather*, are anonymous functionaries in a secret and violent subculture of organized crime.[1] Mrs. Vito Corleone, for example, is barely evident among the hoard of men who surround and define Don Corleone's role as family patriarch.[2] It would appear that Mrs. Corleone is a decent and hard-working woman, but the narrative offers few opportunities by which to detect the scope and depth of her life.[3] Indeed, attributes of Mafia women in the fictional literature are restricted generally to childbearing, marital loyalty, patience, quiet submission and virtuosity. *Una buona femmina* (a good woman) is a normative role type, replete with qualities of life giving, self-sacrifice, toleration and, above all, *sistemata* (a woman who is settled and competent in her role).[4]

More recent films and novels about Mafia family circumstances[5] have enriched the roles of women. Modern fiction enlarges the definitions of conditionalities in women's lives, occasionally evaluating Mafia lifestyle implications or degrees of self-determination.[6] Unquestionably, the men in fictional accounts dominate the decision-making processes for all major family circumstances,[7] but the women appear to demand more information and representation in household dialogues about outcomes. At the margins of literary fantasy, of course, the Mafia woman asserts full self-determination by participating in criminal conspiracy (La Plante, 1991).

An extensive collection of non-fiction literature on organized crime offers a database of information from which fictional characterizations of Mafia women can reasonably be tested. Carefully treated, true accounts based on primary sources and published in autobiographies, biographies or case studies open new lines of inquiry. The objective is to muster sufficient evidence to defend the view that lifestyle conditions of Mafia wives include knowledge and/or direct involvement in some aspects of "family business," abusive and uncaring treatment by Mafia men, and forms of rebellion against the intolerable and often irrational rigors of the Mafioso's double life. Space here does not permit a full accounting of several other propositions about women inside the Mafia lifestyle for which data can be compiled.

Analysis of the circumstances in the lives of Mafia women may have originated with Landesco's (1936) half-century-old article, "The Woman and the Underworld," followed in the same year by a chapter in Van Cise's (1936) *Fighting the Underworld*. In 1951, a chapter ("Ladies Night in Murder, Inc.") in Turkus and Feder's book, *Murder, Incorporated*, described characteristics of the wives of Mafia assassins, the "Ladies Auxiliary." Messick (1968) secured a pathbreaking interview with Ann Drahmann Coppola, wife of "Trigger Mike" Coppola. Three years later, Gage (1971) argued that a Mafia woman's life was circumscribed entirely by family codes.[8] In the past 20 years, small but persistent windows into the lives of Mafia women have been provided by the spate of non-fiction accounts of the American Mafia subculture.

Gage (1971) suggested that the lives of Mafia women were inherently limited by the Mafia code, circumscribed with firm definition. His view of the determined qualities of the lifestyle have received compelling support, even at the margins of the coded life where the consequences of a woman's "infractions" should be less difficult to acquire. Messick (1968) used interview data from Ann Coppola to reinforce the view that Mafia women are subjected to intimidation and violence, even death. Anastasia (1993) injects reality into this proposition when he describes Mrs. Scarfo's reactions to the suicide of her 17-year-old son Mark. Without a systematic arrangement of the non-fiction sources, however, an acceptable case cannot be made for the magnitude of the condition or the diversity of other important conditions. Indeed, a full accounting of the life circumstances of Mafia women cannot proceed without calibration and scrutiny of all available non-fiction literature.

This study regards the collection of non-fiction literature on organized crime as a universe for the purposes of extracting all evidence pertaining to the lifestyles of Mafia women. Unlike other bodies of literature in subtopics of criminology, the organized crime collection is extensive but not unruly. Three propositions were considered: (1) Mafia women have significant insight into and awareness of the criminal activities of male relatives; (2) abusive and insensitive treatment occur with substantial frequency over the life course of Mafia domestic relationships; and (3) rebellion by Mafia women against intolerable domestic conditions occurs on significantly more occasions than has been popularly believed, and forms of rebellion benefit the women and change their relationships with the men. In general, evidence shows that popular, fictional impressions of Mafia wives, daughters, mothers, nieces, and sisters are incomplete and miscast. Mafia women, it will be argued, have real lives significantly more complex and eye-opening than the lives portrayed in fiction. Indeed, it is no longer acceptable to define them as mere passive, tangential and inconsequential functionaries in the subculture of Italian-American organized crime.

STUDY METHODS

Universally, organized crime research encounters methodological hurdles. Insider information is anecdotal, disjointed and uneven (Kelly, 1986).[9] Therefore, researchers either avoid altogether the risks of challengeable inquiry or rely heavily upon government records,[10] such as investigative reports and trial transcripts.[11] Exploratory research may proceed, however, by acknowledging that all forms of qualitative research, especially research which depends upon access to severely restricted populations, is subject to charges of inaccuracy and unreliability.[12] The alternative is unpleasant to consider: no further research progress. By tapping into non-fictional fragments of the lives of Mafia women, as recorded by professional authors and researchers, we may be provided with new opportunities for developing other questions about the inner realities of mob life. We may also rekindle discussion about research strategies for penetrating the veil of secrecy around organized crime.

The author screened all known commercially published autobiographies, biographies and case studies of persons associated with Italian-

American organized crime. This material was then read for its content concerning Mafia women.[13] Data elements, defined as discrete accounts or account fragments of factual circumstances in the lives of Mafia wives, daughters, mothers, nieces, and sisters, were extracted and categorized according to their topical relevance to the propositions under investigation.[14] Categories included insights into and awareness of criminal activities, realities of daily life, and rebellion against traditional role expectations. Author errors or distortions of fact were incalculable.[15]

FINDINGS

Proposition 1: Mafia women have significant insight to and awareness of the criminal activities of their male relatives.

Ianni and Ianni (1972) analogized criminal organizations to social systems in which a code of rules governs expected behaviors having discernible forms. Codes are presumed to pass from generation to generation (Barzini, 1971; Hawkins, 1969). The most vital rule of the Mafia subculture is the code of secrecy, and common sense would suggest that the gender of an insider holding information with potentially damaging value would not matter. Gage (1971) concluded from the observations of Salerno and Thompkins (1969) that, indeed, Mafiosi include women in the circle of insiders who must not reveal operational details of crime family affairs. Salerno and Thompkins (1969) offer three reasons for female secrecy. First, substantial internal conflict can erupt if divorce actions between a Mafioso and his wife introduce risks of retaliatory leaks or forced legal discovery. Second, if women have no knowledge of details, then police investigators will ignore them as informants or investigative targets. And, finally, Mafia operating policy separates "business" from home. Secrets withheld from women may also serve as fragments of control over house and home life, or of puffery in support of machismo.

But despite Gage's (1971) view that criminal organizations make purposeful efforts to compartmentalize women, withholding from them vital information about operations, there is substantial historical evidence to the contrary. Angiolillo (1979) reported that Italian noble bandits in earlier times often included women. Hobsbawm (1969) reported that a Bavarian woman robber was born into a family in which her father, sister, and 20 of her relatives were criminals, and in which there was a 200-year tradition of crime. In 1951, Anna Genovese calmly told investigators working for Senator Estes Kefauver, "If you don't know, you got no business in this business" (Messick and Nellis, 1973:131). In recent times, Nicky Scarfo's sister, Nancy Scarfo Leonetti, was believed to have controlled her brother's enterprises when he went to prison. Later, she was tried and convicted for embezzling union funds (Cox, 1989). Police often assume that Mafia women have valuable information about gangland activities (Gage, 1972), thus making leaks possible despite paternalistic strategies.[16]

Female knowledge of criminal matters can result from personal choices to participate in crimes, or to stand by and benefit from the profits. In an early account of "Ladies of the Mob," Booth (1927) observed: "They were the girls who made their livelihoods 'off' thieves: never definitely entering into crime, but helping to spend a major portion of the money" (p.399). In terms of proactive choices, Joe Valachi reported that his sister went along by choice with a friend on a commercial burglary (Maas, 1968).[17] When Valachi's criminal record prevented him from holding a liquor license, he created a tax dodge by drawing up a private agreement with his business partner's wife to open a restaurant (Maas, 1968). Carlos Marcello turned over management of his liquor store to his wife, Jacqueline Todaro Marcello, while he managed a bar and a marijuana-growing facility (Davis, 1989). Loretta Costello, Frank Costello's first wife, was a partner in a jukebox enterprise along with Carlos Marcello, and it is difficult to reason from the circumstances that she was unaware of how her profits amounting to $16,000 per year were acquired (Katz, 1973). Later in life, the U.S. Internal Revenue Service (IRS) filed tax liens against Carlos and Mrs. Marcello (Davis, 1989).[18] Demaris (1969) discovered that the wives of several Chicago Mafiosi were involved in a stolen-auto scam wherein they were titleholders of vehicles that disappeared from a Ford agency.[19] Sam DeCavalante's wife, Mary, was consulted when Sam wanted to remove associate Bobby Occhipinti as his business manager (Zeiger, 1970). And when Sam's brother, Sal DeCavalente, became deeply in debt and needed $10,000 for his failing restaurant, he brought his wife, Marie, with him to ask Sam for money. Sam threw them out, claiming that Marie's family had called Sam a "racketeer" and a "gangster" (Zeiger, 1970).

Some Mafia women have published their participation in criminal enterprises. During divorce proceedings, Mrs. Genovese told the court that she knew all about the numbers rackets, "because I myself ran the Italian lottery" (Maas, 1968:239). Jewel Fratianno and her daughter, Joanne, were chief operating officers in Jimmy Fratianno's company. Near the end of their marriage, Jewel told Fratianno in front of social guests at their home, "I'm president of this company and if you want to throw away your own money, that's fine, but go to Joanne to ask her to sign checks on the company" (Demaris, 1981:161). A witness to the argument over money later told Fratianno, "Don't ever make a president out of a fucking housekeeper" (Demaris, 1981:161). Shortly thereafter Jewel Fratianno divorced her husband.

Across the non-fiction literature, the degree of cooperative criminal venturing by Mafia women varies with family circumstances and how individual relationships evolved. There is little direct evidence in non-fiction, contrary to Richard Condon's (1982) fictional impression, that women participate in murders or other violent crimes.[20] Women can learn about Mafiosi criminal ventures through persistent questioning and stubborn determination to get answers. Contrary to popular assumptions, Mafiosi are often put on the spot to explain their enterprises to their women, and most live to tell about it. Sam DeCavalente's wife insisted on information about her husband's businesses, and, on learning about them, made Sam promise that he would earn $40,000 to $50,000 legitimately, presumably to resolve his family situation (Zeiger, 1970). Maryann DelGiorno married Philadelphia Mafioso Tommy DelGiorno without knowledge of his bookmaking and numbers businesses, but the marriage deteriorated several years later as she became increasingly ambivalent about the lies and deceptions of her husband (Anastasia, 1993).

Repeated media exposure of criminal entanglements are sources of information for Mafia women. But publicity conjures up three possible emotional reactions which may occur individually or in combination: ambivalence, resignation, and/or media-aimed hostility. An ambivalent reaction toward press exposure may reflect the full acceptance of a lifestyle that a wife or a daughter has chosen to lead in the Mafia subculture, as well as a passive statement of her place in a group of people worthy of media attention. Resignation may reveal a woman's toleration of her role—a quiet but conscious toleration of a life course mainly beyond her control. Media-aimed hostility, an occasional reaction, may reflect media intrusions and revelations which are perceived to threaten a Mafia woman's economic situation, especially if they can result in banishment from the household. Angeline DeTolve Giancana, for example, learned early in her marriage that demanding answers from Sam Giancana about his work was dangerous, yet she lived in lavish surroundings and was frequently in the social company of the most notorious gangsters in the country (Giancana and Giancana, 1992). Rosalie (Profaci) Bonanno was aware of Bill Bonanno's criminal activities: "I couldn't understand why he needed such a gorgeous office at a warehouse. I thought maybe there was something going on there that I had no knowledge of...And I still didn't know why he traveled so often and for such long periods of time" (Bonanno and Donofrio, 1990:81). She feared that the lease on her rented home would be canceled following publicity of Bill Bonanno's "gangland activities" (Talese, 1971). Years after her marriage, and with knowledge of her husband's criminal involvement, she was forced to testify falsely in many federal courtrooms about her knowledge of the Bonanno business income and operations (Bonanno and Donofrio, 1990). In contrast, some women engage in animated verbal denial by lashing out at press reports. Frank Costello's second wife, Bobbie, denied the veracity of news stories which alleged that Frank was a heroin trafficker: "It just isn't fair. They shouldn't be allowed to print those awful stories about Frank" (Katz, 1973:21). And when "insiders" go public, as when Virginia Hill testified before the Kefauver Committee (Moore, 1974), women like Anne Fischetti, wife of Chicago mobster Charlie Fischetti, become enraged (Edmonds, 1993).

There may also be occasions when a Mafia woman is aware of her involvement in business operations, but may not comprehend any intended criminal results. Joe Valachi, for example, involved his wife Mildred in fronting race horses, but he was never convinced she understood the methods for fixing races (Maas, 1968). Mildred told suspicious neighbors that Joe owned the Lido Restaurant, but she never pressed Valachi for an answer to how he could muster large amounts of cash to buy a house (Maas, 1968). It is doubtful that Vito Genovese's wife knew that Vito ordered the death of Steve Franse, Mrs. Genovese's business partner and bodyguard (Maas, 1968). In the Nicky Scarfo case, evidence was produced to indicate that Bobby Rego's wife, Gloria, deposited a check for $1,200 from a man named D'Arbo in the couple's personal account seemingly without any questions as to the source of the money (Cox, 1989). [21]

A variation on naivete occurs when the Mafia woman, knowing well the criminal world in which her man works regularly, misses all the indicators of a criminal conspiracy taking place virtually under her nose. Jimmy Fratianno's wife and daughter, associating on a regular basis with Mickey Cohen and other Los Angeles tough guys, witnessed an attempted assassination of Cohen and the murder of Hooky Rothman without contemplating that Jimmy was the conspirator (Demaris, 1981).

The final source of information is the expected appearance in trial courts when husbands, fathers, brothers or uncles are in trouble. In the legal probings of the public courtroom, women may be forced to recall their reasons for becoming involved with the men on trial. All must endure the embarrassment of witnessing their men in a weakened position, either in handcuffs or seated at the defense table; all must wait for their men to be released on bail; and, intellectually, all must find some mental space to file the charges brought by prosecutors, the coldness of jury verdicts, and the surgical precision of judges' sentences (Alexander, 1988). Jeffie Gallo, wife of Joey Gallo, often experienced the appearance of police or federal investigators at her front door, remained behind in tenuous living conditions and endured occasional beatings when Joey Gallo returned from jail (Goddard, 1974). However, Jeffie Gallo compartmentalized all the intrusions of the justice system in her husband's life, and she refused to leave their troubled marriage until days before Gallo was murdered.

Still other women exhibit passive-aggression toward the criminal justice system, calculating perhaps that their men have the power to overcome the odds of conviction. The matriarch of the Marcello family, Louise Marcello, gathered up all the women in the family to form a "compact phalanx" around Carlos (Davis, 1989:179). Carlos's wife shed crocodile tears at his 1981 trial while his daughters, Florence Robards and Jacqueline Dugas (two of three Marcello "Mafia princesses"), sat in the front row in support (Davis, 1989:492, 508).

On the question of insight into and awareness of criminal activities, a combination of factors appeared during the U.S. Federal Bureau of Investigation (FBI) inquiry into the activities of Paul Castellano. Mrs. Castellano recognized agents Kurins and O'Brien when they rang her doorbell to present Paul with a subpoena, since such visits were not uncommon. She had distanced herself from her husband's associations as a way of bringing some control to her life: "What my husband's friends do is no concern of mine...Don't bother me about my husband's friends" (O'Brien and Kurins, 1991:98).

O'Brien and Kurins consider an important question: Why do "proud and presumably religious women" get involved with Mafia men? Their answers suggest that such women become victims of bad luck and circumstances they cannot control. They languish outside the knowledge of their husbands' work because Mafia protocol prohibits their involvement; they are expected only to take care of home and hearth; they pretend that their husbands are not criminals; or they believe the love they have for their husbands has trapped them in a farce or tragedy. It is possible, of course, that some Mafia women are ambivalent but willing pawns in the links between factions of the "business" (Cook, 1966). O'Brien and Kurins (1991) conclude, however, that "Mafia wives had what amounted to a prenuptual agreement guaranteeing that their children would be given quality educations and kept away from Mob associations" (p.97). All the while, there were sources of information and overt indicators of involvement in major criminal activities.

Proposition 2: Mafia women encounter significant abuse and insensitivity to their human needs.

Popular impressions of the Mafia home include contented wives and daughters who perform domestic chores and raise children in blissful ignorance to Mafiosi business dealings. The wife is not employed outside the home, and her in-home experiences are portrayed as pleasant and free of the harshest forms of domestic conflict. Rosalie Bonanno characterized her early thoughts about marriage thusly:

> Men would make the decisions and it was our duty to have faith in these decisions and to support them. A woman was to keep her body desirable for her husband only, and her home clean...I began another notebook in which I jotted down my mother's recipes...I dreamed of the day I'd have my own kitchen, and took pride in keeping my mother's house spotless and the floors polished to a gleam [Bonanno and Donofrio, 1990:45].

But such fantasies stand in sharp contrast, for example, to the statement of Antoinette Giancana: "...I was in a prison from which there was no escape..." (Giancana and Renner, 1984:235).

According to popular impressions, Mafiosi are family providers. Vinnie Teresa claimed that "the most important thing to a mob guy is his family. [The prosecutors] got to show the mob guy that they'll take care of that family, protect them, provide for them. I guess it boils down to this; we got to be shown a little respect" (Teresa and Renner, 1975:75), presumably because of their high family values. John Roselli was known to his friends and relatives as sincerely interested in family life and children, perhaps as a substitute for the family he secretly supported (Rappleye and Becker, 1991). For all that was known of Roselli's values, other Mafia leaders marked the Los Angeles Don as an exceptional provider (Rappleye and Becker, 1991). Sam DeCavalente claimed to have provided for his family and to have respected his wife and children.

Material objects and other strategies are used to confirm provider characteristics. Bobbie Visconti, a small-time mobster and acquaintance of Vincent Teresa, ordered a new Oldsmobile for each of his daughters as they reached the age of 16 (Teresa and Renner, 1973). Joe Iannuzzi's recent autobiography reveals the self-serving paternalism that lies at the root of some Mafiosi intentions. When Bunny Iannuzzi complained about Joe's frequent disappearances, Joe responded, "I bought you this house. We have an expensive piece of property. You have your own car, jewelry, money in the bank. What the fuck more do you want from me?" (Iannuzzi, 1993:42-43). Naturally, in Joe's mind Bunny and his children loved the possessions that came from Joe's successes (Iannuzzi, 1993).

Mafia men are believed to have the respect of their wives and daughters. Jimmy Fratianno told John Rosselli, "sometimes [my daughter Joanne would] come from school crying but she never said nothing to me about all that bullshit in the papers" (Demaris, 1981:122). Carlos Marcello was known for his violent temper, yet he was believed to be a "loyal and affectionate family man, devoted to his six brothers, two sisters, four children, ten grandchildren, and numerous nieces and nephews" (Davis, 1989:66). Vinnie Teresa once counseled that mob guys do not generally want their kids to be "involved with the rackets" (Teresa and Renner, 1973:91).

Dissatisfaction with the abusive and insensitive conditions of life among Mafiosi appears in the literature. To illustrate, Los Angeles mobster John Rosselli's brief marriage to actress June Lang ended when Lang insisted upon continuing her career; Rosselli insisted upon keeping Lang in the kitchen while he conspired with mob associates (Rappleye and Becker, 1991). Consider, also, Nicky Scarfo's household manner when his wife cooked and served a spaghetti dinner for friends: "[Scarfo] tasted it, winced and then threw the whole plate against the wall in an outburst of displeasure, saying that it tasted terrible" (Cox, 1989:35). Joseph "Joe Dogs" Iannuzzi (1993), an insatiable womanizer, passed off his escapades as an inconsequential sport of men, all the while empathizing with his wife's plight in life. Mrs. Iannuzzi, however, was not above joining Joe in a false insurance claim for a diamond ring which they said had been stolen from their home during a burglary (Iannuzzi, 1993).

The relative and comparative frequencies of Mafiosi infidelity cannot be determined, but marital disloyalty is one of the most frequently mentioned sideshows of family life. Under any circumstances, it suggests domestic instability. Its presence in Mafia families contradicts the propaganda about honor, "family" loyalty and continuity of interpersonal values.[22] Mafiosi, it seems, spend as much time with mistresses as they do in their jobs, thus becoming shadow lovers, husbands and fathers in a manner consistent with all other parts of their lives. Charles Luciano once estimated the frequency of Frank Costello's marital disloyalty: "[I]f you had all the dough Frank spent on broads—I mean in addition to his wife—and what later on he give to one particular girlfriend, you could go around the world for the rest of your life on your own steamship" (Gosch and Hammer, 1974:155).[23] Joe Valachi took his first mistress, "May," in 1929, setting her up in an apartment in the Bronx. May's girlfriend was the mistress to Frank Livorsi, Ciro Terranova's chauffeur and bodyguard (Maas, 1968).[24] Later, when Valachi discovered that May had played around on him, he ended the relationship unceremoniously (Maas, 1968). Finding himself bored with staying at home, Valachi set up another woman in her own apartment, taking care of her health and buying her clothes (Maas, 1968). According to Sam Giancana's son, Don Giancana was fanatical in his compartmentalization of carnal pleasure and marital duties (Giancana and Giancana, 1992).

Available data suggest that Mafia women endure repeated situations in which deception underlies the relationship. In some cases, they have information about the intrigues that affect them (Blumenthal, 1988; Taylor, 1989). Sam DeCavalente regularly hustled other women, frequently calling his wife to lie about absences and infidelities, and telling her how much he loved her (Zeiger, 1970). The plot thickened when Decavalente became jealous of secretary Harriet Gold's husband, Dave, who apparently paid too much attention to his wife (Zeiger, 1970). Meanwhile, Harriet discovered from another man that Sam's "girlfriend" of many years was a woman who had a daughter in her twenties (Zeiger, 1970). Confusion of family loyalties reached new levels of absurdity when Sam was heard to say that he couldn't trust anyone 100%, "and that includes Harriet" (Zeiger, 1970:192).

Uncertainty about infidelity is yet another dimension of family intrigue. The Decavalente investigation wiretaps were enlightening in this regard. Mary DeCavalente wondered why Sam spent so much time in New York City, even though she had information about his activities with other women and she used arguments to extract confirmation (Zeiger, 1970). Without any confirmation, she called him a "playboy" and lived to tell about it (Zeiger, 1970). Had wiretap information been available to her, Mary would have heard Sam's conversations with a woman named "Honey" and special rooms set aside in a New York hotel. Perhaps she would have been sickened by Sam's calls to her to say how much he loved and missed her: "I'm sick from missing you," then later, "I got you under my skin." She would have known of similar calls to Sam's secretary, Harriet Gold, to feed her essentially the same lines (Zeiger, 1970:165). And, had she been a fly on a wall when Sam described her to Joey Bayonne, she would have been warmed by the description, "stocky, white hair" (Zeiger, 1970:173).

Hypocrisy and double standards show up in the dialogue of Mafiosi husbands and fathers. Sam DeCavalente counseled one of his associates, Jerry Quarino, concerning Jerry's domestic difficulties. Sam asked Jerry if his wife had ever cheated on him and whether his wife was a "good wife and a good housekeeper." Jerry admitted that he gave his wife only $30 a week to feed the children and that he had "slugged her in an argument over a loaf of bread." DeCavalente called Jerry a "playboy." Sam frequently gave advice on matters of domestic harmony (Zeiger, 1970). To deepen the mystery, Sam found out from a Gambino informer that Bobby Basile was having an affair with a woman on the Jersey shore. Bobby covered up by telling DeCavalente that "he was very discreet, then added that he was only known at Basile in New Jersey and used his real name of Occhipinti in Brooklyn" (Zeiger, 1970:229). In all this, the daughters, mothers, nieces, sisters, and wives are abstract and distant concerns. The beneficiaries are the mistresses, many of whom spend their days sipping Perrier and enjoying the dresses and jewelry—precisely the situation of Jackie D'Amico's lover (Blum, 1993).

Hypocrisy in the family relationship takes different forms. Vito Genovese intervened in trouble Joe Valachi had in proposing to Mildred Reina, telling Mildred's uncles to stay out of the matter: "[I]f [the uncles] are fit to marry their wives, Joe is fit to marry Mildred. If Joe ain't fit, none of us are fit" (Maas, 1968:127). Of course, Joe Valachi kept his wife from learning about his infidelity two months after their marriage by going straight home after his first contract assassination (Maas, 1968). Vincent Teresa was considered by Vito Genovese to be one of the most vicious Mafia rulers, yet his daughter's parochial school honored him for the regular financial support he provided (Teresa and Renner, 1973). Such piety and citizenry had no application in Teresa's other life. He also gave financial assistance to a mistress, including a home and other luxuries (Fopiano, 1993). Sam DeCavalente had numerous affairs, yet he warned other men of the dangers of their marital delinquencies. This is the same man who was regularly consulted to arrange weddings for daughters and nieces, and who was requested to control the costs of weddings for friends (Zeiger,

1970). Paul Castellano, referring to himself as an honorable man in business dealings, carried on an affair with his maid in his home and under the nose of his wife, Nina Manno, Carlo Gambino's sister-in-law and Castellano's cousin. When the maid questioned Paul's intentions to separate from his wife, Castellano said: "You don't believe it's because I'm honorable that I act like that?...You don't believe it's because I'm honorable I don't throw [Nina] out, I don't insist?" (O'Brien and Kurins, 1991:249).

The so-called sense of honor is further distorted when the crime boss falls in love with a soldier's wife; sometimes the soldier dies (Maas, 1968). Joe Valachi admitted to assassinating a soldier who found himself in this situation, and the event took place in front of his wife: "It's too bad the wife had to see him go" (Maas, 1968:103). The observations of a jury member in the Nicky Scarfo case may serve as the unifying principle in repeated examples of Mafiosi hypocrisy. Referring to defendants Nick Caramandi, Tom DelGiorno and Nicky Scarfo, she said they "were nothing but gangsters who would stab you in the back. They were all out for themselves and would sell out their mother for $10" (Cox, 1989:129-130).

Women are often relegated to secondary status in the pecking order of Mafiosi family priorities. Arlyne Weiss, a mob mistress with years of firsthand experience, reports that wiseguys in the Mafia spend little time at home with their wives and family (Carpenter, 1992). FBI agents O'Brien and Kurins (1991) concluded that Mafiosi think little of "parking spouses in tenement apartments or, at best, forlorn sidebyside duplexes filled with garish furniture, too many televisions, ashtrays from Las Vegas, and terrifying reminders of the Crucifixion" (p.96). Wiseguys like Henry Hill almost always had girlfriends on the side:

> ...you didn't leave a wife or abandon a family for one, but you did swank them around, rent them apartments, lease them cars, and feed them regularly with racks of swag clothes and paper bags of stolen jewelry. Having a steady girl was considered a sign of success, like a thorough-bred or powerboat but better: a girlfriend was the ultimate luxury purchase" [Pileggi, 1985:140].

John Rosselli, his biographer described, was "a man governed by stern, brittle ideas....," and women were "baubles, objects upon whom he could work techniques and test his skill; if things progressed beyond the initial conquest, he invoked the old, Catholic, Italian ideas of a woman's role" (Rappleye and Becker, 1991:97). For some Mafiosi, divorcing a wife and retaining a common-law wife serves as a compromise where appearances of a settled home life must be maintained. Both Gennaro Angiulo and Aniello Dellacroce took common-law wives (O'Neill and Lehr, 1989; Blum, 1993), and in the latter case the woman held the stature and decorum of a true Mafia princess.

Women of the mob are regularly treated to the possibility that their economic security will be injured by the decisions of Mafiosi. John Gotti's visits to bars, social clubs and jails strained his marriage to Victoria (DiGiorgio) Gotti, resulting in frequent separations (Mustain and Capeci, 1988). Jacqueline Marcello lived in constant fear that her husband, Carlos Marcello, would be sent to jail or exiled from the U.S. (Davis, 1989). Maria Franzese, wife of "yuppie Don" Michael Franzese, was forced to get a job when denied a monthly income of $7,500 during her husband's imprisonment (Franzese and Matera, 1992). Vinnie Teresa imposed danger upon his mother's home, hiding out for several days following a street fight with a bad-tempered mob "headhunter" and telling his wife not to answer the door and to "just do what I tell you" (Teresa and Renner, 1973:115). Nina Castellano experienced repeated FBI appearances at her front door, expressing indignity and fear that the FBI knew and had interviewed her son: "My son Joe's a good boy....I don't know why you had to talk to my Joe" (O'Brien and Kurins, 1991:110). Mrs. Castellano appeared to have wished for a settled life in Brooklyn, "married to the neighborhood butcher, living in a cramped apartment. No big house. No Cadillacs. No maids. Just big family meals on Sundays, and plenty of grandchildren to spoil" (O'Brien and Kurins, 1991:110-111).

Economic or other insecurities produce defensive reactions toward outsiders or toward the basis of the insecurities. Joseph Salerno's wife, Barbara, had little patience for her husband's associations with the Scarfo mob, warning him that he would bring trouble to his family upon deeper involvement (Salerno and Rivele, 1990). The Marcello women and children rallied around Carlos when he was exiled to the Dominican Republic in 1961. According to Davis (1989), "their emotional and financial dependence on Carlos was absolute" (p.102), since none of the other Marcello brothers commanded the same degree of respect in their criminal activities. Rosalie Bonanno, on the other hand, took courses in computer programming to build a career option, and to prepare herself for employment on the chance that Bill Bonanno would be convicted of credit card fraud (Talese, 1971). Genovese soldiers were taxed $25 per month to provide for defense lawyers and expenses for wives and children if a soldier went to prison (Maas, 1968). Angry with Nick Caramandi, the women of the Narducci family located the federal protected witness at a resort in Ocean City, MD. They harassed Caramandi verbally on the beach, scream- ing epithets about his traitorous actions against Nick Scarfo and Frankie Narducci (Anastasia, 1991).

Wives and daughters experience emotional and physical abuse. Some- times death is an option for meddling in business affairs or in creating organizational friction. Joe Valachi testified that death was the penalty for a Mafioso who told his wife about business activities (Maas, 1968). Although documentation is limited, some cases of wife murder have been publicly revealed. A healthy Doris Coppola died under mysterious circum- stances after childbirth, and after she and her father were indicted for perjury. Doris refused to discuss what she had learned about "Trigger Mike" Coppola's gangster activities (Messick, 1968). Before committing suicide, Coppola's second wife, Ann Drahmann Coppola, was convinced that Doris had been murdered to keep her quiet. Helen Nafpliotis, common law wife of Nick Melia, was harassed and beaten on several occasions, and even the protection of the FBI was insufficient to guarantee her future (Renner and Kirby, 1987). Boston mobster Frank Cucchiara shot his wife, then killed himself at their home in Belmont, MA in 1976. Dominick Cataldo told Joe Iannuzzi that his solution to his wife's threats to leave him over infidelities was to threaten to kill her mother and father (Iannuzzi, 1993). Connie (Castellano) Catalonotti, Paul Castellano's daughter, was regularly lied to, betrayed and beaten by her small-time hood husband, Frank Amato. Castellano swore revenge (Mustain and Capeci, 1992), despite the hypocrisy in his own life. Following her divorce from Amato, and his subsequent disappearance, Connie remained under her father's thumb when she remarried and was required to live next to her father's house (O'Brien and Kurins, 1991).

Finally, Mafia women can contract diseases from men whose infidelities are often numerous. Evidence for this outcome is limited also, but Al Capone and Willie Moretti were both syphilitic (Maas, 1968). Both con- tracted the disease from prostitutes several years before they died and while they remained married. No evidence of HIV or AIDS infections transferred from Mafiosi and their mistresses has yet appeared. But given the frequency of infidelities, the probability of impact on wives and offspring is substantial. A hint of this probability, though unproven, appeared in a recent New Jersey mob trial (Rudolph, 1992).

Proposition 3: Female rebellion against male Mafia members occurs often.

Talese reported that Bill Bonanno regarded *The Godfather* as a fairly accurate portrayal of the Mafia "secret society" (Talese, 1971). Bonanno accepted the rule that Mafia women must not resist male authority, and in public they must never display any form of rebellion. Apparently, however, Maria Testa Muzio, Sal Testa's sister and only surviving member of the Phil Testa family, did not subscribe to such rules. She announced publicly that she was insulted by the fact that Sal Testa's longtime friends did not attend Sal's funeral. Later, she testified that the mob had killed her brother (Cox, 1989). Equally uncharacteristic was Mrs. Thomas DelGiorno's retort to her husband's taped statement that her stepmother should be killed because "she was related to Harry Riccobene," a Scarfo family competitor: "Then why don't you get your machine gun and just kill everybody" (Cox, 1989:324). A defiant Anna Genovese told federal investigators that she didn't mind talking with them: "...he can't do anything to me. I'm going to divorce him, anyway" (Messick, 1973:130).

A Mafia woman's rebellion is a rational defensive reaction to physical abuse, deception, infidelity, neglect and secrecy. Evidence indicates that many Mafia women are unwilling to be controlled or manipulated completely by male relatives. When Nicky Larosso stole $650 from his ex-wife, she filed charges against him. Larosso was arrested and the ex-wife refused to drop charges. Even Sam DeCavalente could not persuade her to drop the charges, explaining to a friend, "the woman involved was related to a deceased Cosa Nostra member" (Zeiger, 1970:245). Connie Castellano had no difficulty in divorcing her abusive husband, and, moreover, she was not afraid to stand toe to toe with an FBI agent to tell him to leave her mother's property (O'Brien and Kurins, 1991).

Perhaps Jeffie Gallo's relationship with Joey Gallo is instructive for learning how some Mafia women bring a measure of self-determination to their lives:

> Though she had yielded to Joey as the dominant partner in their marriage, it was a highly qualified surrender. She would abide by his decisions only if she approved of them. Mutual respect was her watchword, and if, on minor matters, she did sometimes give way against her better judgment, she would always make it clear to him that this was without prejudice (Goddard, 1974:117).

Forms of rebellion vary with the personalities, positions and histories of the women involved. Sam DeCavalente's wife went to social events and stared at DeCavalente's secretary, Harriet. Harriet "couldn't have a good time when she was together with Sam and her husband, Dave" (Zeiger, 1970:80). Sam and Harriet had been carrying on an affair for years under Mary's nose. Harriet expressed jealousy of Mary (Zeiger, 1970). The deception worsened when Sam stayed at Harriet's house until three in the morning talking to Dave about how much Sam loved Harriet (Zeiger, 1970). Even more ironic, Harriet's jealousy was aimed at other secretaries in Sam's office, and she found little ways to control all the female staff (Zeiger, 1970). In sharp contrast to these women, Karen Hill (wife of wiseguy Henry Hill) had a different strategy for maintaining control. Believing that Henry was a good provider, she resolved, "Why should I give him up to someone else? Never! If I was going to kick anybody, it was going to be the person who was trying to take him away from me. Why should she win?...The way I began to see it, she was getting the worst side of him and I was getting the best" (Pileggi, 1985:151-152).

Another form of rebellion is disloyalty to male relatives, perhaps through sexual betrayal or betrayal of confidence. The wife of Los Angeles underboss Girolomo "Momo" Adamo was seriously wounded by her husband when it was discovered that she had been having affairs with the boss of the Los Angeles Mafia, Frank Desimone. Sam DeCavalente's cousin Bobby once cautioned him that Vito Genovese's wife had betrayed Genovese. Anna (Vernotico) Genovese committed adultery on several occasions, in the marital bed, when she learned that Vito Genovese had murdered her first husband (Stuart, 1985). The response was, "What a wife did, a girl friend might be more apt to do" (Zeiger, 1970:71). Joe Adonis's daughter, Marilyn Doto, was a mob informer with a "wild reputation" in a certain New York club (Katz, 1973). Bootsie Marcello, wife of Joe Marcello, had an affair with FBI agent to whom she fed information about Marcello family operations (Davis, 1989). Public announcement of the affair offended Marcello's honor, especially since the infidelity arose from the actions of a family member's wife and "in the arms of a deadly enemy" (Davis, 1989:323).

Rebellion can be systematic and rationally pursued by a woman determined to prove her independence of mind. Josephine Profaci, for example, married her husband outside the Catholic Church, despite the fact that her older sister, Rosalie, wished for a Catholic life like the one they experienced in their youth. Gay Talese speculated that part of

Josephine's rebellion related to her dislike of Bill Bonanno and his treatment of Rosalie (Talese, 1971). Sam DeCavalente once discussed Bill Bonanno's oppression of Rosalie: "It's a shame; the girl wanted to commit suicide because of the way he treated her. His father [Joe Bonanno] knows that and he gave him the *consiglieri* job" (Zeiger, 1970:133). Josephine Bonanno, however, was an entirely different type of woman, "a product of another time. She was the first daughter to finish college, and without being feminist, she undoubtedly identified with the cause of modern women seeking greater liberation..." (Talese, 1971:308).

Rebellion includes rejection of patterns of demeaning male behavior. Paul Castellano's wife, for example, was not afraid to argue with her husband, the onetime top boss of the Gambino family, over matters like picking his own pants off the floor. She told him forthrightly that she would not take his clothes to the cleaners or get him aspirin for his headaches (O'Brien and Kurins, 1991). Despite her husband's blustering about running his own house, Nina Castellano moved her children into her house.[25] Bill Bonanno, jealous of Rosalie's professional career, locked Rosalie in the house until she had washed every dish and laundered all the clothes: "For you working's a privilege. You want to do it, you'll have to work twice as hard for the opportunity" (Bonanno and Donofrio, 1990:190). Not long after, Rosalie decided to divorce Bill, concluding "that she did not want to live as the ignored and used wife of Bill Bonanno" (Bonanno and Donofrio, 1990:191).

ART AND LIFE IN THE MAFIA

Responding to interview questions from CBS's Mike Wallace, Joseph Bonanno spoke of the reverence paid to the women of his family: "They [are] revered and, till this day...and if anything should enter into their eyes that might be a little bit discolored or a little bit harmful, they're protected from it."[26] In his autobiography, Bonanno wrote that his wife, Fay, "...had to restrain herself, keep a stiff upper lip and bravely carry on..." in her role as the mate of a "man of honor" (Bonanno and Lalli, 1983:312). Bonanno's paternalism harmonizes well with that of a French magistrate who, in a ruling concerning the case of a Mafioso who abused his wife, and used bribery and intimidation to gain child custody in a divorce action, stated that: "...a crook can be a good father" (Greene, 1982:26).

This research does not quarrel with the proposition that art may imitate life. Fictional literature can, indeed, reflect conditions inside the Mafia lifestyle. For example, the loyal wife of Al Capone, Mae Capone, paid all the bills for household expenses (Kobler, 1971) and permitted property deeds to be put in her name (Kobler, 1971). She remained steadfastly loyal to Capone until his death in 1947 (Schoenberg, 1992).[27] Capone's mother, known as Mama Teresa, always defended her son; she enjoyed serving him gourmet pasta meals (Kobler, 1971). Charles Luciano's mother once said, "You don't know how to eat anybody's spaghetti sauce but mine" (Gosch and Hammer, 1974:28). In Louisiana, the Marcello women often cooked large spaghetti and meatball dinners on Sunday afternoon for the Marcello brothers, fathers, sons and others (Davis, 1989). And Marcello's grandmother, Louise, always said the grace.

Similarly, Mrs. Salvatore Profaci (mother of Rosalie Profaci Bonanno) was a nurturing mother and protector of her children and grandchildren,[28] and Joe Valachi's mother made bed sheets out of old, used cement bags (Maas, 1968). Mrs. Profaci's daughter, Ann, followed in the lifestyle of her mother, "an efficient homemaker, a wonderful mother, and, while she was intelligent, she deferred to her husband's judgment; her husband was clearly in charge" (Talese, 1971:305). Following his assassination in 1962, Anthony Strollo's wife insisted that he was a "kind person who had no enemies; everyone loved him" (Maas, 1968:282). Protection of the husband's or father's subcultural image may also extend to lashing out at FBI informers, such as when Adeline Narducci berates Nick Caramandi when she happens to spot him at the beach (Anastasia, 1991).

Protection of males even extends to public declarations or appeals for special treatment from the justice system. Johnny Torrio, owner of many whorehouses in Chicago, won his wife's oft-stated appellation, "the greatest husband in the world" (Wolf and DiMona, 1974:80). Al Capone's sister, Mafalda, blamed the Philadelphia police for Capone's 1929 gun-toting arrest, charging that the police needed the publicity (Kobler, 1971). In more recent times, Janice Grande, wife of a Philadelphia Mafioso, approached the federal judge court upon her husband's conviction. She pleaded with the court, "...give my daughter a chance to know her father. I love my husband very much and it has been very hard to be away from him. Please, your honor, let us be a family. Please don't let our lives end like this" (Cox, 1989:396-397). Grande, however, was sentenced to 40 years. When the verdict was read in the Nicky Scarfo case, "several wives and family members of the accused fingered rosaries and held up their hands with fingers crossed in good luck signs for their relatives sitting beyond the fence" (Cox, 1989:196).[29] In a book on Gotti's activities, authors Mustain and Capeci (1988) describe Victoria (DiGiorgio) Gotti as "wife of John Gotti, mother of their five children" (p.xi), highly protective of her husband's image and infatuated with his good looks.

WHEN ART DOES NOT IMITATE LIFE

Cummings and Volkman (1990) described Gotti as Victoria's "hen-pecked" husband: "Only his closest friends kn[o]w that the tough-talking, swaggering hood was often at a loss on how to deal with a wife who clearly had a mind of her own. And when Victoria Gotti did not get her way, she walked out" (p.64). The thought that the head of the Gambino crime organization could have a wife who insisted upon a measure of self-deter-mination indicates that alternative propositions about Mafia women may be in order. In fact, ample evidence suggests, first, that Mafia women do not lead lives of blissful ignorance of the criminal circumstances of their men. They have significant insight into and awareness of criminal affilia-tions, and they have information about criminal conspiracies and ratio-nalizations for criminal actions. Knowledge ranges from mere indicators of suspicious circumstances to participation in conspiracies.

Second, there is convincing evidence that Mafia women do not lead the contented, happy and peaceful lives portrayed frequently in fictional accounts. Mafia men, because of the expectations of their enterprises and their subscription to secrecy rituals, lie, cheat on, dominate, manipulate, and abuse the women they believe are tolerant of subcultural mores concerning loyal submission.[30] Barbara Fuca, wife of "French Connection" kingpin Patsy Fuca, was suspected of carrying messages between criminal associates (Moore, 1969), yet she was left to stand alone in criminal court when the "connection" was uncovered (Moore and Fuca, 1977). Rosalie Bonanno characterized the male view of the woman's place as feudalistic: women are expected to engage in family maintenance activities while the men orchestrate intrigues, make important decisions and do crimes. They must avoid involvement in men's criminal activities. Should they learn of criminal activities, they must remain subservient victims or passive, unquestioning loyalists in a male-driven, economically successful criminal conspiracy. Lack of equal footing means that mistresses rank higher than wives in terms of attention and quality time spent (Dubro, 1988). In addition, verbal dialogues must be suffered for all their double standards and hypocrisies, family activities are charades put on for a Mafioso's presentation of self among colleagues, abuses must be survived and financial insecurities confronted and worried, and disrespect and diseases must be withstood. This cannot be a complete characterization of the plight of Mafia women, but based on evidence of a wide collection of sources, it appears to represent the lives of many of them (Bonanno and Donofrio, 1990).

Third, non-fiction evidence shows also that Mafia women rebel against some conditions of the programmed lifestyle. Rebellion appears in various forms and eventually seeks its own level. It takes place with sufficient frequency to appear in public through accounts of inside observers, and through informants or wiretaps. Arguments, divorces, infidelities, separations and forms of counterviolence occur among Mafia women in ways that appear to be similar to non-Mafia women. Seemingly, the secret subculture is incapable of dictating all actions, thoughts or fantasies of women. Mafia women observe and consider different lifestyle situations. Therefore, intimidation and oppression by Mafia men are inefficient vehicles for controlling women, in contrast to ways that may incorporate respect for a woman's contributions to family life. The form, intensity, and duration of rebellion are determined by the degree of authoritarian or violent behavior of the Mafioso, and most likely emanate from a woman's learned reactions to conflict in her own family.

Mischaracterization of the realities of Mafia women in fictional literature may sustain a mythology that Mafia men continue to believe. Perhaps, however, Homer's (1974) suggestion is correct: "Italians are not 'ideally' suited for organized crime [in the United States]" (pp.75-76). Perhaps the proclivities of the ethnic group, such as strong moral bonds within the family, opposition to drugs and cooperation with other ethnic groups, "may be contradictory or dysfunctional for an organization's goals" (Homer, 1974:76). Over time, fundamental characteristics of what it means to be an Italian-American may have weakened Mafiosi capacity to dominate all aspects of family life, including the actions and thoughts of Mafia women. The diversity and ever-changing nature of American culture also mitigates against the ability of the criminal subculture to sustain an archaic mythology. The non-fiction evidence suggests that Mafia women act and think like other women in American society, a subject about which there is little formal discussion.

There is reason to believe that the traditionally closed lifestyle of Mafia women has been affected by the penetrations of changed gender and family relations in mainstream American culture.[31] Future studies should define the inner and outer limits of change inside Mafia families. Unquestionably, the Mafia woman has participated in the general trend of change in the total Italian-American experience.[32]

□

NOTES

1. I draw from Albini's (1971:319) use of the word "functionaries."

2. She appears in only two scenes, as the insignificant wife of a dominant and powerful patriarch, Vito Corleone.

3. In the original film, only three women have major roles: Connie Corleone, Don Vito Corleone's daughter; Kay Adams, Michael's Irish girlfriend and later wife; and Appolonia Vitelli, Michael's Sicilian lover and wife. Don Vito's wife has no name. She appears in only two scenes: once in the introductory wedding scene where she sings an Italian love song, and once while she awaits the Don's return from the hospital following an assassination attempt. Connie is abused by her husband, Carlo Rizzi, a low-level soldier in the Don's organization. She overeats, complains to her mother about the beatings and spends her days as a housewife. Appolonia is a shy, innocent girl who serves to absorb the bomb blast meant for Michael. Because Kay is Irish, she cannot achieve more than peripheral involvement in family affairs. In the novel, the oldest of the Don's sons, Fredo, cannot control his wife's sexual escapades, and she is cast as a pants-wearing, prostitute-like and usurious shrew.

4. See Gambino's (1974) discussion of "La Serieta—The Ideal of Womanliness."

5. See, for example, Linda La Plante's novel, *Bella Maria* (1991), and the films *Married to the Mob* and *Goodfellas*.

6. In the film *Married to the Mob*, for example, the Mafia wife is an unhappy yet questioning person whose expectations of life are well beyond those of her gangster husband and other women with whom she associates. In *Goodfellas*, women associated with mobsters may be loving wives, but they may also participate in criminal schemes with their husbands. In an old classic, Reeve (1931) referred to these wives or partners by the label "gun molls." Reeve remarked, "A gun moll may be an active member of a gang. She may pack a gun in hold-ups or wear an ornamented smile as a decoy in blackmail. Or, again, she may be only a gangster's sweetheart, sharing his life and his secrets" (pp.141-142).

7. A quotation from a recent novel is in keeping with this theme: "You can make believe you are a member of this family, make believe you are still my daughter, because that's the way your grandfather wants it, or you can get out—you are not in this family, you are not my daughter, and I am going to see to it that you stay an old maid for the rest of your life" (Condon, 1982:18-19). Other useful vignettes appear in Condon (1983, 1988).

8. Gage observed, "In the Mafia a woman may be a means to a profitable alliance with another Mafia "family"; a showcase for displaying her husband's wealth, status, and power; a valuable piece of property; a loyal helpmate; a good cook; a showy and ego-boosting mistress. But what she must never be is a liberated woman." Gage claimed that Mafia women lead dull social lives, friendships are limited to other Mafia wives and spending money is constrained to avoid IRS detection. Furthermore, fear of losing the Mafia husband is persistent, second-class status to mistresses is commonplace and there is no likelihood of achieving "equal footing with a man" (pp.95-96). In support of Gage's view, Katz (1973) learned of intrusions by the IRS to build a net-worth case against Frank Costello by searching every bank account in his or his wife's name. The IRS concluded that Costello had significant material assets, while his wife owned two cars and two fur coats valued at $59,000 (p.196.)

9. Sources, such as anonymous informants or ex-wiseguys, are inaccessible except through the books they may write. Accuracy of reporting and interpretation by insiders, biographers or ghost writers is subject to criticism on grounds of skewed motivations or faulty memory. Reliability and replication, two ordinary and reasonable social science tests, often are not guaranteed. Access and reliability of Mafia women, in particular, are constrained by complex allegiances such persons have with their male relatives and by the potential for harm.

10. See, generally, Calder (1992).

11. Acquisition of government records, of course, is a time-consuming and uncertain endeavor, and the value of their insights depends upon agency cooperation and source integrity. Indeed, even beyond earlier observations by Cressey (1967) of inherent methodological concerns, dependence upon government records can subject the research enterprise to charges of aiding in the construction of a state-controlled criminology of organized crime.

12. This approach, I argue, is no less credible or reliable than the variety of research innovations introduced by investigators like Talese (1971), Eisenberg et al. (1979), Pileggi (1985), Ianni and Ianni (1972), Lupsha (1981), Block (1977, 1980, 1991), Haller (1990), Davis (1989), Hess (1973),

Arlacchi (1986), Albini (1971) and others. All have raised "new questions" (Cressey, 1969) and have expanded the data upon which overall understanding of organized crime can proceed. In each case, creative ways for acquiring information and constructing research propositions about the Mafia subculture were applied.

My defense of this strategy is based essentially on the observation that no published evidence exists to disclaim the great mass of primary- and secondary-source non-fiction concerning inside views of Mafia operations. Naturally, an effort to accomplish such research is fraught with difficulties, but I rely upon the fact that at present there is no social science scholarship offering any significant challenges to autobiographical, biographical or journalistic writings about the lives of Mafiosi and their women.

Huie (1951) pulled off a most creative stunt to acquire inside information on Benjamin Siegel. Through a job placement office, Huie got a job as Siegel's butler. On the job in Siegel's house, he collected information and insights into Siegel's lifestyle and temper. Moreover, he photographed documents from Siegel's file cabinet. This type of original source information is not likely to be repeated.

13. A sample of the most detailed sources employed in this study is reflected in the appended collection of references.

14. Information pertaining to cousins, mistresses, prostitutes, cousins or secretaries of Mafia men was ignored, unless such information bore direct relevance to Mafia women as defined.

15. For purposes of exploratory research, however, the size of the data set and the absence of published challenges to credibility were considered reasonable hedges against error in some accounts. Of necessity, great reliance was placed on the experience, integrity and professional stature of the author's accounts from which data elements were extracted.

16. We are reminded of a *New York Times* article published in January 1947 referring to the disappearance of "Trigger Mike" Coppola's first wife, Doris. Apparently, District Attorney Frank Hogan wanted to ask Mrs. Coppola several questions pertaining to the killing of a Harlem Republican district captain, Joseph Scottoriggio. Hogan announced to the press that Mrs. Coppola "has information of value to us in the Scottoriggio investigation" (p.27). Mike Coppola was being held as a material witness in the killing.

17. Valachi was not averse to introducing his wife to numerous Mafiosi as he began to learn the business of horse-race betting (Maas, 1968).

18. Marcello's secretary, Frances Pecora—the wife of Nofio Pecora, an "ex-convict with a history in heroin traffic and prostitution" (Davis, 1989:64)—operated a call-girl business in several southern states.

19. This group comprised the wives of Sam Battaglia, Fiore Buccieri, and Albert Frabotta, as well as Dolly Pontone, a "guest at the wedding party of [Anthony] Arcardo's daughter" (Demaris, 1969:81).

20. "She went into the john, closed the door, screwed the noise-killer to the piece and went back into the living room and killed Sam Netturbino. *Then* she peed" (Condon, 1982:109).

21. There was no live person with the name of D'Arbo. The name was taken from a deceased tile contractor.

22. No research has been conducted to examine closely the role of infidelity in Mafia marriages in comparison with its representation in the general population.

23. Luciano took a mistress in 1948. Her name was Igea Lissoni. He claimed in his interviews with Martin Gosch that Igea was the only woman he ever loved. She died of cancer in 1958; Luciano was at her side and mourned her passing.

24. Valachi married Mildred Reina, oldest daughter of Gaetano Reina, over the objections of her mother, brother and uncles (Maas, 1968:124).

25. "I want some peace in my own house, woman. I don't like anybody running my house, see? I don't like this, all of a sudden, your kids are here, they're staying over, everything's all rearranged..." (O'Brien and Kurins, 1991:234).

26. Transcript of CBS's *60 Minutes* "Man of Honor," March 27, 1983, p.8.

27. According to Kobler (1971), Mae Capone was always supportive of her husband. In rejecting a book-contract offer for $50,000, she said, "The public has one idea of my husband. I have another. I will treasure my memory and I will always love him" (p.269). She was by his side when he went to prison in 1931, tried to have him moved to a different federal prison, tried to get time off his sentence for good behavior, was with him when he died and sued the CBS network for its characterization of Capone in *The Untouchables*.

28. See Talese's (1971) account of Mrs. Profaci's willingness to take care of her pregnant daughter, Ann, and to help with the cooking and looking after Ann's other children. Also, she assisted her oldest daughter, Rosalie, in her

domestic chores, and guided her youngest daughter, Josephine, through her wedding plans and graduation from the University of California at Berkeley.

29. Other examples abound: (1) "In the old Sicilian family, the man of the house sits at the head of the table and the women wait on him hand and foot." He went on to describe his grandfather's dominance in the household, and his grandmother's and mother's second-class status. His grandfather was not a Mafioso (Teresa and Renner, 1973, 75-76). (2) When Vito Genovese died, reported Teresa, "the women of the neighborhood fingered their rosaries and wept. They had a delegation of nuns come to pay their respects" (Teresa and Renner, 1973:86).

30. The impression of total domination and victimization appears in Chapter 24 of Meskil (1976).

31. The author is fully aware of the need to expand the discussion in this article by placing the changes in Mafia women's lives in the larger context. Space did not permit a lengthy examination of this important topic here.

32. Mangione and Morreale (1992) have provided an excellent point at which to begin research in this area.

REFERENCES

Albini, J.L. (1971). *The American Mafia: Genesis of a Legend*. New York, NY: Appleton-Century-Crofts.

Alexander, S. (1988). *The Pizza Connection: Lawyers, Money, Drugs, Mafia*. New York, NY: Weidenfeld & Nicolson.

Anastasia, G. (1991). *Blood and Honor: Inside the Scarfo Mob—The Mafia's Most Violent Family*. New York, NY: Kensington.

—— (1993). *Mobfather: The Story of a Wife and a Son Caught in the Web of the Mafia*. New York, NY: Kensington.

Angiolillo, P.F. (1979). *A Criminal as Hero*. Lawrence, KS: Regents.

Arlacchi, P. (1986). *Mafia Business: The Mafia Ethic and the Spirit of Capitalism*. London, UK: Verso.

Barzini, L. (1971). *From Caesar to the Mafia: Sketches of Italian Life*. New York, NY: Bantam.

Block, A.A. (1977). "Aw! Your Mother's in the Mafia: Women Criminals in Progressive New York." *Contemporary Crises* 1:5-22.

—— (1980). "Searching for Women in Organized Crime." In: S.K. Datesman and F.R. Scarpitti eds., *Women, Crime, and Justice*. New York, NY: Oxford University Press.

—— (1991). *Masters of Paradise: Organized Crime and the Internal Revenue Service in the Bahamas*. New Brunswick, NJ: Transaction.

Blum, H. (1993). *Gangland: How the FBI Broke the Mob*. New York, NY: Simon & Schuster.

Blumenthal, R. (1988). *Last Days of the Sicilians: At War with the Mafia*. New York, NY: Times.

Bonanno, J. and S. Lalli, (1983). *A Man of Honor: The Autobiography of Joseph Bonanno*. New York, NY: Simon & Schuster.

Bonanno, R. and B. Donofrio (1990). *Mafia Marriage: My Story*. New York, NY: William Morrow.

Booth, E. (1927). "Ladies of the Mob." *American Mercury*, December 27, pp.399-407.

Calder, J.D. (1992). "Al Capone and the Internal Revenue: State-Sanctioned Criminology of Organized Crime." *Crime, Law and Social Change* 17:1-23.

Carpenter, T. (1992). *Mob Girl: A Woman's Life in the Underworld*. New York, NY: Simon & Schuster.

Condon, R. (1982). *Prizzi's Honor*. New York, NY: Coward, McCann and Geoghegan.

—— (1983). *Prizzi's Family*. New York, NY: G.P. Putnam's Sons.

—— (1988). *Prizzi's Glory*. New York, NY: Dutton.

Cook, F.J. (1966). *The Secret Rulers: Criminal Syndicates and How They Control the U.S. Underworld*. New York, NY: Duell, Sloan and Pearce.

Cox, D.W. (1989). *Mafia Wipeout: How the Feds Put Away an Entire Mob Family*. New York, NY: Shapolsky.

Cressey, D.R. (1967). "Methodological Dilemmas in the Study of Organized Crime as a Social Problem." *Annals of the American Academy of Political and Social Science* 374:101-112.

—— (1969). *Theft of the Nation: The Structure and Operations of Organized Crime in America*. New York, NY: Harper and Row.

Cummings, J. and E. Volkman (1990). *Goombata: The Improbable Rise of John Gotti and His Gang*. Boston, MA: Little, Brown.

Davis, J.H. (1989). *Mafia Kingfish: Carlos Marcello and the Assassination of John F. Kennedy*. New York, NY: McGraw-Hill.

Demaris, O. (1969). *Captive City*. New York, NY: Lyle Stuart.

—— (1981). *The Last Mafioso: The Treacherous World of Jimmy Fratianno*. New York, NY: Times.

—— (1986). *The Boardwalk Jungle*. New York, NY: Bantam.

Dubro, J. (1988). *Mob Mistress*. Toronto, CAN: Macmillan of Canada.

Edmonds, A. (1993). *Bugsy's Baby: The Secret Life of Mob Queen Virginia Hill*. New York, NY: Birch Lane.

Eisenberg, D., U. Dan, and E. Landau (1979). *Meyer Lansky: Mogul of the Mob*. New York, NY: Paddington.

Fopiano, W. and J. Harney (1993). *The Godson: A True-Life Account of 20 Years Inside the Mob*. New York, NY: St. Martins.

Franzese, M. and D. Matera (1992). *Quitting the Mob*. New York, NY: HarperCollins.

Gage, N. (1971). *The Mafia is Not an Equal Opportunity Employer*. New York, NY: McGraw-Hill.

Gambino, R. (1974). *Blood of My Blood: The Dilemma of the Italian-Americans*. New York, NY: Doubleday.

Giancana, A. and T.C. Renner (1984). *Mafia Princess: Growing Up in Sam Giancana's Family*. New York, NY: William Morrow.

Giancana, S. and C. Giancana (1992). *Double Cross: The Explosive Story of the Mobster Who Controlled America*. New York: Time Warner.

Goddard, D. (1974). *Joey*. New York, NY: Harper & Row.

Gosch, M.A. and R. Hammer (1974). *The Last Testament of Lucky Luciano*. Boston, MA: Little, Brown.

Greene, G. (1982). *J'Accuse: The Dark Side of Nice*. London, UK: Bodley Head.

Hawkins, G. (1969). "God and the Mafia." *Public Interest* 14:24-51.

Haller, M.H. (1990). "Illegal Enterprise: A Theoretical and Historical Interpretation." *Criminology* 28:207-235.

Hess, H. (1973). *Mafia and Mafiosi: The Structure of Power*. Farnsworth, UK: Saxon House.

Hobsbawn, E.J. (1969). *Bandits*. New York, NY: Delacorte.

Homer, F.D. (1974). *Guns and Garlic: Myths and Realities of Organized Crime*. West Lafayette, IN: Purdue University.

Huie, W.B. (1951). "My Christmas with Bugsy Siegel." *New American Mercury* (Jan.):7-22.

Ianni, F.A.J. and E. Ianni (1972). *A Family Business: Kinship and Social Control in Organized Crime*. New York, NY: Russell Sage Foundation.

Iannuzzi, J. (1993). *Joe Dogs: The Life & Crimes of a Mobster*. New York, NY: Simon & Schuster.

Katz, L. (1973). *Uncle Frank: The biography of Frank Costello*. New York, NY: Drake.

Kelly, R.J., ed. (1986). *Organized Crime: A Global Perspective*. Totowa, NJ: Rowman and Littlefield.

Kobler, J. (1971). *Capone: The Life and World of Al Capone*. New York, NY: G.P. Putnam's Sons.

Landesco, J. (1936). "The Woman and the Underworld." *Journal of Criminal Law and Criminology* 26:901-912.

La Plante, L. (1991). *Bella Mafia*. New York, NY: William Morrow.

Lupsha, P.A. (1981). "Individual Choice, Material Culture, and Organized Crime." *Criminology* 19:3-24.

Maas, P. (1968). *The Valachi Papers*. New York, NY: G.P. Putnam's Sons.

Mangione, J. and B. Morreale (1992). *La Storia: Five Centuries of the Italian American experience*. New York, NY: HarperCollins.

Meskil, P.S. (1976). *The Luparelli Tapes*. New York, NY: Playboy.

Messick, H. (1968). *Syndicate Wife*. New York, NY: Macmillan.

—— and J.L. Nellis (1973). *The Private Lives of Public Enemies*. New York, NY: Peter H. Wyden.

Moore, R. (1969). *The French Connection*. Boston, MA: Little Brown.

—— and B. Fuca (1977). *Mafia Wife*. New York, NY: Macmillan.

Moore, W. H. (1974). *The Kefauver Committee and the Politics of Crime 1950-1952*. Columbia, MO: University of Missouri.

Mustain, G. and J. Capeci (1988). *Mob Star: The Story of John Gotti*. New York, NY: Franklin Watts.

—— (1992). *Murder Machine: A True Story of Murder, Madness, and the Mafia*. New York, NY: Dutton.

O'Brien, J.F. and A. Kurins (1991). *Boss of Bosses, the Fall of the Godfather: The FBI and Paul Castellano*. New York, NY: Simon and Schuster.

O'Neill, G. and D. Lehr (1989). *The Underboss: The Rise and Fall of a Mafia Family*. New York, NY: St. Martin's.

Pileggi, N. (1985). *Wiseguy: Life in a Mafia Family*. New York, NY: Simon & Schuster.

Puzo, M. (1969). *The Godfather*. New York, NY: G.P. Putnam's Sons.

Rappleye, C. and E. Becker (1991). *All American Mafioso: The Johnny Rosselli Story*. New York, NY: Doubleday.

Reeve, A.B. (1931). *The Golden Age of Crime*. New York, NY: Mohawk.

Renner, T.C. and C. Kirby (1987). *Mafia Enforcer: A True Story of Life and Death in the Mob*. New York, NY: Bantam.

Rudolph, R. (1992). *The Boys from New Jersey: How the Mob Beat the Feds*. New York, NY: William Morrow.

Salerno, J. and S.J. Rivele (1990). *The Plumber: The True Story of How One Good Man Helped Destroy the Entire Philadelphia Mafia*. New York, NY: Knightsbridge.

Salerno, R. and J.S. Thompkins (1969). *The Crime Confederation*. Garden City, NY: Doubleday.

Schoenberg, J. (1992). *Mr. Capone: The Real—and Complete— Story of Al Capone*. New York, NY: William Morrow.

Stuart, M.A. (1985). *Gangster #2: Longy Zwillman, the Man Who Invented Organized Crime*. Secaucus, NJ: Lyle Stuart.

Talese, G. (1971). *Honor Thy Father*. New York, NY: World.

Taylor, N. (1989). *Sins of the Father: The True Story of a Family Running from the Mob*. New York, NY: St. Martin's.

Teresa, V. and T.C. Renner (1973). *My Life in the Mafia*. New York, NY: Doubleday.

—— (1975). *Vinnie Teresa's Mafia*. Garden City, NY: Doubleday.

Turkus, B.B. and S. Feder, eds. (1951). *Murder, Inc.: The Story of the Syndicate*. New York, NY: DeCapo.

Van Cise, P.S. (1936). *Fighting the Underworld*. Boston, MA: Houghton Mifflin.

Wolf, G. and J. DiMona (1974). *Frank Costello: Prime Minister of the Underworld*. New York, NY: William Morrow.

Zeiger, H.A. (1970). *Sam the Plumber: One Year in the Life of a Cosa Nostra Boss*. New York, NY: New American Library.

Use and Avoidance of RICO at the Local Level: The Implementation of Organized Crime Laws

by

Donald J. Rebovich

Abstract: *A survey of local prosecutors in the U.S. who had made use of state RICO laws to prosecute organized crime indicated that district attorneys, particularly in metropolitan areas, were engaged in more organized crime prosecutions than ever before because of: (1) a prevalence of crimes committed by loosely organized criminal enterprises that federal authorities view as minor and leave unaddressed, (2) improvement in prosecutorial skills, and (3) a willingness by a select group to experiment with newly provided "hammers" like state RICO laws. To date, use of state RICO laws on a local level tends to show modest results. Like earlier assessments of the use of RICO on a federal level, the present study of state RICOs and local prosecutors confirms the natural hesitancy to use such a new and complex law.*

PURPOSE AND SCOPE OF THE STUDY

In 1967, The President's Commission on Law Enforcement and Administration of Justice concluded that the implementation of enforcement and prosecution strategies more progressive than those existing at the time was necessary if organized crime was to be effectively controlled. Probably the most noted, and controversial, control mechanism developed since the late 1960s has been the Racketeer Influenced and Corrupt Organization Act (RICO; 18 U.S.C., 1961-1968 [1988]), a law that leaves the "crime" to other laws and addresses the idea of being "organized."

The perception of enhanced control fostered by new statutory tools can be quite divorced from reality. While much has been written about the potential impact of RICO, little attention has been paid to its actual use, particularly at the local level of government in those 29 states that have adopted their own versions of RICO. We are still largely unaware of how willing prosecutors have been to relinquish use of the timeworn "attrition" strategy of organized crime prosecution—the attempt to control such crime by prosecuting key figures in criminal enterprises—and to avail themselves of the purported benefits of RICO.

The purpose of this chapter is to provide much-needed information on the extent of the implementation of RICO prosecutions at the local government level. A study of this nature is both timely and important considering that most indications are that prosecutors in local jurisdictions still appear somewhat ambivalent about RICO and its use. Local jurisdictions traditionally carry the brunt of most prosecution activity, and now possess the capacity to fill the void created by the reallocation of federal resources (i.e., multi-jurisdictional task forces, federal funds, specialized prosecution units). Yet, according to findings presented here, they continue to rely primarily upon traditional conspiracy statutes and forfeiture provisions within their respective criminal codes to prosecute racketeering cases.

System variables inevitably affect the implementation of any new public policy; therefore, the impact of system and other related variables upon RICO implementation, and the outcome of that implementation, become important focal points for analysis. The study this article is based on—a national survey of local prosecutors' offices—suggests that while state RICOs may be an appealing prosecution tool in the ideal, system and organizational realities may have served to limit the application of these statutes (Rebovich et al., 1993). Organizational and environmental constraints (e.g., budgets, training, criminal justice capacity variables, judicial and legislator perceptions) that typically confront local prosecutors can have a pronounced affect on the choices that are made to vigorously implement new public policy on organized crime. These factors have joined with prosecutors' perceptions of potential public response, levels of their own specialized expertise, internal office policies and political commitment to further dissuade prosecutors from active use of RICO.

This project was built on the early work of the National Association of Attorneys General (civil RICO prosecutions) and the U.S. Department of Justice (federal criminal RICO prosecutions), which identified the requisite policy criteria as well as some environmental and organizational factors that facilitate or obstruct the successful prosecution of criminal RICO violations at the local level. Specific attention was paid to: jurisdiction-specific criminal RICO statutes and provisions; other applicable conspiracy and forfeiture laws within the criminal codes; requisite resources; training and expertise; decision-making criteria and processes; organizational structure and commitment; crimes (i.e., type, duration, frequency, intensity); workload volume; and outcome (disposition) measures.

The data collected in this research project can be an asset for prosecutors and others contemplating the use or modification of RICO and its provisions to fight organized criminal activity, particularly drug trafficking, in their jurisdictions. Analyzing public policy from a systems perspective allows an analysis of "policy in action." It examines how decision makers determine the policies to implement, strategies to employ, resources and expertise to develop, and organizational structures to adopt based upon their jurisdiction-specific needs. Public policy analysis, using methodologically sound research methods, provides a comprehensive explanation and evaluation of RICO laws and prosecutions at the local level. These data, collected from a large, diverse group of prosecutors' offices, provide information for policymakers and prosecutors who need to know "what works" in combating organized criminal activity.

PREVIOUS RESEARCH

In 1970, Congress and President Nixon gave federal prosecutors around the country a powerful new legal weapon in the fight against organized crime: RICO. RICO's criminal and civil components assisted prosecutorial efforts against organized crime in two ways: (a) RICO was designed to be flexible through its loose construction; and (b) it provided new and severe criminal and civil sanctions. At the time of its enactment, RICO's primary purpose was to serve as a legal device to remove and prevent organized crime elements from infiltrating legitimate businesses.

Over the past 20 years, however, the role of RICO in American law enforcement evolved in substantial and sometimes controversial ways. First, using the federal RICO statute and experience as a model, states sought to empower their own prosecutors and advance their criminal justice objectives by passing RICO-style laws, known as "little RICOs." Indeed, by 1992, 29 states had enacted such laws. Second, federal RICO and little RICOs increasingly have been used to prosecute criminal cases, such as public corruption, securities fraud, and obscenity cases, that go beyond the more traditional RICO organized crime target.

Paralleling the growth in the use of RICO by prosecutors has been a growth in the literature on the subject. RICO has been the object of special attention, as evidenced by the existence of RICO newsletters, its own American Bar Association committee, a special review unit in the Department of Justice, a set of guidelines for federal prosecutors and several procedural manuals. Despite all this attention, scholars such as Dombrink and Meeker (1985) have pointed out that "little data has been presented reflecting the overall cases of this controversial and potentially powerful statute." Law and criminology journal articles have centered on the implications of the use of civil RICO provisions and the issues associated with it—evolving RICO case law and legislative histories. There are only a handful of studies that deal directly with state and local RICO laws and their use, or with the state-federal RICO nexus.

An area that demands thorough exploration is the utility that experiences with federal RICO can have for state and local RICO prosecutors. Insight into federal experience with RICO may aid local prosecutors in their efforts to discover the elements of successful RICO prosecutions, and to avoid the organizational and prosecutorial quagmires already discovered by their federal counterparts. Perusal of the current literature yields no substantive empirical studies that apply, on a national basis, to federal RICO experience with the little RICOs. There are a host of studies, however, that have examined the legal controversies associated with RICO. Using the several representative studies described below, one can gain a clear sense of the dynamics of RICO and the implications of these findings for state and local prosecutors.

Common Elements: Linkage of Federal RICO to State RICO

The central elements of the federal RICO law form a common thread tying together the 29 state RICO statutes. Although many of the state RICO laws have similar key components, each has its own unique composition. Several common elements evolving from the federal statute can be identified.

The first common element involves the definitions of the criminal acts that can be considered predicate offenses. Specifically, definitions are provided for what constitutes the two essential parts of a RICO violation: "enterprise" and "pattern." Second, like the federal statute, a criminal section outlining prohibited activities and penalties, and a civil section including a provision for a private cause of action, is usually contained in the state statutes. Third, most states include a forfeiture guidelines section subjecting to seizure all property intended, derived or realized from the prohibited activity. Specific provisions regarding revolving funds and other procedures are provided in many state RICO statutes.

The close relationship between the structure of the federal RICO law and the state statutes is one reason to believe that some of the problems and successes encountered at the federal level can be applied to the state level. By isolating relevant information from the sphere of federal experience, state and local prosecutors can enhance their effectiveness using their own RICO statute. For example, the legal controversies over two elements of federal RICO—the definitions of "enterprise" and "pattern"—are easily applicable to the state statutes, almost all of which incorporate these central elements in some form.

One of the few analyses directly applying the federal experience to state RICO was done by Blakey and Walker (1989). The authors apply the legal experience of federal RICO to an assessment of the Colorado Organized Crime Control Act (COCCA). The authors point out that since COCCA was modeled on many of the features of federal RICO, federal decisions interpreting RICO provisions and language are relevant to COCCA issues. Case law from other states with versions of RICO were also applied to the COCCA analysis.

Blakey and Walker (1989) describe how four RICO issues relate directly to the Colorado statute: the debate over the "pattern" definition, the uncertainty over the applicable period of limitations, the nuance of suing corporations and suits for a conspiracy to violate COCCA. They point out that in interpreting COCCA, Colorado judges, like their counterparts in other states, refer to federal jurisprudence for guidance. Blakey and Walker (1989) found it relevant, therefore, to explore the current federal case law on RICO, with the aim of understanding and predicting COCCA developments.

Another study that explored aspects of the federal-state RICO relation was completed by Castillo (1985) for the National Governors' Association. Castillo asked state representatives about the existence and purpose of their RICO statutes, the number and type of state RICO prosecutions, and the strengths and weaknesses of their state RICO laws. At the time of the study 17 states had enacted such laws. The report's findings, however, are useful beyond the drug trafficking orientation of the analysis. Castillo found that all of the states used their state RICO for purposes similar to the federal statute; namely, the elimination of criminal organizations. Specifically, Castillo states that RICO laws "may be the only effective means of prosecuting principals of criminal organizations involved in drug trafficking" (1985:107).

The difficulties with the state RICO laws, as described by Castillo (1985), seemed to parallel problems with federal RICO. State and local prosecutors reported that the sometimes vague terms in statutory language, such as "pattern of racketeering activity" and "predicate act," were an occasional obstacle to successful use of state RICO statutes. Other problems encountered were judicial inexperience with RICO-related issues, prosecutors' and investigators' inexperience with RICO, prosecutors' perceptions that the state RICO law is difficult to use, and "an overall lack of resources to implement the RICO provisions effectively" (Castillo, 1985:102).

As of 1985, according to the report, state and local prosecutors apparently have not used corresponding state provisions as often or as successfully as their federal counterparts. Financial constraints and limited investigative resources were found to be primary obstacles to the use of RICO laws, but "the nature and extent of the criminal organizations engaging in drug trafficking operations, a state's ability to seize the assets of such organizations, and other state interests" were cited as additional considerations influencing a prosecutor's decision to launch a RICO prosecution (Castillo, 1985:93).

Additional instructive analysis for state and local prosecutors is provided by Martinez and Richards (1985), who, like Blakey and Walker (1989), approach their study of New Jersey's RICO provisions contained in its 1977 Casino Control Act (CCA) by referring to the federal RICO experience. They assert: that "CCA-RICO, as a direct offspring of the federal RICO statute with little legislative history of its own [,] will inherit most of the major interpretive issues currently besetting the federal statute" (p.655). Four of federal RICO's interpretive issues were identified as likely to arise in connection with the New Jersey statute: (a) necessity of a prior criminal conviction; (b) necessity for injury beyond that caused by the predicate acts of racketeering; (c) the two personal-act rule, i.e., what a defendant must do, or consent to do, to join a RICO conspiracy; and (d) whether a RICO-defined "enterprise" also can be considered a defendant in a civil suit. In 1981, New Jersey legislators enacted a general state RICO statute, which was designed to protect itself from some of the legal controversies facing federal RICO. Martinez and Richards (1985) contend that the general statute made the older RICO-CCA provisions obsolete.

Controversy Surrounding Innovative Applications of RICO

A key interest of state/local prosecutors centers on how RICO has been used creatively in federal courts as well as in other state jurisdictions. Over the past two decades, particularly beginning in the 1980s, some prosecutors began to use RICO for cases that were unlike the more traditional organized crime syndicate prosecutions. These innovative applications include prosecutions of securities fraud, of public corruption and of street gang crimes. A number of scholarly articles have been written analyzing the legal issues associated with these new and often controversial prosecutorial applications of RICO.

RICO prosecutions using obscenity violations as the predicate offense are a prime example of this controversy. After federal RICO was amended in 1984 to include obscenity violations in the list of predicate offenses, several states also included such a provision in their RICO statutes to combat sexually explicit material. Several articles have examined the subject from a legalistic perspective. For example, Indiana's use of its state RICO law's obscenity provision was critically explored by Melnick (1989).

In his detailed legal analysis, Melnick (1989) identified two major constitutional issues raised by the recent trend to use RICO for obscenity cases: (a) whether RICO's pre-judgment provisions (i.e., temporary restraining orders, seizures, padlocking orders) violate defendant's first amendment rights of freedom of speech and press; and (b) whether RICO's judgment remedies, including forfeiture, constitute an impermissible prior restraint under the first amendment's freedom of speech and press guarantees when applied to criminal obscenity violations. These issues are raised in an Indiana case appealed to the U.S. Supreme Court. The state of Indiana alleged that Fort Wayne Books had engaged in a pattern of racketeering activity by repeatedly selling obscene materials. On the basis of this assertion, the state obtained the court's permission to seize all of Fort Wayne Books' real and personal property used, intended to use, derived from or realized through the alleged racketeering activity. After finding probable cause of a RICO violation, the court ordered the immediate padlocking of the bookstore and seizure of its contents. Melnick (1989) described the rationale of the Supreme Court's decision that struck down the Indiana law by declaring that pre-judgment provisions to seize expressive materials from bookstores were unconstitutional. The court left open, however, the constitutionality of post-judgment seizures.

The same legal issues were discussed in an earlier article by Eggenberger (1988), who related the prior restraint standard to RICO forfeiture sanctions applied to obscenity violations. Eggenberger concluded that such sanctions are an unconstitutional form of prior restraint. Relevant case law was also discussed and applied to this controversy.

Essentially, the debate about the legality of these new areas of RICO prosecution arises from a fundamental difference in interpretation. Those who subscribe to a conservative view of this law regard many of the unprecedented applications as dangerous "abuses" of RICO laws. Those who have a more liberal interpretation see RICO as sufficiently flexible to be used for new types of prosecution applications, such as street gang and securities fraud prosecutions.

The state experience has been shown to mirror the federal experience on this issue. For example, in Blakey and Walker's (1989) analysis of the Colorado RICO law, COCCA, conclusions about the state law were based on legal challenges to federal RICO. During the early federal experience of RICO, some critics contended that the statute was meant only to apply to "traditional" organized crime entities, e.g., La Cosa Nostra. The federal courts, including the U.S. Supreme Court, rejected this claim. The courts found no evidence in RICO's text or in its legislative history to support the argument constricting its applicability. Using the legal antecedent, Blakey and Walker (1989) conclude that COCCA, too, is not limited to traditional organized crime entities.

Other Legal Challenges to RICO

In addition to the controversy regarding the application of RICO to new prosecutorial areas, a lively debate had been waged in the courtrooms and in law journals about specific provisions of the RICO statutes. State and local prosecutors are particularly sensitive to these more "technical" issues. Asset forfeiture is often the focus of critical analysis. Some legal scholars and defense attorneys have challenged the constitutionality of asset seizures.

Another contested practice is the forfeiture of attorneys' fees in RICO cases. In addition to asset forfeiture, the provisions providing a private cause of action and setting penalties have been subject to intense review. The federal statute allows for treble damages, and many states have replicated this provision. Some claim that such severe penalties are too harsh.

RICO and Prosecutorial Discretion

Dombrink and Meeker (1985) conducted a study of criminal RICO litigation reaching appellate review between 1970 and 1983. The focus of their study was to present data as to the types of RICO cases and whether there has been any congruent variation in conviction rates. Eighty federal RICO cases reaching the appellate level were selected for analysis. It was concluded that appellate courts have not found RICO white collar crime prosecutions to be "problematic," as some critics suggest. Of the 11 cases involving white collar crimes, nine were affirmed unanimously, with one case reporting a dissent and concurrence and one a dissent. Fifty-one of seventy-one cases (72%) that could be classified were considered traditional organized crime cases by the authors. Dombrink and Meeker (1985) also tested the charge by critics that forfeiture provisions are overused and abused. The controversial criminal forfeiture provision was used infrequently in the sample; only 12% of the cases studied involved forfeiture. On the basis of their study, Dombrink and Meeker assert that criminal RICO has "been used in a conservative manner without systematic abuse or creative extension"— a conclusion at variance with the criticism that RICO has been used recklessly.

As to prosecutorial discretion, Dombrink and Meeker (1985) note that the "dilemma between flexibility and unbridled discretion is at the root of much of the criticism of RICO" (p.589). The authors further note that to curtail the abuse that may arise from uncontrolled prosecutorial flexibility and to maintain uniformity of enforcement policy, the Department of Justice created the Organized Crime and Racketeering Section (OCRS) in 1980. Using specific criteria as its guide, OCRS is the "quality control" phase of federal RICO prosecutions.

A description of the OCRS case selection process, provided by Coffey (1990), bears closer review. At the outset, all RICO prosecutions—including civil RICO complaints—initiated by the Department of Justice must be reviewed and approved by the OCRS. The prosecutor must submit a prosecutive memorandum and a draft indictment. OCRS staff examine the memorandum to determine whether the underlying crimes meet the Criminal Division's policy and legal criteria for RICO prosecutions. At the initial screening stage, OCRS will screen memoranda for risky or inappropriate cases. Coffey (1990) noted that the easiest cases to review are those that deal with crimes of violence and/or narcotics trafficking by organized crime groups. The most difficult are cases involving frauds by white collar suspects with no discernable connections to traditional organized crime groups. OCRS pays particular attention to two of the most controversial areas of RICO prosecution: obscenity and securities fraud cases. Some critics charge that obscenity-based RICO prosecutions have an unfairly negative impact on the financial industry. Even the cases that appear to show a clear-cut case of RICO violations may not be approved for RICO prosecution, however. For instance, in cases where the pattern of criminal activity consists entirely of narcotics trafficking, extortion, and gambling, it would be better prosecutorial strategy to use the relevant felony statutes rather than RICO. Such an approach eliminates unnecessary complication for a trial jury and avoids the potential for restrictive case law arising out of an overextension of RICO, Coffey (1990) explained.

OCRS will search and identify any major legal issues that might arise in the case, as well as ensure that the memorandum meets the list of criteria for prosecution. If a memorandum passes the first reading, several steps follow. OCRS reviews the final draft of the indictment. If a RICO restraining order will be requested, approval will be withheld until the effect of the restraint on the defendant and his or her interests can be determined. If the prosecutor wants to seek forfeiture, OCRS will assess whether it is proportionate. Finally, OCRS will usually conduct, if asked, an informal conference with the defendant's attorney to discuss the RICO recommendation and forfeiture request, if there is one. According to Coffey (1990), the OCRS conducted 12 of these conferences in 1990. These meetings give the defendant's attorney the chance to persuade the prosecutors that the RICO charge and/or forfeiture prosecutions can sometimes be overbroad and inimical to legitimate business. Coffey (1990) concluded by stating that the "Washington review and approval of federal RICO prosecutions is a wise precaution" (p.1043).

Conclusions of Previous Research

State and local prosecutors are discovering the power of RICO to destroy criminal enterprises which harm their communities; before RICO these criminal enterprises were often able to evade the reach of prosecution. With a greater reliance on state RICO laws comes a greater demand for information. Yet, although the body of empirical literature dealing with federal RICO is growing, there is very little research on criminal RICO prosecutions at the local level. Indeed, as Dombrink and Meeker (1985) note, the promulgation of state RICO statutes may yet fulfill the predictions and fears of the critics (that the law is abused). Whether or not this is the case or is likely to occur requires further systematic observation and investigation.

The lack of analysis of state RICO issues is particularly noticeable since state and local law enforcement entities have had to assume some of the cases formerly handled by federal agencies. Responsibility for the prosecution and investigation of mid-level criminal organizations, for instance, is increasingly shifting to state and local agencies due to the reduction and reallocation of federal resources. Studies such as Blakey and Walker's (1989) analysis of the Colorado RICO law (COCCA) and the National Governors Association report demonstrate that state and local prosecutors are dealing with the same kinds of legal, organizational, and procedural experiences as federal prosecutors underwent in the 1970s and 1980s. On its face, the nexus between the federal and state/local experiences can be found in at least three major areas: criminal justice needs for RICO provisions, obstacles to RICO prosecution and procedures/methods used for successful RICO prosecution. The nature and level of such parallelism of experience can be tested by surveying prosecutors' offices around the country.

Prosecutors can benefit from empirical studies that can answer the basic questions of "what is being done?" and "what works?" These apparently simple questions require a cluster of complex answers. Under the rubric of the local RICO prosecution process, attention needs to be paid to such aspects as policy criteria, decision making, organizational factors, legal issues and resource requisites. Research and evaluation using a multi-faceted analysis can provide these kind of comprehensive findings.

STUDY DESIGN

The research design for this study blends aspects of mailed self-administered questionnaire surveys with telephone interviews of local prosecutors. Prosecutors' offices representing local counties, districts and cities (N=2,703) were partitioned into six strata, based on jurisdictional population size, from which a representative sample of 368 offices was drawn. The survey yielded a response rate of 150, or approximately 40%. Subsequent telephone contact was made with a select group of prosecutors' offices identified as having prosecuted state RICO cases and/or "RICO-like" cases. The respondents elaborated on their organized crime prosecution experience, including; (1) *the type of case* in which RICO was used, (2) *reasons for using, or respective use of*, the state RICO statute and (3) *improvement suggestions*. The survey attempted to identify all types of local prosecution of organized crime activity between January 1, 1989 and January 1, 1992, including the use of traditional criminal code alternatives to RICO (i.e., "RICO-like" cases).

SURVEY FINDINGS

The total number of offices that conducted *any* type of organized crime prosecutions during the study period was 47, or 31% of the sample. Thirty-seven of these offices reported using RICO statutes in the prosecution of the case. Thirty-two of the offices prosecuting organized crime represented jurisdictions with populations over 250,000. An examination of the offense categories of RICO prosecutions within the study's sample, and their frequency of occurrence, help peel back some informational layers to expose the key characteristics of these types of prosecutions. The plurality of 174 cases (27%) were narcotics cases, i.e., cases in which the primary offense(s) was identified as involving narcotics trafficking/distribution; 16% were gambling offenses. An additional 16% of the cases *were* classified as fraud, i.e., consumer fraud, investment fraud and bank fraud, with *consumer fraud* being the most common type within this category. Prostitution/obscenity cases accounted for 9% of the total.

Equally informative were offense distributions of RICO alternative prosecutions conducted by the reporting local prosecutors' offices *not* using RICO. The total number of these cases exceeds the number of RICO cases prosecuted for the same time period (i.e., 199 to 174), with offense categories of narcotics offenses making up significant portions of the total offenses prosecuted (i.e., 59% and 29%, respectively); this represented a sharp departure from the earlier distributions for RICO narcotics and gambling prosecutions.

The original 37 offices reporting the use of RICO were found to report over 700 cases in which the use of RICO was rejected in favor of traditional state statutes. Most of these cases were for narcotics offenses (476, or 63%), more than four times the number of narcotics-related RICO prosecutions conducted by the same offices. In addition, RICO alternative prosecutions for gambling offenses represented more than three times the number of RICO gambling prosecutions in the 37 offices.

INTERVIEW FINDINGS

The national mail survey conducted on local RICO prosecutions furnished the researchers with insight into the frequency with which local prosecutors utilize state RICO statutes and RICO-like statutes, and the criminal categories within which they fall. However, more contextual data are required to examine why local prosecutors may find their RICO statutes to be helpful, or why they may avoid their use. For this information, the researchers turned to telephone interviews of select jurisdictions identified through the mail survey as having experience with prosecuting local RICO/RICO-like cases.

A sample of jurisdictions that had prosecuted cases using either state RICO statutes (i.e., criminal and/or civil), RICO-like statues, or a combination of both (i.e., criminal and/or civil) were selected for telephone contact to supply further explanatory data on statute use, advantages, and obstacles. Interviews were conducted with 35 assistant prosecutors from 13 jurisdictions: Ventura County, CA; Alameda County, CA; Englewood, CO; Denver, CO; Orlando, FL; Live Oak, FL; Ramsey County (St. Paul), MN; Essex County, NJ; Union County, NJ; Franklin County, OH; Philadelphia County, PA; Montgomery County, PA; and Lawrenceburg, TN. The questionnaire for the telephone survey was divided into the following areas: (1) types of cases in which RICO prosecutions have been conducted, (2) reasons for using the state RICO statute, (3) reasons for not using the state RICO statute, and the alternatives used, and (4) recommendations for improvement. In keeping with methodological direction provided through other qualitative criminal justice studies (see, for example, Gibbs and Shelley, 1981; Miles and Huberman, 1984), the flexibility of the interview's application was stressed to complement the exploratory nature of the study. In effect, the questionnaire served as more of an interview guide than an interview schedule.

Types of Cases

Types of cases in which the respondents employed the use of state RICO statutes or RICO-like statutes fell into the general categories of white collar offenses, narcotics offenses, gambling, sex offenses and homicide.

The most common prosecution category was white collar offenses. Ten of the thirteen site representatives indicated that from 1989 to 1991 they used the state RICO statute in the prosecution of offenses that included embezzlement, telemarketing fraud, investment fraud, public corruption, theft by extortion and fencing. The next most common category was narcotics offenses, most of which involved narcotics-related forfeitures. One Orlando, FL narcotics prosecution overlapped with the white collar offense area, while the next most frequently cited offense area was gambling (bingo operations run by criminal organizations were used to "front" for the laundering of funds gained from drug trafficking). RICO gambling prosecutions centered primarily on illegal lottery/bookmaking operations. Both of the two sex offense prosecutions were for the promotion of prostitution, and the single jurisdiction reporting use of their state RICO statute in a homicide case—Philadelphia County, PA—involved homicides committed by a narcotics-related criminal enterprise: the "Junior Black Mafia" street gang in which 45 individuals were killed as a result of gang "turf wars."

Reasons For RICO Statute Use

The reasons for turning to state RICO statutes on the local level ranged from enhancing the local prosecutor's capacity to apply relatively strict sanctions—or threatening to use that application—to directing prosecution resources toward offenses that could fall into the "gaps" between local and federal enforcement.

By frequency of citation as a reason for applying the RICO statute, the sample was distributed as follows:

Table 1: Reasons for Use of State RICO Statute

Severity of penalties	43%
Plea bargaining leverage	15%
Forfeiture strength	7%
Statute-of-limitation strength	7%
Simplification of case for jury	7%
Street gang eradication	7%
Inter-jurisdictional application	7%
Filling federal gap	7%

As indicated in Table 1, local prosecutors reported that the key attribute prompting them to use their state RICO statutes was the belief that the statutes had the potential for the administration of stiff penalties not provided through other legal avenues. One of the primary positive impacts of state RICO was that the local prosecutor could bring serious penalties to bear on what many may consider relatively minor criminal activities. This was particularly stressed by respondents from Columbus, Orlando and Denver. The Columbus prosecutor found that employing RICO for certain white collar offenses proved more productive than aggregating the individual offenses. In Orlando, escort services catering to prostitution rings were closed and funds forfeited through the use of Florida's RICO, and the owners received what was considered significant prison sentences. The Orlando respondent noted that it would have been likely that the offenders would have been allowed to quickly return to their unlawful behavior had prosecutors chosen to rely on local prostitution statutes. A similar use of a state RICO statute was reported by the assistant prosecutor from St. Paul, MN, in which a RICO conviction for promotion of prostitution resulted in the forfeiture of two buildings worth $260,000 that harbored the prostitution enterprise, and of illegal profits totaling $200,000.

Denver's deputy district attorney viewed Colorado's state RICO statute as a source of high versatility in employing sanctions not available through other means for a wide variety of offenses. One case involved the interstate "selling" of kitchen equipment in which the offender defrauded customers of deposits ($90,000) on merchandise never delivered. Other reported cases included a moving company that stole rental trucks to transport its customers' possessions, a mortuary that illegally billed the state's Department of Social Services and two telemarketing fraud cases accounting for $600,000 in illegal gains. COCCA, Colorado's RICO law, was described as being closely modeled after federal RICO. A reported advantage to COCCA was that it could be used to obtain injunctions to prevent RICO violators from further business activity in which the criminal operation was focused (the injunction can be sought upon conviction or a civil finding), and that it could be used as a prosecution "hammer" in criminal cases.

COCCA also offered prosecutors an attractive prosecution framework and sharp penalties in contrast to standard criminal statutes. For example, with regard to telemarketing fraud, the regular applicable state statute requires that a case involve over $15,000 of allegedly stolen funds in addition to other criteria. COCCA, on the other hand, permits the prose-cutor, in the respondent's words, to "...pick a small number of transactions and get a bigger penalty."

In the area of plea negotiations, the prosecutor using COCCA can start with "more chips in the middle of the table" since the act targets Class 2 felonies, and the prosecutor can threaten its use against a defendant to obtain a guilty plea to a lesser charge. Extensive use of state RICO as a plea bargaining tool was also cited by the interviewee from Norristown, PA. In this jurisdiction, the threat of RICO was so successful in achieving the local prosecutor's desired outcome that actual RICO prosecutions were rarely followed through, leaving no documented record of the actual impact of state RICO statute presence.

Additional prosecution staff in the Denver office perceived COCCA as being valuable in cross-jurisdictional criminal cases and in extending the statute of limitations for predicate offenses. One reason given for the local use of COCCA in interstate criminal activity was the conclusion that federal enforcement/prosecution authorities were failing to seriously pur-sue complaints in areas of telemarketing fraud and other types of com-puter fraud. As one Denver prosecutor stated:

> There is a huge gap in terms of federal enforcement...There is no systemwide enforcement of these types of consumer fraud cases. Since the federal entities turn away complaints, and keep no record of it [sic], they are unable to detect a pattern of criminal activity in a particular area or case. These could be likely candidates for RICO prosecu-tion...The complainants then turn to the local and state prosecutor for assistance. Thus, these criminal enterprise cases are being handled by local prosecutors by default of federal prosecutors.

According to this respondent, criminals based in Colorado engaging in telephone or mail consumer fraud focus their illegal activities on out-of-state victims because they are aware that the state will refer the case to the "feds" where there is "no real threat of [federal] enforcement."

Surprisingly—considering the accounting of reasons for RICO *non-use* reported later in this report—state RICO statute use was reported as providing a much-needed degree of simplicity for jurors. For example, Columbus's assistant prosecutor maintained that embezzlement and public corruption cases "fit neatly" into the Ohio RICO legal framework, and, consequently, allow for an easier presentation to the jury of what would normally be a highly complicated case. As previously stated, Philadelphia's deputy district attorney reported a high degree of satisfaction with Pennsylvania's RICO statute in enabling his office to make significant inroads in eradicating street gang "turf wars."

Reasons for Avoiding the Use of RICO

The characteristic that stands out above all others when considering reasons for avoiding the use of RICO is the frequency of reasons for choosing not to use state RICO statutes. There were 29 such instances of avoidance, falling into ten separate categories. Incidence of RICO avoidance was not only confined to those interviewed who had completely rejected RICO, but also included those having used RICO under certain conditions.

Reasons for RICO avoidance by local prosecutors interviewed can be categorized as follows:

Table 2: Reasons for State RICO Avoidance	
Fear of failure	27%
Statute complexity	17%
Light penalties	17%
Other laws more effective	10%
Handled by state/federal prosecutor	10%
Vulnerability to constitutional attack	7%
Lack of resources	3%
Potential for press/public backlash	3%
High standard of proof	3%
Narrow court application	3%

Half of the prosecutor respondents indicated that an obstacle to the successful application of their state RICO statute—one that could be instrumental in the decision to reject use—was the fear that chances were slim for achieving a successful disposition. Pessimism over obtaining convictions under RICO was attributed to three problem sources: lack of familiarity by local prosecutors, potential confusion for jurors, and potential confusion for judges.

The respondents from Ohio and Florida were particularly outspoken on this subject. The Ohio respondent underscored the impact that the relative newness of that state's RICO statute has on the selection of cases. Local prosecutors in this jurisdiction are said to be especially discriminating about selecting cases because they are cognizant of their role in forming case law; only strong cases that fit a rigid "in-house" criteria are selected.

The respondents from Live Oak, FL contended that in the 3rd Judicial Circuit, "many prosecutors were intimidated by RICO—including judges." According to Orlando's assistant prosecutor, this intimidation can go beyond the prosecutor and the judge, to affect jurors in state RICO prosecution cases.

> Many of my colleagues generally use several individual statutes to address crimes that could be prosecuted wholly under the RICO statute. This is done out of fear of losing the case and fear that the jury would not adequately understand the elements of the RICO statute...In instances where the prosecutor fears losing the case, charges may be slightly downgraded to avoid application of RICO provisions.

The Englewood, CO and Union County, NJ respondents added that their respective drug and forfeiture statutes are "simpler to present to juries" and carry stiffer penalties, another frequently cited reason for state RICO avoidance.

Specifics on why local prosecutors in some RICO states turn to other statutes with more attractive penalty structures were provided by respondents from Minnesota and Florida. Minnesota's sentencing guideline for RICO was described as being ranked as a probationary offense which severely limited judicial discretion in administering more severe sentences.

The assistant prosecutor in Live Oak, FL described RICO penalties as not being any greater than sentences associated with regular criminal statutes. According to this respondent, that fact, coupled with the perceived complexity of RICO, results in a strong disincentive to use Florida's RICO. The Live Oak respondent indicated that local prosecutors often opt for Florida's habitual offender statute since it offers the prospect of tougher penalties and is seen as being more straightforward. Orlando's respondent concurred: in his experience, Florida's RICO statute was generally not applied in certain cases because the state's drug offense statutes were found to be more appropriate or to carry stiffer penalties (e.g., Florida's Continuing Criminal Enterprise statute was characterized as being more desirable due to its maximum life-term penalty, with a 25-year mandatory minimum). This respondent also reported that in some instances the local prosecutor would be more interested in the length of sentence than in the assets that can be seized, making the local drug statute more attractive.

In New Jersey, local prosecutors have been turning to statutes other than state RICO that actually mirror some of the underlying principles of RICO. New Jersey's Leader of Criminal Enterprise statute was described as targeting drug organizations/networks with high levels of trafficking and distribution in the community, and with a significant amount of property and assets (i.e., other than motor vehicles and cash, which we earlier reported as being easily forfeited under New Jersey drug and forfeiture statutes). In addition, the Essex County, NJ prosecutor's office also reported that "organized crime-type" cases involving gambling are typically prosecuted on the local level using state gambling statutes (e.g., promotion of gambling, criminal usury, theft by extortion) that are more than sufficient to address these cases.

Judging from interviewee responses, local prosecutors have also distanced themselves from civil RICO statutes as a foundation for seizure and forfeiture of illegal funds/property. Florida respondents indicated that the civil provision of that state's RICO statute was rarely used by local prosecutors. For narcotics-related forfeitures, local prosecutors tend to rely on the Florida Uniform Contraband Forfeiture Act because it is "simpler than civil RICO." Similarly, local prosecutors from Colorado felt that the Colorado Public Nuisance Law was more appropriately utilized than the civil features of COCCA for narcotics-related forfeitures, but indicated that this could change in the near future: the state legislature has recently passed a new forfeiture law—distinct from COCCA civil provisions—which shifts the burden of proof to the prosecutor and affords the defendant a right of continuance. It is predicted that this could motivate local prosecutors to gravitate to the forfeiture power of COCCA if the prosecutorial burden is less under the act.

Remaining reasons cited for avoidance of use of state RICO statutes by local prosecutors included: (1) "overbroad" RICO statute language that opened the door for constitutional attack; (2) unreasonably high standards of proof; and (3) the perception that judges would apply the statute narrowly, ruling out a practical application of the statute to white collar offenses. One of the Florida respondents described that state's courts has having narrowed the application of RICO statutes over the past few years in a number of different ways:

For instance, it is very difficult to bring a RICO action against one or two individuals despite evidence of ongoing criminal activities in more than two predicate areas. Also, the forfeitable property definition for RICO forfeitures has been narrowed. A recent homesteading ruling disallowed individuals' homes from being forfeited subsequent to RICO conviction. Only businesses or homes actually used in the commission of the offense are now eligible for forfeiture.

In at least one instance, a respondent indicated a hesitancy to use RICO for fear that its application may be interpreted by the public and media as an unreasonable application of the statute to what may be seen as non-organized criminal offenses.

Somewhat surprisingly, in only three cases did respondents state that RICO cases were handled by state or federal prosecution authorities—and in only one case was this attributed to a lack of resources. In Essex County, NJ, local prosecutors were found to occasionally provide physical surveillance to the State Attorney General's office on state RICO cases, but rarely prosecuted them at the local level. According to Essex County's representative:

> New Jersey's RICO statute is strong, but my office simply does not have the resources to conduct the investigation and the protracted litigation that these cases could entail. Such cases are usually handled by the State AG'S [Attorney General's] office. They have the required manpower and time to devote to these cases, something a smaller local prosecutor's office—even a metropolitan local prosecutor's office—may not be able to supply. We feel we'd operate under a handicap from the beginning, so we simply don't attempt it.

In Tennessee, local prosecutors were described as advocating collaboration with U.S. Attorneys on RICO cases for reasons less to do with resource needs and more to do with high standards of proof in Tennessee's civil RICO that were said not to apply to federal RICO. As reported by Lawrenceburg's representative, local prosecutors in Tennessee must prove beyond a reasonable doubt that any party of interest to the assets (e.g., business partner, wife) had knowledge that criminal activity had been present in order for assets to be forfeited.

Recommendations for Improvement

Recommendations for improvement were clustered primarily in the following categories: (1) RICO training for local prosecutors, (2) substantive changes in state RICO law, and (3) the exercising of cautious discretion in the selection of RICO cases at the local level (in two cases, actually advocating formal "in-house" criteria for this selection process).

These recommendations, as well as others, were distributed as follows:

Table 3: Recommendations for Improvement	
RICO training for DAs	23%
Substantive changes in law	23%
Discretion in case selection	23%
Stiffer penalties	9%
Increased federal collaboration	9%
Wider applicability	4%
Earlier prosecution involvement	4%
Increased resources	4%

In five jurisdictions, training of local prosecutors in understanding appropriate application and litigation using state RICO statutes was seen as critical to facilitating the use of the statute, and to help ensure effective results. According to these assistant prosecutors, RICO training for DAs is either lacking or virtually non-existent in their states. Consequently, this was viewed as being the nexus of the problem of RICO avoidance locally. The five respondents believed that a more comprehensive understanding of the utility of RICO and the pitfalls of prosecution using the statute could help ameliorate other associated problems, such as "fear of failure" in the use of the statute. Training was characterized as not only making local prosecutors aware of RICO as a potentially powerful tool against organized crime—an awareness that the respondents believed was sorely absent—but also permitting prosecutors to overcome their understandable hesitancy of RICO use, and to instill a sense of confidence in actively utilizing the statute.

The same number of respondents indicated that substantive changes needed to be made in their respective RICO statutes if there was to be any chance that local prosecutors would increase their frequency of turning to the statute. Recommendations here included: (1) widening the scope of predicate offenses, specifically recommended by the Philadelphia respondent to include "aggravated assault" because of the offenses associated with violent "street gang" activities, (2) simplifying language, and (3) weakening provisions dealing with private claims of action to prevent abuse of the statute by private-sector plaintiff attorneys. The last recommendation applied specifically to COCCA. The respondent from Englewood, CO explained that private parties currently file claims for damages under COCCA, using it as a bargaining chip for settlement. Overuse of this provision was described as "lessening the credibility of COCCA with judges and the public."

Detailed recommendations for substantive change were offered by the respondent from Alameda County, CA, who asserted that the statute is probably unconstitutional as currently written. This was primarily because it lacks due process protection (i.e., guidelines on seizure and defendant notification). The respondent suggested the following revisions to strengthen the statute:

- **Separate conviction from California's forfeiture proceedings.** Under the current law, a criminal conviction must be obtained before a court will entertain a forfeiture proceeding. This implicitly places a "beyond-a-reasonable-doubt" standard on the prosecutor seeking forfeiture. The respondent said a lesser standard would be more effective from a prosecutorial standpoint (e.g., preponderance or probable cause).

- **Include specific procedural provisions to protect the statute from constitutional challenges, and to provide the defendant with defined rights.** The current statute is vague on the subject of procedural protection. In fact, a recent case (eventually settled out of court) in the jurisdiction highlighted the considerable discrepancy between the procedural safeguards contained in California's Narcotics Asset Forfeiture Act and the absence of similar protection in the California RICO statute. The respondent suggested that provisions for defendant notification, fair hearing rules and more narrowly drawn language be included in a revised version of the statute.

  Also recommended was inclusion of an "early-release" provision which gives the defendant the right to ask, within ten days, that the court review the government's request for forfeiture. The government must prove its case by a preponderance of the evidence.

- **Replace the current in rem forfeiture standard with in personam jurisdiction and substitute asset provisions.** Currently, California prosecutors can only "forfeit what [they] seize" (i.e., an *in rem* standard); the prosecutor can only seek forfeiture on the assets that can be located. Instead, it was suggested that California adopt the federal RICO standard, *in personam*, and allow for substitute asset forfeiture; Arizona has such standards in its Little RICO law. This would permit California prosecutors to seek forfeiture of assets not directly linked to the criminal activity if the direct proceeds of the crimes cannot be located. As exemplified by the respondent:

Assume that a narcotics distributor saved his income from legitimate employment, but spent the proceeds derived from his criminal enterprise in liquid transactions. If the prosecutor can show that his income from dealing drugs totaled $50,000, the court can order that his bank account be forfeited even though the cash balance was obtained by saving legitimate paychecks. The defendant's illegal income was fungible and allowed him to accrue such a savings account. This kind of forfeiture maneuver would be permitted under the *in personam* and substitute asset standards.

- **Include an "administrative" forfeiture provision.** According to this provision, if a defendant does not contest the state's forfeiture claim within ten days, the prosecutor can invoke an administrative forfeiture. The respondent pointed out that this provision would also place less burden on the courts.

Five respondents recommended that the utilization of state RICO statutes could be improved if local prosecutors were more cautious in how they applied them. Lack of good judgment was feared as having the potential for creating a "backlash" among the media and the general public. This apparently was a fear generated not only by inappropriate application of RICO to what may be widely considered "non-organized" crime, but also by the controversy and press coverage of extreme instances of seizure/forfeiture of assets. To help in limiting application of RICO, several respondents suggested the use of "in-house" selection criteria and the development of "model indictments." The Franklin County, OH prosecutor's office currently employs RICO case selection criteria that include the following:

- amount of criminal activity
- time span of criminal activity
- number of individuals involved
- appropriateness of case to state RICO framework

Although similar, the Jefferson County, CO prosecutor's office has developed in-house selection criteria emphasizing consideration of:

- nature of offense

- extent of offense
- existence of criminal enterprise
- number and types of individuals involved
- evidentiary advantages possible (e.g., inclusion of predicate acts)
- budgetary constraints: staff requirements

Two respondents contended that the local district attorney's use of state RICO statutes could be improved through a greater collaboration between these individuals and their federal counterparts. A Denver respondent lamented that there was no coordination or liaison between his office and the U.S. Attorney's office on RICO prosecutions, although he noted that a task force in Denver was recently established to coordinate state-federal activity against telemarketing fraud. Reported members of this new task force included representatives from the U.S. Federal Bureau of Investigation, the State Attorney General's office, the local prosecutor's office and the U.S. Attorney's office.

The assistant prosecutor respondent from Tennessee strongly recommended involvement of federal prosecutors at the earliest possible stages of the RICO prosecution (i.e., the planning stage). Such involvement could help to ensure that the possible disparities between federal and local investigative, legal, and procedural rules are considered (e.g., differing search warrant standards/procedures), and could improve interagency "spirit."

In a related comment, another respondent declared that a key ingredient to surmounting local prosecutor obstacles in prosecuting RICO cases is the inclusion of prosecutorial involvement at the earliest possible stages of the investigation. This respondent maintained that earlier involvement from the local prosecutor would provide better legal guidance for a complicated offense category, improve evidence collection procedures, and generally enhance the ease with which the prosecutor could use investigative information and evidence collected by law enforcement officers. To underscore his point, the respondent offered the following example:

> This particular case involved a drug organization that operated a "buy" house, a "stash" house and several inconspicuous "pick-up" locations, along with a sophisticated communications and delivery network. The purchaser paid for the drugs at one house, a call was made to the stash house indicating how much to courier to the pick-up house and the buyer would then go to the pick-up rendezvous point to receive the drugs. This operation was charged under RICO as an ongoing criminal

enterprise with significant assets...In this instance local law enforcement had made a number of smaller "buy-busts" outside the house, but had failed to conduct phone toll analysis or several other investigative procedures that eventually revealed the organizational infrastructure. The prosecutor had a better knowledge of what types of information and evidence would best support a RICO prosecution, and conveyed this knowledge to the law enforcement officers involved in the investigative process.

DISCUSSION

It is understandable that the topic of the *local* prosecution of organized crime activity is likely to be greeted with more than a bit of skepticism by those most familiar with other works on organized crime prosecution. The common perception is that organized crime is apt to be prosecuted on a federal government level, on which prosecutors are seen as possessing the requisite experience as well as the legal tools and broad jurisdictional authority demanded by such cases. The local prosecutor, on the other hand, is often characterized as having few such crimes falling into their relatively narrow jurisdictional authority, and, if they do, lacking the skills and/or the resources to tackle such complex cases.

The present study takes some major steps in helping to dispel these conclusions about local prosecutors and organized crime. The data reveal that district attorneys, particularly in metropolitan areas, are engaged in more organized crime prosecutions than ever before because of: (1) a prevalence of crimes committed by loosely organized criminal enterprises that federal authorities view as minor and leave unaddressed, (2) improvement in prosecutorial skills, and (3) a willingness by a select group to experiment with newly provided "hammers" like state RICO laws.

Given the fact that local prosecutors appear to be facing the prospect of prosecuting these types of cases more often, there is clearly a need to enhance their skills to facilitate their rise to this new professional challenge. The introduction of RICO as part of 29 states' criminal codes has furnished local prosecutors in these states with an extraordinary means to commence this enhancement. The results of the extent to which local prosecutors have taken advantage of this new tool are mixed, however, and are to some degree incongruous. Certain aspects of the utilization results are promising. Unlike findings derived from Dombrink and Meeker's (1985) study of federal RICO prosecutions, local prosecutors who used state RICO statutes did so in a progressive fashion, breaking away from what can be considered conservative application patterns reserved exclusively for traditionally defined organized crime cases. By and large, experience with the use of RICO statutes by these prosecutors was positive. Nevertheless, this was overshadowed by the sheer numbers of cases in which local prosecutors chose to reject RICO application in favor of more conventional, proven white collar crime statutes.

It is commonly known that through the use of wide discretionary powers, the local prosecutor can decide which cases will be prosecuted and which charges will be made against the defendants. Key elements that are factored into this decision-making process typically include the prosecutor's appraisal of public sentiment on the level of criminality of certain social behavior, and the cognitive powers of both judges and jurors in the courtroom to understand trial proceedings. Weighing these factors when considering the application of RICO appears to have presented many prosecutors with a dilemma. On one hand, prosecutors recognize that RICO can fortify them with strengthened plea negotiation positions and sharp penalties for organized criminal activity for which the local populace demands action (e.g., prostitution rings). By using RICO successfully in these cases, local prosecutors can effectively attack offense areas that may ordinarily fall through the cracks between federal/state and local prosecutorial authorities, and help set public policy that accurately reflects community attitudes. Conversely, the scale can easily be tipped in the direction of RICO rejection by lack of experience with the laws; their high level of complexity for prosecutors, judges, and jurors alike; and anxiety over being publicly accused of imprudent zeal in their application.

Alert to the "overbroad-application" controversy associated with RICO at the federal level, local prosecutors are sensitive to the risks of being portrayed by the media as overstepping reasonable bounds in their use of RICO, and, therefore, are prone to resort to the safety net of more traditional statues. In a work environment where failure and success are frequently judged by rates of conviction, the added dimension of a heightened risk of "looking bad" while losing a case can be more than enough to dissuade the average prosecutor from turning toward relatively untested RICO statutes. At first blush, it appears that the efforts of respective state legislatures to enact state RICOs are laudable, for when used they open the door to creative prosecutorial strategies heretofore unavailable on the local level. But upon further investigation, it becomes evident that the failure to match the substance of newly developed RICO laws with prosecutorial needs and a lack of attention to practitioner orientation to the implementation of the laws have combined to block RICO from reaching its full potential at the local level.

Matching Statute Substance with Prosecutorial Needs

Without a doubt, the legislative process can prove to be a fertile ground for the redefining of original policy goals of *any* new law. Goal renegotiations will inevitably occur during this stage, which can lead to the implementation of criminal justice policy bearing remote resemblance to original intents. We are not broadly aware of the results of state RICO legislation process evaluations conducted in the "little RICO" states, for if the states have attempted to assess the results of RICO enactment, they have gone unreported. Desire for substantive revisions in some "little RICO" statues, expressed by interviewed prosecutors, would hopefully serve as a clarion call for a revisiting of RICO enactment processes, comparisons between original intent and current state of the laws, and comparisons between state RICO statutes and traditionally available alternatives.

Value judgments associated with long-term targets of the dismantling of organized crime entities and the deterrence of criminal infiltration of legitimate businesses through prosecuting enterprises may have been imposed during the legislative process without adequately accounting for the more immediate organizational targets of criminal justice practitioners—targets like achieving punitiveness greater than that which could be achieved through existing statutes. It is unclear how removed local prosecutors were from the legislative evolution of the state RICO statutes, but the separation between policy creators and policy implementers is not uncommon in the enactment of new criminal laws. This is a phenomenon that can end in a final product that does not necessarily correspond to mandates of agencies responsible for implementation, unintentionally steering them toward the use of alternative devices (Berk et al., 1977).

Implementation of RICO at the Local Level

Besides a separation between policymakers and implementers in the enactment of new law, there can be a failure by policy drafters to recognize the level of feasibility in carrying out the law; that is, to what degree can policy practitioners be expected to realistically comply with the wishes of policy drafters? Further, in the temporal sequences between law enactment and implementation, there can be a slighting of the availability of statute education for practitioners. There is fairly strong evidence that local prosecutors suffer from a neglect by state governments to pay necessary attention to raising not only the local prosecutors' knowledge level of RICO, but, correspondingly, a neglect to raise the confidence level in effectively prosecuting RICO cases. Local prosecutors may have been presented with the basic tools to progressively prosecute organized crime offenses through "little RICO" enactment, but they were not always supplied with the fundamental training necessary to fully understand statue rationale, effective application methods, common defense strategies, and pitfalls. These can all be contributing factors to fostering a lack of confidence in risking experimentation with a dramatically different approach to organized crime prosecution—an approach that could result in losing cases due to inexperience, or public criticism raised by "inappropriate" applications of the statute to the offense. These potential costs to RICO prosecutions can easily outweigh potential *benefits* for a local prosecutor uncomfortable with the degree of guidance provided on effective RICO use. Chief recommendations for rectifying this problem come from local prosecutors themselves: effective training, and the development of internal application criteria based on a substantive analysis of the case characteristics of successful RICO prosecutions.

After years of thoughtful consideration, developing consensus, and the building of a federal RICO statute, most states have argued for and compromised on additional periods of time and finally adopted state versions of that statute. For now, the implementation of these laws on a local level tends to show modest results. What may be viewed as gains for any new criminal justice legislation can take considerable time to accrue, and the changes may well be counter-intuitive; that is, the results of efforts may well indicate directions other than those predicted. Like earlier assessments of the use of RICO on a federal level, the present study of state RICOs and local prosecutors confirms the natural hesitancy to use such a new and complex law. Results of the local implementation of state RICO laws remind us that the criminal justice system is a creature of its professionals, and their level of satisfaction with and confidence in new laws can be critical to the laws' implementation.

❑

Acknowledgements. Research upon which this chapter is based was supported through a cooperative agreement with the Bureau of Justice Statistics, Office of Justice Programs under cooperative agreement 91-BJ-CXK034. Points of view expressed are those of the author and do not necessarily represent those of the U.S. Department of Justice.

REFERENCES

Berk, R.A., H. Brockman and S. Lesser (1977). *A Measure of Justice: An Empirical Study of Changes in the California Penal Code, 1955-1971.* New York, NY: Academic Press.

Blakey, G.R. and G.A. Walker (1989). "Emerging Issues Under the Colorado Organized Crime Control Act." *Colorado Lawyer* 2077(10):2077-2085.

Castillo, E. (1985). "Disrupting Criminal Organization Activity: Use of Conspiracy Law and RICO Statutes." In: *State Laws and Procedures Affecting Drug Trafficking Control: A National Overview.* Washington DC: National Governors' Association and National Criminal Justice Association.

Coffey, Paul E. (1990). "The Selection, Analysis and Approval of Federal RICO Prosecutions." *Notre Dame Law Review* 65:1031-1049.

Dombrink, J. and J.W. Meeker (1985). "Racketeering Prosecution: The Use and Abuse of RICO." *Rutgers Law Journal* 16(3/4):639.

Eggenberger, T.R. (1988). "RICO Dealers v. Dealers in Obscene Matter: First Amendment Battle." *Columbia Journal of Law and Social Problems* 22:71-113.

Gibbs, J.J. and P.J. Shelly (1981). "Life in the Fast Lane: A Retrospective View by Commercial Thieves." *Journal of Research in Crime and Delinquency* 19(2):299.

Martinez, R.P. and P.R. Richards (1985). "CCA-RICO: Reflections on a Sleeper." *Rutgers Law Review* 16:655-672.

Melnick, A.J. (1989). "A Peep at RICO: Fort Wayne Inc. v. Indiana and the Application of Anti-Racketeering Statutes to Obscenity Violations." *Boston University Law Review* March:389-434.

Miles, M.B. and A.M. Huberman (1984). *Qualitative Data Analysis.* Newbury Park, CA: Sage.

Rebovich, D., K. Coyle and J. Schaaf (1993). *Local Prosecution of Organized Crime: The Use of State RICO Statutes.* Bureau of Justice Statistics Discussion Paper Series. Washington, DC: Bureau of Justice Statistics.

Money Laundering:
A Preferred Law Enforcement
Target for the 1990s

by

Margaret E. Beare

Abstract: *A review analyzes the recent law enforcement focus on money laundering, particularly in North America. Tracing the illicit proceeds of crime, and seizing these profits, is currently viewed as an ideal way to destroy the economic base of criminal operations. While the emphasis in this chapter is on trends and legislation in the U.S. and Canada, the issues, treaties, conventions and facilitating institutions and professionals are international in scope. Money-laundering legislation and enforcement require the same high level of international cooperation that is demonstrated by the criminal enterprises. However, to date, criminal organizations appear better equipped than law enforcement agencies to operate in the international arena.*

"The term 'money laundering' has become one of the buzz phrases of crime in the 1990s, and a 'money launderer' conjures up the image of an extremely sophisticated professional person based in a tax-haven who can instantly generate shell companies, nominee directors, electronic wire transfers, client accounts, back to back loans and all the other almost legendary paraphernalia of the 'new Criminal.' [Gold and Levi, 1994:7]

In many large organized crime groups, criminals must continually turn their illicit proceeds into some non-suspicious, spendable form that has the appearance of legitimate earnings; this is the process called "money laundering." Failure to successfully process their criminal proceeds, can result in detection, conviction, and the potential seizure and forfeiture of the illicit profits. This money laundering "industry"—an industry from the perspectives of both the criminal *and* law enforcement—is changing quite rapidly. This chapter will identify those professionals who facilitate money laundering, the business and financial institutions that are particularly vulnerable to the laundering schemes, the legislation that enables the police to engage in this particular police strategy, changing trends in the laundering schemes, and cross-jurisdictional issues that remain to be resolved. The main focus will be on developments in the U.S. and Canada, with some comments on the global and international implications.

DEFINITIONS OF MONEY LAUNDERING

The following definition of money laundering, adapted from the 1988 United Nations Convention Against Illicit Traffic in Narcotic drugs and Psychotropic Substances, emphasizes that money laundering involves a multi-stage process:

- the *conversion* of illicit cash to another asset, possibly involving the placement of the funds into a financial institution;
- the *concealment* of the true source or ownership of the illegally acquired proceeds, possibly through a technique referred to as "layering" whereby a series of otherwise legitimate transactions are carried out which due to the frequency, volume or complexity of the transactions create a paper-trail that is hard or impossible to follow;
- the *creation* of the perception of legitimacy of source and ownership. By this stage the funds may be integrated into the legitimate economy so thoroughly as to be interchangeable with legitimate earnings [United Nations Convention Against Illicit Traffic..., Article 3, paragraph 1(b)]

Future monitoring of money-laundering enforcement may determine that this UN definition has become too narrow. Recent 1993 and 1994 U.S. cases show that the term money laundering can be used quite broadly. For example, money-laundering legislation is being applied to situations involving nothing more complex than the stealing of funds that are then deposited or otherwise mingled with legitimate earnings. Technically, according to U.S. legislation, depositing the proceeds of white-collar crime qualifies in certain circumstances as money-laundering conduct. For example, the ex-president and several executives of the United Way of America have been charged with various offenses, including money laundering, based on evidence that funds had been allegedly siphoned from the United Way Campaign, disguised as legitimate consulting fees, and then ended up being spent for private use. Similarly, a chiropractor and his wife were charged with four counts of money laundering for hiding funds derived from allegedly fraudulent health claims within company accounts and subsequently using them to pay company bills (*Money Laundering Alert*, Oct. 1994, p.6). The conviction of a California attorney is cited as the first case in which a laundering law was used to prosecute a lawyer allegedly involved in a personal injury scam. The government argued that paying "cappers" (runners who direct accident victims to corrupt doctors and lawyers for a share of the settlement) with criminal proceeds served to conceal the nature of the illegal money and perpetuated referrals (*Money Laundering Alert*, Nov. 1994, p.6).

The U.S. Financial Crimes Enforcement Network (FinCEN) (U.S. Department of the Treasury, 1992) refers to money laundering as being an *integral support function* common to all profit-producing criminal activities, including robbery, fraud, extortion and, of course, drug trafficking. While this may be true, the laundering requirements of criminal operations such as drug trafficking are quite different from the requirements of other less consistently lucrative criminal activities. The trafficker is faced with the task of laundering large amounts of money on a continuing basis, rather than the mere laundering of sporadically acquired criminal profits. Laundering enters a realm of "professionalism" when the laundering mechanisms is designed to hide a continual accumulation of illicit proceeds.

The greater the volume of proceeds and the more frequent the laundering transactions, the more sophisticated the scheme that must be developed. One way to add complexity to a laundering process is to cause the illicit proceeds to flow through a number of jurisdictions. Adding this international aspect to the laundering scheme automatically assists in camouflaging the paper-trail by adding cross-jurisdictional complications. Thus, research in Canada (Beare and Schneider, 1990) has indicated that 80% of the laundering cases had an international dimension. This international aspect is often not a mere transiting of funds into and out of bank accounts, but may involve a more in-depth presence in the various jurisdictions. For example, the U.S. Drug Enforcement Administration (DEA) has chosen to target well-organized "kingpins" who become entrenched in the international financial network and in some cases are a part of the political establishment (U.S. DEA, 1992b).

RECENT LAWS

The notion of taking the property and other proceeds of crime away from criminals is not new, but it had fallen out of favor for over 100 years. In Anglo-American common law, conviction of a felony offense resulted in the forfeiture of the lands and chattels of the offender (Donald, 1989; Finkelstein, 1973). The offender was therefore vulnerable to lose all of his or her possessions, with no distinction made between those gained legally and those acquired through criminal means. Given the large number of offenses falling under the felony category, this meant that significant numbers of offenders were rendered destitute by these provisions. The offenses in some cases were minor in comparison to the sanctions imposed, and critics feared that the creation of a destitute class might inevitably lead to greater criminality. As a result, Canada's Forfeiture Act of 1880, which was incorporated into the 1892 Criminal Code, abolished the forfeiture of a convicted felon's property (Donald 1989). During the next 100 years, the emphasis in Canadian punishment practices was on imprisoning or fining the offender, with little attention being paid to the offenders' property.

Law enforcement in North America has recently turned its attention again to the financial gains of criminal operations, primarily because of the growing perception of "threat" from organized crime. The perception that a nationwide crime syndicate known as the Mafia was operating freely in many large cities was nurtured at the 1951 hearings of the U.S. Senate's Kefauver Committee, and culminated in the reports of the 1967 U.S. President's Commission on Organized Crime (cf. Albini, 1988; Ianni, 1972; Moore, 1974; Rogovin and Martens, 1990). The consensus of this rhetoric—which may have been driven by political platforming, law enforcement resource needs, and ethnic/ racial competition and discrimination—was that the financial power of criminal organizations enabled them to corrupt officials, create monopolies, take over legitimate businesses through a combination of legal purchases and criminal means, and undermine urban centers with drug-related violence and, more recently, AIDS.

In 1970, the Racketeer Influenced and Corrupt Organizations Statute (RICO) came into force as part of the U.S. Crime Control Act. This legislation served as a model for other countries, including Canada, the U.K. and Australia. Eventually versions of this type of legislation were enacted that focused specifically on organized crime (Meagher, 1983,

Howard League, 1984; Canada. Solicitor General, 1982 and 1983; Canada. Department of Justice, 1983).

Focusing on the proceeds of crime was also seen as a way to identify the higher echelon criminal members. U.S. Financial Crimes Enforcement Network (FinCEN) calls the laundering stage the "choke point" of narcotics trafficking. According to the DEA, tracing the proceeds through the laundering schemes and the seizure and forfeiture of assets:

- links kingpin violators to the criminal drug conspiracy;
- serves to destroy the economic base of the criminal organizations;
- serves to create dissension in the criminal organizations due to the disruption caused by the seizure of the assets [U.S. DEA, 1992a, p.14].

Internationally, countries have responded in a manner similar to the U.S. and Canada. The international community expressed its intolerance of drug-related money laundering by adopting the 1988 United Nations Convention against Illicit Traffic in Narcotic Drugs and Psychotropic Substances. In November 1990, after the required number of countries (20) had ratified the convention, it came into force. The convention outlined a model Mutual Legal Assistance Treaty (MLAT) that facilitates the international sharing of intelligence and provides a legal mechanism for assisting prosecutions that cross jurisdictions. The convention required that participating countries have in place:

- legislation to make money laundering an offense;
- legislation that allows for the confiscation of proceeds derived from drug offenses; and,
- procedural tools and cooperation in the investigations necessary to identify, trace, and secure proceeds of crime.

The cooperative work of the Group of Seven nations' Financial Action Task Force (FATF) is another excellent example of an international initiative against the use of the banking system and financial institutions for money laundering. Since 1989, the task force has encouraged the adoption of appropriate legislation and enforcement capabilities in the seven original nations plus eight additional countries. FATF participants were the U.S., Japan, Germany, France, the U.K., Italy, and Canada (as well as the Commission of the European Communities). The eight additional participating countries are Sweden, Netherlands, Belgium, Luxembourg, Switzerland, Austria, Spain, and Australia.

The initial FATF report outlined a 40-point legislative, regulatory, and diplomatic approach to money laundering. The 1994 *Annual Report of the*

Financial Action Task Force On Money Laundering emphasized the need for banks to identify customers, particularly in cases where there is no face-to-face contact between the institutions and the customers. A second focus of the 1994 report was to direct attention to money laundering at non-financial institutions and to bring their accountability requirements in line with those imposed on financial institutions. The U.S. Money Laundering Suppression Act of 1994 (to come into force in 1995) emphasizes this concern with non-traditional financial institutions, and extends coverage to "money transmitters" that provide services such as check cashing, currency exchange and travelers' checks. It is estimated that this new law will make it mandatory for 200,000 non-bank financial institutions to register with the government (*Money Laundering Alert*, October, 1994 p.3).

Similarly, in Canada An Act to Facilitate Combatting The Laundering of Proceeds of Crime came into force June 21, 1991, and the implementing regulations became effective in spring 1993. The main target of this legislation is likely to be the foreign currency exchange houses that previously had not been subject to adequate regulation and accountability.

While various countries have responded with slightly different components in their legislation, in general, attempts to counteract money laundering by criminal organizations involve:

- legislation that facilitates taking the profit away from the criminal via processes of seizing/freezing and eventually forfeiting these proceeds. These provisions target the criminal proceeds, rather than/or in addition to the criminals;
- legislation that acknowledges that the money laundering process is critical to organized crime and must be treated as a criminal offense; and
- legislation that facilitates the gathering of cross- jurisdictional evidence and the development of cases in cooperation with foreign jurisdictions.

As Gold and Levi (1994:24) note, there is strong "moral and political pressure" on countries to enact the agreed-upon measures. In addition to the legislation, case-based literature is now available on the schemes and techniques involved in "cleansing" criminal proceeds. For example, within the last four years, the U.S., Australia, England and Canada, as well as

U.S. Federal Legislative Tools Against Organized Crime and Money Laundering:

- *Racketeer Influenced and Corrupt Organizations Statute* [RICO] (Title 18, USC Section 1961)
- *Continuing Criminal Enterprise Statutes* (CCE)
- *Money Laundering Control Act* (Title 18, USC Sec. 1956)
- *Transactions in Criminally-Derived Property* (Title 18, USC Sec. 1957)
- *Illegal Money Transmitting Businesses* (Title 18, USC Sec. 1960)
- *Bank Secrecy Act* (Title 31, USC 5311-5330)
- *Cash reporting by Trades and Businesses* (Title 26, USC Sec. 60501)
- *Right to Financial Privacy Act* (Title 12, USC Sec. 3401)
- *Willful Violation of Banking regulations* (Title 12, USC Sec.1956)

Canadian Legislative Tools Against Organized Crime and Money Laundering:

- *Mutual Legal Assistance in Criminal Matters Act* (R.S.C. 1985, Chap. 30, 4th Supp.)
- *Proceeds of Crime Legislation* (cc R.S.C. 1985 as amended, Part XII.2 [S.462.3-S.462.48])
- *Act to Facilitate Combatting the Laundering of Proceeds of Crime* [Proceeds of Crime (Money Laundering) Act] (SC, 1991, Chap. 26)
- *Seized Property Management Act* (Bill C-123; SC 1993, Chap. 37))

the Group of Seven Financial Action Task Force, have all studied and written on this subject (cf., Australia. National Crime Authority, 1991; Beare and Schneider, 1990; Commonwealth Secretariat, 1992; Zagaris and Castilla, 1993; and Financial Action Task Force on Money Laundering reports).

ENFORCEMENT ISSUES

Large laundering operations must be targeted as if they were multi-national corporations. However, the resources available to the large-scale launderers provide an enormous advantage to these criminals. For example, Norm Inkster, Commissioner of the Royal Canadian Mounted Police (until 1994), noted in a 1994 address at Queens University that wealthy Colombian cartels operating in Canada were able to buy cellular phones by the hundreds, thus nullifying the ability of the police to determine the telephone numbers required for wiretaps.

In addition to the latest in technology, traffickers can also afford the most highly-paid expertise. As noted in the 1992 U.S. Fincen *Assessment of Narcotics Related Money Laundering* report:

> among law enforcement representatives, there was an almost universal perception that traffickers and cartel related money launderers can usually afford to hire the best lawyers, accountants, etc., an advantage which provides them with additional sources of expertise in avoiding detection by the government [FinCEN 1992:29].

The size and resources available to some organizations permit them to employ full-time specialists who may operate out of "cells" with strict task separation between responsibilities. As Edelhertz and Overcast state:

> This approach to specialization within organized crime is exactly what one would expect to find in an organization devoted to maximizing profits through increases in the efficiency of its workers. Specialization is deliberately adopted in the legitimate business world for exactly the same reasons, and there is no reason to expect organized crime to operate differently [1993:44].

While all organized crime groups do not operate with the same degree of sophistication or complexity, the procedures used by transnational groups tend to be quantitatively and qualitatively different from those used in the past. Particularly in drug-trafficking cartels, the laundering operations are often kept completely separate from the narcotics operations (FinCEN, 1992). Such bifurcated operations allow for greater control and some check on intra-organizational corruption. As a 1992 U.N. report observes:

> The evolution of organized crime can be regarded as a process of rational reorganization on an international basis of criminal 'enterprises' following the same pattern as legal enterprises. ... Criminal organizations are being structured like major corporations, with an operational arm to move the 'goods and services' and a financial arm to manage the proceeds. The two arms tend to be kept quite separate with quite different people working on each. This separation of activities again renders detection more difficult [United Nations, 1992:5].

Thus, a typical cartel organization might involve *operational* people with responsibility for running the money laundering, stash houses, couriers; *support* personnel involved in the details relating to the holdings, transportation and bank accounts; *customer service* people concerned with customer satisfaction, pickups / payments / deliveries; and other inactive or miscellaneous categories of "employees."

Previously, law enforcement officials have assumed that, while the major traffickers might not directly touch the trafficked drugs, they always touched the money (FinCEN, July 1992:4). This view may change if criminal organizations become successful at distancing themselves from all but the "cleanest" of illicit proceeds. Officials are beginning to see the development of a new industry of "insurance brokers" who bid for drug shipments, pay approximately 90% of the value to the drug baron in Colombia, and "earn" the difference by absorbing all of the laundering risks (*Money Laundering Alert*, July, 1993). The result is that the drug cartels may become insulated from the money trail that circulates around the sale of a large drug shipment. Before the drugs reach the street, the cartel will already have received full payment. Law enforcement must constantly adjust to these changes in the criminal operations.

Money-laundering investigations require imaginative undercover pro-jects often involving the offering of money laundering services. There have been several large successfully prosecuted cases that have illustrated the ability of countries to work collaboratively on these projects. Green Ice is one such example. The DEA referred to this case as the "first" operational international task force formed to combat money laundering (U.S. Depart-ment of Justice, 1992b). DEA personnel worked with officers from Italy, Spain, Costa Rica, Colombia, the U.K., the Cayman Islands and Canada to infiltrate money-laundering enterprises run by the Colombian cocaine cartels. Undercover officers posed as money launderers and set up leather shops which also served as laundering operations. The Royal Canadian Mounted Police (RCMP) carried out parallel operations in Canada to dovetail with the U.S. project. Law enforcement officials reported that seven top money managers of the Colombian Cali drug cartel were arrested in this operation.

Role of Professionals

There never has been an easily generalized image of the money laun-derer. Former U.S. Attorney General Meese equated a professional money launderer to a "fence" utilized by a burglar: "It takes a professional—a lawyer, an accountant, a banker, with all the trappings of respectability—to manipulate these sophisticated schemes" (*Organized Crime Digest*, June 1985:1). Some of the most notorious and sophisticated cases have involved a lawyer (or lawyers) involved in both the creation and implementation of the schemes—and of course at the stage of defending the suspect if charged. The lawyers can operate either knowingly as accomplices in the laundering scheme or as an innocent facilitator. Following are some of the laundering "services" offered by lawyers (cf., Beare and Schneider, 1990; Australia. National Crime Authority, 1991):

- providing a nominee function;
- incorporating companies;
- conducting commercial and financial transactions;
- managing and physically handling illicit cash;
- coordinating international transactions; and
- buying and selling real estate.

While each of these functions is important, the authority of a lawyer to act on behalf of a client in a nominee role is extremely useful. This nominee function can be combined with the ability of the lawyer to conduct commercial and financial transactions with the illicit funds. Hence, it is no one function, but rather a combination, that facilitates the criminal operation.

Lawyers are a powerful lobby group that has been granted special privileges argued to be necessary in order to protect the legitimate relations between lawyers and their clients. Nevertheless, in October 1989, the U.S. Internal Revenue Service launched a national operation that targeted lawyers for failure to provide details to the government about their cash-paying clients. In this "Attorney's Project," certified letters were sent initially to more than 2,400 lawyers notifying them that failure to file a Form 8300 is a felony offense. The lawyers claimed that this action violated their attorney-client privileges (*Money Laundering Alert*, 1989, Vol.1, #3).

Lawyers have offered similar resistance in Canada. In 1991, the Council of the Canadian Bar Association (CBA) passed a resolution urging the federal government to withdraw the newly introduced *Money Laundering Bill* because the requirement that lawyers maintain certain records would: "...seriously undermine the independence of the legal profession and the integrity and confidentiality of the lawyer-client relationship ..." (Canadian Bar Association, 1991:47). The legislation, passed after negotiations with the CBA, requires that records be kept of transactions involving more than $10,000 in cash being "paid or transferred on another's behalf."

Even with appropriate legislation in place, police investigations involving lawyers are particularly problematic. The U.S. President's Commission on Organized Crime (1986a) spoke of the need for "sting" operations, undercover agents, and electronic surveillance to break through the attorney-client privilege that otherwise would be "an impenetrable shield protecting lawyers who engage in a wide variety of criminal actions" (Beare and Schneider, 1990:331). In Canada, Supreme Court Charter decisions during the early 1990s have increased the difficulty of carrying out these types of operations. For example, Duarte v. The Queen (1990, 53 C.C.C. (3rd) 1 (S.C.C.)) specifies that authorizations are required for the police to conduct electronic surveillance of certain private communications even when one of the parties to the communication consents to being taped. Police fear that these authorizations will be harder to obtain when targeted against lawyers.

However, there is some evidence that the legal profession has reached a point of wanting to eliminate criminal or compromised lawyers from its midst. For example, since the early 1990s the Canadian Law Societies have called more frequently upon external persons to review the behavior of some of their members (Beare and Schneider, 1990).

Vulnerable Business and Financial Institutions

Studies of the case material from Canada, Australia and the U.S indicate that virtually every type of business and financial institution can be used to launder money. However, certain businesses are particularly useful to the laundering process. The following types of vulnerable businesses have been identified in the Canadian *Tracing of Illicit Funds* report (Beare and Schneider), the Australian *Taken to the Cleaners: Money Laundering in Australia* (NCA report), and separate U.S. reports including the *Assessment of Narcotics Related Money Laundering* (Fincen):

- deposit-taking institutions
- currency exchange houses
- the securities industry
- the insurance industry
- real estate firms
- the incorporation and operation of companies
- gold market/ precious gems/ jewelry stores

- casino operations
- the travel industry
- the luxury goods industries

In order for organized crime to exercise control internationally, it is essential to have businesses serving as fronts, as laundering mechanisms, and, in some cases, as channels for importing illicit commodities. Laundering schemes often involve both legitimate and illegitimate transactions. The "criminal enterprise" therefore consists of the continuing criminal and legitimate activities, plus the structures and agreements used in order to perpetuate the illicit gain. Law enforcement strategies, therefore, must follow the trail that links into legitimate businesses, locate the placement of funds overseas, and identify the complex investment structures. This enforcement approach is advanced by the Australian Transaction Reports Analysis Centre (Coad and Richardson, 1993).

"Banking" the Illicit Funds

The initial stage in the laundering process is particularly risky for the criminals because it requires them to dispose of large amounts of suspicious looking cash, often in small denominations. This is the conversion or placement stage in the laundering process. Small denomination bills are not only bulky, but also are surprisingly heavy. The U.S. General Accounting Office (1994) estimates that 450 paper bills weigh one pound; many operations require the conversion of thousands of bills. That is why the cooperation of "front-line" personnel—bank tellers, car dealers, brokers and casino operators—is critically important to controlling money laundering. U.S. and Australian legislation requires them to *report* transactions over $10,000; Canadian legislation requires them to *record* similar transactions. All three countries have a "suspicious transaction" process whereby law enforcement can be notified of any transaction that seems "peculiar." As important as this enforcement tool may be, it is also highly discretionary. As laundering schemes change, so must the awareness of the public as to what is "suspicious." The U.S. Office of the Comptroller of the Currency issued new guidelines in fall 1993. However, these mechanisms have not stopped structuring or "smurfing," whereby money is deposited in numerous transactions all under the $10,000 threshold. Nor does it prevent the smuggling of currency out of the country. Accordingly, the 1994 the Police Foundation of Wales study (Gold and Levi 1994) concluded the U.K.'s suspicion-based transactions-reporting system has had only a limited impact to date.

Underground Banking

In addition to formal or official banks, the launderer has several other options. Operating parallel to the banking network are underground operations that transfer money around the world with no paper or records being generated. According to the DEA, the *hawala* or *hundi* underground banking systems originating in Pakistan and India, and similar underground banking systems being used by the ethnic Chinese criminal organizations, are assuming increasingly important roles (U.S. DEA, 1993). These operations are now used throughout China, Hong Kong, South-East Asia, Middle Eastern Countries, East Africa, Europe and North America. The benefit of dealing with these brokers is the speed, simplicity and confidentiality of the transactions. While the money transferred may be tainted, the families that operate the hawala systems tend to be well-known and trusted. Faxes are sent acknowledging the crediting of accounts even though no money has actually been physically transferred. The hawala brokers often maintain ledgers in code so that no official paper trail is created. In situations where the flow of currency credits is one-sided, the accounts can be balanced via other activities such as the smuggling of gold, silver, currency or other valued commodities into countries with import restraints.

Working from small import-export businesses, manipulation of invoices is an effective method of laundering money through the hawala brokerage system. In the U.S. and Canada, hawala brokers could be held accountable under the existing legislation; however, they are seldom identified (U.S. Department of Justice, 1993). International cooperation, shared intelligence and intimate knowledge of the domestic ethnic communities are required in order to impede the hawala system.

Smuggling

Even if all domestic banking-related money laundering problems could be solved, illicit proceeds would still move around the world. Customs officials in Canada and the U.S. have acknowledged that large amounts of cash are smuggled over the borders for laundering abroad and then eventually brought back into North America. That is why U.S. Customs initiatives such as Operation Buckstop targeted passengers and cargo leaving the U.S. In the four-year period ending September 1992, customs agents seized more than $170 million in unreported currency. But they acknowledge that it is only a small percentage of what is leaving (U.S. General Accounting Office, 1994). Canadian officials are handicapped further by the absence of border cash reporting or recording requirements.

CROSS-JURISDICTIONAL ENFORCEMENT ISSUES

Any discussion on money laundering requires acknowledgement of the limitations of cross-jurisdictional or international law enforcement and policing. Legislation in one jurisdiction must compliment, or be complimented by, companion legislation elsewhere. That is why "transaction oriented" laws (Harmon, 1988) are designed to "follow" criminal proceeds throughout the world and discard the older limitations of jurisdiction. New sovereignty issues are arising as countries attempt to bring other nations "into line" with their own internal laws, policies and procedures. For example, the Kerry amendment to the U.S. Anti-Drug Abuse Act of 1988 specified that the Secretary of the Treasury would enter into negotiations with 18 countries whose financial institutions facilitated the laundering of U.S. drug-sale proceeds. Countries that do not cooperate with U.S. policies may be prevented from using U.S. dollar-clearing systems.

As stated by the United Nations (1992):

In the fight against organized crime any divergence from a concerted international response will be readily and effectively exploited by organized criminal groups. It is widely accepted that a chain is as strong as its weakest link. This maxim should guide international action against organized crime and all countries should assist to ensure that weak links are eliminated where they exist."(p.12)

Joint force operations, use of the Mutual Legal Assistance Treaties and the international sharing of assets are all part of this new enforcement focus. There are still many improvements required in these areas, and procedures are yet to be made uniform across jurisdictions.

CONCLUSIONS

To date, the balance tilts in favor of the criminal organization that is able to move illicit commodities and criminal proceeds across borders with greater ease than has been demonstrated by law enforcement's cross-border efforts. Criminals have proven themselves infinitely capable of adjusting their activity to avoid risks as law enforcement efforts are enhanced.

While there is an increasing emphasis on sharing intelligence and on other forms of cooperation in multi-jurisdictional cases, formal mechanisms to facilitate this sharing are relatively new and somewhat primitive in comparison to the sophisticated cross-border money laundering networks. However, on the positive side, countries are moving toward global strategies, and there is now international agreement that the illicit proceeds should be removed from the criminal organizations.

REFERENCES

Albini Joseph L. (1988) "Donald Cressey's Contributions to the Study of Organized Crime: An Evaluation." *Crime & Delinquency* 34(3):338-354.

Australia. National Crime Authority (1991). *Taken to the Cleaners: Money Laundering in Australia.* 3 volumes. Canberra, AUS.

Beare, M.E. and S. Schneider (1990). *Tracing of Illicit Funds: Money Laundering in Canada.* Ottawa: Solicitor General Canada, User Report #1990-05.

Canada, Solicitor General (1982). "Proceedings of the 1982 Symposium on Enterprise Crime." Unpublished. Ottawa.

—— (1983). "Proceedings of the Reparative Sanctions International Consultative Workshop." Unpublished. Ottawa.

Canada. Department of Justice (1983). *Enterprise Crime Study Report.* Ottawa.

Canadian Bar Association (1991). Council resolutions of mid-winter meeting held in Regina. Legal and Governmental Affairs.

Coad, B. and D. Richardson (1993). "Reducing Market Opportunities For Organized Crime." Paper delivered at the Australian Academy of Forensic Science, Sydney, 20 May.

Commonwealth Secretariat (1992). *Basic Documents on International Efforts to Combat Money Laundering* and *Action Against Transnational Criminality.* (2 volumes).

Donald, P. (1989). "A Commentary on the Provisions of C-61 Canada's New Proceeds of Crime Legislation (S.C. 1988, c.51)." *Advocate* 47:423-431.

Edelhertz, H. and T.D. Overcast (1993). *The Business of Organized Crime.* Loomis, CA :Palmer Press.

Financial Action Task Force on Money Laundering Reports (1990; 1991; 1992; 1993; 1994). Produced by the Organization for Economic Co-

Operation and Development, Directorate for Financial, Fiscal, and Enterprise Affairs.

Finkelstein, J. 1973. "The Goring Ox: Some Historical Perspectives on Deodands, Forfeitures, etc." *Temple Law Quarterly* 46(2):169-290.

Gold M. and M. Levi (1994). *Money Laundering in the UK: An Appraisal of Suspicion-Based Reporting.* Cardiff: The Police Foundation of Wales and Griffin Press.

Harmon, J.D. (1988). "United States Money Laundering Laws: International Implications." *New York Law School Journal of International and Comparative Law* 9(1):1-45.

Howard League for Penal Reform (1984). *Profits of Crime and Their Recovery.* Produced as a final document by the Hodgson Forfeiture Committee from the *Consultative Paper,* London, UK.

Ianni, F. (1972). *A Family Business.* New York: Russell Sage Foundation.

Meagher, D., Q.C. (1983). *Organized Crime: Papers Presented to the 53rd ANZAAS Congress.* Perth, Western Australia, May 16-20.

Money Laundering Alert (1989). 1(3).

—— (1991). 2(5). February.

—— (1991). 2(11). August.

—— (1993). 4(10). July.

—— (1993). 4(11). August.

—— (1994). 6(1). October.

—— (1994). 6(2). November.

Moore, W.H. (1974). *The Kefauver Committee and the Politics of Crime 1950-1952.* Columbia, MO: University of Missouri Press.

Organized Crime Digest (1985). "D.O.J. Proposes Comprehensive Money Laundering Law Seeking Stiff Civil/Criminal Penalties." 6:6.

Ragano, F. and S. Raab (1994). *Mob Lawyer.* New York: Charles Scribner's Sons.

Rogovin, C. and F. Martens (1990). "The Invaluable Contributions of Donald Cressey to the Study of Organized Crime." Paper presented at the Academy of Criminal Justice Sciences Annual Conference, March.

United Nations (1988). *Convention Against Illicit Traffic in Narcotic Drugs and Psychotropic Substances,* (Article 3, paragraph 1(b)). Vienna: E/CONF.82/15 of 19 December.

—— (1992). *The Strengthening of International Cooperation in Combating Organized Crime.* 47th Session Social Development: Crime Prevention and Criminal Justice, September.

U.S. Department of the Treasury, Financial Crimes Enforcement Network (FinCEN) (1992). *An Assessment of Narcotics Related Money Laundering.* Washington, DC. July.

U.S. Drug Enforcement Administration (DEA), Operations Division (1992a). *Financial Investigations: A Guide To Proprietary Undercover Money Laundering and DEA Financial Strategy*. Washington, DC. September.

—— (1992b). "Operation Green Ice." News release, September 28.

—— 1993. *Money Laundering in Southwest Asia*. Washington, DC: DEA Publications Unit, Intelligence Division, September.

U.S. General Accounting Office (1994). *Money Laundering: U.S. Efforts to Fight It Are Threatened by Currency Smuggling*. Washington, D.C. March.

U.S. President's Commission on Organized Crime (1986a). *The Impact: Organized Crime Today*. Washington, DC.

—— (1986b). *America's Habit: Drug Abuse, Drug Trafficking, and Organized Crime*. Washington, DC.

Zagaris, B. and S. Castilla (1993). *Implementation of a Worldwide Anti-Money Laundering System: Constructing an International Financial Regime*. Washington, DC: Police Executive Research Forum.

Motor Fuel Tax Fraud and Organized Crime: The Russian and the Italian-American Mafia

by

Richter H. Moore, Jr.

Abstract: *In the 1980s, Russian immigrants to the U.S. joined with members of the Colombo organized crime family to operate a scam which made it appear that the motor fuel excise tax had been paid when it had not. Because motor fuel tax evasion is difficult to investigate, organized crime members have labeled it the "perfect crime." Estimates of the loss in tax revenues range up to $5 billion per year. Despite recently passed legislation, the problem appears to be growing.*

Origins of Gasoline Bootlegging

Gasoline bootlegging by criminal organizations goes back to the days of World War II, when gas was rationed and customers would pay a premium for a few extra gallons to go joyriding, engage in some money-making illegal enterprise, or just get around. However, in the past few years, the manipulating and bootlegging of gasoline and diesel fuel for the purpose of perpetrating fuel tax fraud has become a multibillion dollar business for organized crime.

The early 1960s saw the rise of gasoline bootleggers, mostly Greek and Turkish immigrants based in New York. They operated service stations, collecting gasoline and diesel fuel tax at the pump. These operators would pocket the tax money and disappear before the U.S. Internal Revenue Service caught them (Friedman, 1993). By the 1970s things began to change.

Change in the 1970s

In the early 1970s, the Soviet K.G.B. began emptying its jail of hard-core criminals, sending them to the U.S. Almost all were Jewish, and this became the first wave of Soviet Jewish immigration after World War II. Many of these individuals were well-educated professionals with advanced degrees in the sciences and in economics, medicine, engineering, and mathematics. Most settled in the Brighton Beach section of Brooklyn (Friedman, 1993).

They had developed their skills in the Soviet black market and in circumventing the Communist bureaucracy (*Organized Crime Digest*, 1994). Observing the small-time tax scam of the Greeks and Turks, the Russians put their talents to work to turn this operation into one of the greatest tax frauds in American history. In addition, their crime counterparts, the Italian-American Mafia, were also becoming involved.

Franzese (1992), a self-described member of the Colombo organized crime family, entered into the gas tax fraud business in 1981. Larry Iorizzo was in the wholesale gasoline business, Vantage Petroleum, and was being shaken down by a group of thugs. One of his employees went to the Franzese crew to solve the problem. The problem was eliminated, and Iorizzo paid Franzese by taking him into the gas tax fraud scheme (Franzese, 1992).

The inability of the federal, state and county governments to collect the 27¢-per-gallon gas tax was the major key to the success of the tax fraud scheme. Franzese saw the potential for major profit. He reported making a deal with Iorizzo, essentially taking over the operation, with 20% of the profits going to the Colombo family and the rest split equally between the two of them (Franzese, 1992).

Problems of Collection

Prior to 1982, in New York and in other states, individual gas stations were responsible for collecting fuel taxes, which could amount to as much as 28¢ per gallon (Friedman, 1993). This method of tax collection made cheating easy. Some, like Greek and Turkish groups, would sell gasoline and diesel fuel, fail to file tax returns, and go out of business and disappear before revenue officials sought to collect the tax due. Other small-time cheats would merely turn back the counter on the pump and underreport the amount of taxable fuel sold. The tax collection systems were cumbersome, understaffed and lacking in individuals with expertise in fuel tax fraud investigation. The Russian and American organized crime groups saw a golden opportunity and immediately began to take advantage of it.

Attempting to close the tax collection loss loopholes, in 1982 New York enacted legislation which placed the collection responsibility on the distributor (Block, 1994). The Russian mafia and Franzese met the challenge easily and found it provided an opportunity for even greater profits. They began to set up their own distributorships. The distributorships were supplied with gas and diesel fuel purchased from both U.S. refineries and overseas suppliers, particularly those in Africa and in South America (Seper, 1991).

When fuel is obtained, it must eventually be sold to a retailer who the paper records will show has received fuel, gasoline or diesel, on which the excise taxes have been paid. The Russians and the Franzese-Iorizzo group of the Colombo crime family used their distributorship to operate a scam which made it appear that the motor fuel excise tax had been paid when it had not.

HOW THE SCAM WORKED

The typical scam set up a series of companies through which the gasoline or diesel fuel moved on paper. It began when a licensed company purchased a barge or tanker load of gasoline. The gasoline was passed on paper to another company, and then to another in the "daisy chain." The daisy chain may have encompassed as many as a dozen fake companies. One of the dummy companies in the illegal chain became what is called the "burn company," the one that was supposedly responsible for paying the applicable taxes. Documents showing transfer of the gasoline or diesel fuel from the burn company to another distributor, or to service stations, would show that the tax had been paid. The price of fuel to the service station would include the amount of the tax. However, since the tax was never paid, the bogus company could sell the gasoline to the service station several cents cheaper than a legitimate distributor who has paid the tax. The retailer was then able to sell the gasoline or diesel cheaper than his competitor and still make a substantial profit. When tax officials went to the bogus company to collect the tax, they found that the company was actually a mailbox, an empty store, or a vacant lot—that did not exist or had disappeared (*Organized Crime Digest*, 1993).

Another form of the scheme involved the purchase of diesel fuel, supposedly for home heating, which is not taxable. The fuel moved through the chain of paper companies, and somewhere along the line a phony company would show an invoice for highway diesel fuel with tax paid. The retailer bought the fuel at a reduced rate and paid the tax to the bogus company, which then pocketed the tax money and disappeared (Kiely, 1992). The Russians established networks of buyers nationwide, particularly among independent stations in New York, New Jersey, Pennsylvania, Texas, California and Florida (*Oil Express*, 1992).

THE RUSSIAN-FRANZESE SCAM

The Franzese-Iorizzo operation expanded across New York into New Jersey, Connecticut and Pennsylvania, purchasing independent petroleum marketers and their wholesale distributors' licenses to be used in the daisy chains (Franzese, 1992). Franzese and Iorizzo were splitting two to four million dollars a week and still delivering from $250,000 to $500,000 to the Colombo family (Franzese, 1992). The operation was expanded to Florida through a company called Houston Holdings. Observing the success of the Russians and the Franzese operation in fuel bootlegging, the New York-based Genovese and Lucchese crime families became secret partners with the Russian bootleggers in the early 1980s, imposing a 2¢-per-gallon "family tax," or, as some refer to it, a "mob tax" on the Russian bootleggers. The Colombo family, through Franzese-Iorizzo, took over one of their operations (Franzese, 1992).

"When the mobsters discovered there were millions in illegal profits to be made, they simply muscled in on the bootleggers," said Edward A. McDonald, the head of the Justice Department's Organized Crime Strike Force in the Eastern District of New York State. "And the bootleggers, who are making millions, won't complain to us because that would kill the goose that lays the golden egg [Raab, 1989:B7]."

Lawrence Iorizzo, the tax-fraud artist credited with inventing the daisy chain, testified in his 1988 gasoline tax evasion and money laundering trial that he had paid $360 million in stolen taxes to the Colombo family from 1980 through 1984 (Raab, 1989).

Franzese became involved with the Russian crime figure Michael Markowitz, who was running his own billion-dollar gasoline scheme. He said he cut a deal with Markowitz to take over the operation for 75% of the action, with the Russians receiving the remaining 25%. Shortly after this arrangement was made, however, Markowitz was shot to death in Brooklyn in his Rolls Royce (Raab, 1989). In 1986, John Gotti was told about the scheme by an associate. Wiretapped conversations indicate that he declared that the family had to get involved in this activity immediately (Friedman, 1993). Today, tribute from the Russians' fuel tax fraud operation is paid to four of the five New York Italian crime families. It is estimated that this brings the New York Italian-American Mafia $42 million a year, second only to drugs as a source of income. Moreover, this estimate may be quite low according to figures cited by some members of the mob (Friedman, 1993).

INVOLVEMENT BEYOND THE "MOB TAX"

The Italian crime families have been more involved than merely receiving the "mob tax." They were particularly active in Florida and some other states. Florida was described as a fuel bootleggers' heaven in the 1980s. In his book *Quitting the Mob* (1992), former Mafia Don Michael Franzese, now in prison, describes how profitable his operation was:

> Houston Holdings and its fifty different paper subsidiaries were moving 300-500 million gallons of gasoline a month in five states. Figuring that they offered discounts of five to ten cents a gallon to monopolize the market, a ballpark estimate is that they were stealing twenty cents a gallon. That's $60-100 million a month in stolen taxes alone, not considering legitimate profits [Franzese, 1992:179].

In 1987, the first concrete details on how the fuel bootleggers paid off the Italian Mafia came in a conversation with an informant recorded by federal undercover investigators. Brooklyn gasoline wholesaler Philip Moskowitz said each bootlegger was under the umbrella or protection of one of the New York Mafia families (Raab, 1989). Shortly after Moskowitz talked with undercover agents, he was found strangled to death in New Jersey (Raab, 1989). The full picture of how the tax evasion scam really worked was obtained from Moskowitz. Petroleum carriers controlled by mob front companies had been transporting untaxed fuels into a number of states extending from North Carolina to Canada. Invoices for gasoline and diesel fuel from New Jersey distributors had shown up at truck stops in North Carolina. In 1992, North Carolina Department of Transportation Secretary Thomas Harrelson said that the department estimated the state was losing between $40 and $60 million a year through fuel tax evasion. North Carolina began to notice that something was wrong in 1990 when tax-paid sales of diesel fuel and gasoline began declining after years of steady growth, when at the same time vehicle miles traveled were going up at highway counters throughout the state (Stith, 1992).

Fuel tax evasion schemes have begun to appear in more and more states. Often the supplier of untaxed fuel can ultimately be traced to Russian crime groups. In addition to the New York, New Jersey and Pennsylvania areas, fuel tax bootleggers have been active in Texas, Oklahoma and especially California (Seper, 1991). Operating under a variety of names, Russian bootleggers in California have expanded their operations to Nevada, Colorado, Wyoming, Utah and Nebraska (*Oil Express*, 1991).

In general, the Russian crime groups in the East, the Southwest and the Far West have all had easy access to fuel arriving at ocean ports, as well as from terminals and refineries. Alleged Russian Mafia leader Marat Balagula, described as the dominant fuel tax bootlegger in America, controls seven terminals, a fleet of trucks and over 100 gas stations (Friedman 1993). Consequently, there is a ready supply of motor fuel obtainable before tax is collected. From the ports and terminals the fuel can be shipped easily to buyers around the country. It may be offered to a legitimate marketer by a bootlegger who just happens to drop by the office with the explanation that he has an oversupply and must move it at a discount. Appearing legitimate, the bootlegger says he must have the marketer's 637, a form that identifies the recipient as one eligible to receive untaxed fuel. When the bootlegger gets the 637, he opens a mail drop or office in the name of the marketer's company, and, without his knowledge, uses it to purchase untaxed fuel and begin a daisy chain (*Oil Express*, 1992).

"COCKTAIL DIESEL"

Not only are the fuel bootleggers making money selling legitimate gas and diesel without paying the tax, but some are selling "Cocktail Diesel"—a mixture of truck diesel and old crankcase oil (Murphy, 1992). Others are selling various mixtures sold as gasoline, which include 10% distillate, 5% alcohol and 2.5% MTBE. A mixture in California sold as diesel contained a product call transmix and light cycle oil (*Oil Express*, 1991).

The Gambino, Lucchese, and Genovese families are thought to be involved in collecting waste oil from service stations, industrial concerns and tank cleaning waste, which is supposed to be treated as required by environmental regulations. These waste oils are mixed with clean oil and sold as fuel. Inevitably, they have picked up contaminants like heavy metals, which can emit dangerous pollutants. But of as great importance to truckers and the motoring public, these fuels can ruin engine parts and lead to costly repairs. A yearlong investigation in New Jersey determined that more than 8 million gallons of contaminated oil was sold to an unsuspecting public (Sullivan, 1993). Using hazardous waste, the fuel bootleggers are able to make even more money. Not only are they paid to collect and dispose of the waste, but by mixing it with clean oil and selling it for fuel, they receive the price of the fuel as well as the fuel tax money.

CONNECTIONS TO LEGITIMATE BUSINESS

Phillip R. Chisholm, Executive Vice President of the Petroleum Marketers Association of America, has said that organized crime involvement in gasoline and diesel bootlegging is costing legitimate marketers millions of dollars a year. Bootleggers underselling legitimate marketers and service stations have caused the bankruptcy of a number of gas retailers and distributors over the past decade, simply because they cannot compete with the prices offered by stations dealing with fuel bootleggers or by distributors who are bootleggers (Chisholm, 1992).

Assistant U.S. Attorney General Shirley Peterson, who in the early 1990s was in charge of the federal government's prosecution of tax law violations, has said, "By obtaining a 40¢-per-gallon advantage through evasion of fuel taxes, a wholesaler can gain an almost insurmountable edge over legitimate dealers" (Martinez, 1991:1). In 1990, Peterson made fuel tax evasion one of the major initiatives of her division. Although the problem was initially linked to organized crime, she said investigations revealed a growing involvement among legitimate businesses (Gardner, 1990). The conviction of Getty Petroleum Company officials and of two independent gasoline wholesalers for conspiring to evade payment on more than one million dollars in gasoline excise tax illustrates the involvement of legitimate dealers (Pearson, 1990). Nevertheless, the Russian mafia was also involved in the Getty conspiracy.

THE CRIMINAL JUSTICE RESPONSE

By 1991, the fuel tax evasion problem had become so serious that the U.S. Justice Department assigned prosecutors full time to deal exclusively with motor fuel tax fraud. Deputy U.S. Assistant Attorney General James Burton said that more than 100 federal investigations were underway in 18 cities (BNA Daily Report, 1990). A number of states have set up special task forces or established motor fuel tax evasion specialists in their Revenue or Attorney General's office (Gray, 1989).

In 1993, indictments were issued in states ranging from New Jersey to Nebraska to California. A 101-count federal indictment was issued in New Jersey against members of the Gambino family and Russian mafia for depriving the federal and state governments of $60 million in tax revenue in only five quarters (Strum, 1993). In Philadelphia, tax fraud cases were brought against two firms and 15 people, most of whom were Soviet emigres operating in Pennsylvania, New Jersey and Florida. They were charged with depriving the states of $14.8 million in tax revenue (Cohn, 1993). Actions were taken against 13 gas stations and a number of people in Nebraska, Colorado, and Wyoming. Tax losses to the federal government in Colorado and Nebraska amounted to $4.6 million. Colorado's loss was $2.7 million and Nebraska's, $1 million (O'Hanlon, 1993).

Because motorfuel tax evasion is so difficult to investigate, organized crime members have labeled it the "perfect crime." Some in the petroleum business, such as marketers and truck-stop operators, declare that if something is not done soon there will be no reputable motor fuel market left (Journal of Commerce, 1992). Every time there is a gas tax hike, the criminal organizations cheer. The 1990 5¢-per-gallon increase was described by the Mafia as an early Christmas present (Vincini, 1990).

In 1993, Congress enacted legislation that changed the method of diesel fuel tax collection but still left some loopholes. It also enacted a color code for diesel fuel which went into effect on January 1, 1994 (Wines, 1994). This code is supposed to prevent the use of untaxed home heating oil on the highway or at least make it easier to detect violations. However, the law is so complicated that it is causing confusion at the moment. Once the dust settles, and the law's provisions are clarified, most in the petroleum industry believe the code will help reduce fraud.

State and federal authorities are understaffed, and most law enforcement agencies do not have personnel qualified to investigate motor fuel tax fraud (Chisholm, 1992). The prosecutions that have taken place in the past few years have been only a drop in the bucket. The fuel tax is so easy to evade that more and more independent operators around the country are getting involved. The chances of getting caught are small. There is a distinct possibility that organizations (criminal and otherwise) will develop and spread with new means of evading the motor fuel tax.

LEGITIMATE BUSINESS MIMICS ORGANIZED CRIME

Already, North Carolina has discovered that some petroleum transport operators are purchasing gas in Georgia from legitimate dealers at the regular marketers' price, with all taxes paid. These operators are then transporting it to North Carolina for sale to independent dealers. In so doing, they are evading the North Carolina state gas tax, which is higher than that of Georgia (Stith, 1992). The profit is not as great as those evading all federal and state taxes, but it is sufficient to take the risk of hauling loads from nearby states. As new gas taxes are proposed, the problem will increase rather than decrease. Independent entrepreneurs are learning from organized crime groups how easy motor fuel tax fraud is, and there are new groups springing up nationwide to take advantage of this quick and reasonably safe money maker.

Motor fuel tax revenue continues to drop, and, despite increasing efforts, governments appear unable to stop the hemorrhaging of tax dollars to the underworld through motor fuel tax fraud. As early as the mid-1980s, authorities were speculating that as much as a billion dollars in gasoline tax revenue was being funnelled into the hands of organized crime in the New York area alone (Raab, 1989). In 1990, the U.S. Justice Department reported that a multiagency investigation estimated that the U.S. was losing a billion dollars a year from gasoline and diesel fuel tax evasion (Ostrow, 1990). In a 1992 congressional hearing on the shortfall in Highway Trust Fund collections, Eugene McCormick of the Federal Highway Administration told Congress that the level of diesel fuel tax evasion was between 15 and 25% of the total gallons consumed (*BNA Daily Report*, 1992). It was estimated that the evasion of federal excise taxes on gasoline and diesel fuel was costing the Highway Trust Fund a billion dollars a year, with a total loss of federal and state tax revenue of over $2.5 billion annually (*BNA Daily Report*, 1992). By the spring of 1993, a U.S. attorney estimated the tax evasion conspiracy was costing the federal government alone more than $2 billion per year (Strum, 1993). Others in 1993 estimated that as much as $5 billion per year in tax revenue on gasoline and diesel fuel was being lost by the states and federal governments (Friedman, 1992).

Until the 1980s, neither federal nor state governments had investigators in their revenue departments assigned exclusively to fuel tax fraud investigators who understood the intricacies of gasoline and diesel fuel excise tax evasion. As more budget cuts take place, fewer people will be available in government to try to stop this fraud. As legitimate businesses see themselves going under, many will join the outlaws rather than become their victims. Changes in the tax laws may help, but already major violations of the 1994 diesel fuel act have been discovered. The problem grows, and no end appears to be in sight.

REFERENCES

Block, A.A. (1994). "Racketeering In Fuels: Tax Scamming by Organized Crime." In: A. A. Block, ed., *Space, Time, and Organized Crime* (2d. ed.). New Brunswick, NJ: Transaction Books.

BNA Daily Report for Executives (1990). "Justice Department Steps Up Enforcement of Gas Tax Evasion." December 18, p.G-2.

—— (1991). "DOJ Announces Five Indictments For Gas Tax Evasion and Conspiracy." January 31, p.G-10.

—— (1992). "Recent Gas Tax Increases Invite More Evasion, Burton Says." February 24, p.G-4.

—— (1992). "Fuel Tax Evasion Costing Highway Trust Fund As Much as $1 Billion, Official Says." May 6, p.G-5.

Chisholm, P.R. (1992). Personal communication with the Executive Vice President, Petroleum Marketers Association of America, Arlington, VA.

Cohn, G. and J.G. Martinez (1993). "Two Firms, 15 People Accused of Tax Fraud." *Philadelphia Inquirer*, March 30, p.B1.

Franzese, M. and D. Maters (1992). *Quitting the Mob*. New York, NY: HarperCollins.

Friedman, R.I. (1993). "Brighton Beach Goodfellas." *Vanity Fair* (Jan.):27-41.

Gardner, L. (1990). "Justice Officials Launch Crackdown on Gasoline Excise Tax Evasion Scheme." *Oil Daily*, December 18, p.1.

Gray, T. (1989). "Fuel Tax Evaders Siphoning From Highway Trust Fund." *Tax Notes*, October 30, pp.5-23.

Journal of Commerce (1992). "Truck Stop Operators Seek to Snuff Out Fuel Tax Cheats."p.3B.

Kiely, E. (1992). "Gas Tax Fraud Costing N.J. $40M a Year." *Hackensack Record*, May 6, p.1.

Martinez, J.C. (1991). "Soviet American Mobsters Join Forces in Fuel Tax Scam." *Journal of Commerce* (Nov.):1.

Murphy, M. (1992). "Soviet Immigrants Involved In Latest Motor Fuel Tax Scams." *Oil Daily*, January 16.

Murphy, M. (1992). "Soviet Immigrants Involved In Latest Motor Fuel Tax Scams." *Oil Daily*, January 16.

O'Hanlon, R. (1993). "Tax Probe Targets 13 Stations." *Omaha World Herald*, April 7.

Oil Express (1991). "CIA Told Prosecution to Back Off Russian Bootlegger." April 1, p.1.

—— (1991). "Dealer Taken at Gunpoint, Held For Seven Hours." April 1, p.4.

—— (1991). "State Officials Battle Khrimian Silverline and Its Marketing Network." April 8, p.103.

—— (1991). "Armenian Marketer and His Companies The Focus of Much Marketer, Law Enforcement Attention." March 18, p.4.

—— (1991). "Tax Scams, Pipe Bombing, Linked to Oil Marketer's Network." March 25, p.1.

—— (1992). "States Say Bootlegging Rampant, Call For More Help From IRS Uncle Sam." May 18, pp.4-5.

Organized Crime Digest (1990). "Gas Tax Fraud on the Rise: Cost U.S. $1 Billion A Year." December 26, p.1.

—— (1993). "Gas Scheme: Gambinos and Russians Team Up." May 12, p.5.

—— (1994). "Russian Gangsters: Spreading Their Operation Throughout U.S." February 23, pp.1-4.

Ostrow, R.J. (1990). "Justice Dept. Launches Probes of Gasoline Tax Evasion." *Los Angeles Times*, December 18, p.A29.

—— (1990). "U.S. I3 Investigating $1Billion Fraud in Gasoline, Diesel Taxes." *Los Angeles Times*, June 21, pp.D1, D15.

Pearson, A. (1990). "Government Tracking Gas Tax Thieves." *Houston Chronicle*, December 18, p.1C.

Raab, S. (1989). "Mafia Aided Scheme Evades Millions in Gas Taxes." *New York Times*, February 6, p.B1.

—— (1989). "Mob-Linked Business Man Killed in Brooklyn." *New York Times*, May 3, p.B3.

Seper, J. (1991). "The Soviet Mafia: An American Success Story." *Washington Times*, September 29, p.A1.

Stith, P. (1992). "Fuel Tax Scams Burn State." *Raleigh News and Observer*, September 21, p.1.

Strum, C. (1993). "13 Indicted in Oil Scheme Laid To Mob." *New York Times*, May 6, p.B6.

Sullivan, J.F. (1993). "12 Held in Trucking of Untaxed and Contaminated Oil." *New York Times*, May 28, p.B5.

U.S. House of Representatives. Committee on Ways and Means, Subcommittee on Oversight (1987). *Compliance With Federal Gasoline Excise Tax Provisions: Hearings*. Washington DC: U.S. Government Printing Office.

Vincini, J. (1990). "U.S. Probe Targets Gas-Tax Fraud." *Philadelphia Inquirer*, December 18, p.A3.

Wines, M. (1994). "What's Red, Blue, or Clear in the Diesel Tank"? *New York Times*, January 9, p.B1.

The Potential for the Growth of Organized Crime in Central and Eastern Europe*

by

Matti Joutsen

Abstract: *The recent fundamental changes in Central and Eastern Europe have changed many aspects of everyday life and increased the potential for crime and organized crime. This chapter looks at some of the recent trends in Central and Eastern Europe that have contributed to the growth of crime in general, and organized crime in particular.*

INTRODUCTION

In the previously socialist states of Central and Eastern Europe, the shift to a market economy and the rush towards adoption of a capitalist ethic have brought with them, for the first time, widespread unemployment and (officially recognized) rapid inflation. A 1992 survey showed that the average purchasing power of Russians had dropped by more than half in two years. Because of rising prices and inflation, the average Russian family must spend from 75 to 80 % of its income on food alone (*International Herald Tribune*, 1992b). The life savings of many have been wiped out because of inflation.

The changes have also affected social welfare, health and education. The Central and Eastern European countries have prided themselves on the standard of their cradle-to-grave system. All children were assured a basic education, and many were offered a free academic education. Also, the basic medical and dental services were free, and everyone was supposed to be protected by the safety net of the social services. (However, this glowing portrayal of the system was at odds with reality. Though health care was free, its quality was not very high, and the social services could not provide more than a modest level of support.) Now there are

---

* Parts of this chapter have previously appeared in M. Joutsen, "Organized Crime in Eastern Europe," *Criminal Justice International* 9(2):11-18.

clear signs of a worsening in public health. For example, according to the Ministry of Health of the Russian Federation, only one of every seven children can be said to be in good health (*New York Times*, 1992).

The discrediting of the previous political system and the immense problems in day-to-day survival have also had their effect on crime. With the virtual collapse of formal and informal social control in Central and Eastern Europe, the rates of reported and, presumably, hidden crime have increased considerably. This has come as a shock to many, since these countries have long been vaunted as societies that have been succeeding in preventing and controlling crime.

The media, seeking to provide the public with Western-style reporting, has focused on the increase in crime. This marks a considerable change in coverage. Up to the mid-1980s, the mass media in most Central and Eastern European countries had dealt with crime only in passing, as an educational matter. The standard crime news item allowed to appear had been a report of individuals who had been found guilty of a crime and sentenced to punishment. Some of the reasons for the crime may have been mentioned: abuse of alcohol, bad company or other bad influences, unwillingness to work, and so on.

Today, crime—and in particular the increase in crime—have become standard fare in the mass media. The news is no longer limited to reports of offenders brought to justice and given their deserved punishment. Now we also see reports about crimes that are not solved and that appear to exceed the ability of the criminal justice system to deal with them.

The increase in reporting sends several subconscious messages to the public: crime has suddenly increased enormously; since many offenders are not apprehended and indeed may be making enormous profits, crime obviously *does* pay; and finally, the criminal justice system appears to be failing in its job.

This is a lesson that has proven irresistible to many. While the majority of the population has joined the "new poor," a counterpoint is provided by the successful entrepreneurs who have taken advantage of the new market economy to buy and sell wherever there is an opportunity. Despite the deregulation, some price controls remain, for example in Russia on raw materials such as oil, wood and scrap metals. Those with the right contacts and capital can buy up huge stocks of these raw materials and sell them either at home or abroad for an enormous profit.

Entrepreneurs, however, come in many shapes and sizes. The push of poverty, the pull of hitherto unheard-of riches, the enormous uncertainty over what is possible and what is not under the new precepts of capitalism, and the collapse of formal and informal social control have led to a considerable expansion of organized crime.

ORGANIZED CRIME BEFORE "PERESTROIKA"

Organized crime and its related phenomena, as such, are not new to Central and Eastern Europe. According to largely anecdotal evidence, economic crime and corruption were largely built in to certain facets of the Soviet model. Drug trafficking and organized crime appear to have been minimal, except in the Central Asian republics. As for environmental crime, most of the considerable despoliation that has occurred in for example former Czechoslovakia, Poland and the Russian Federation had occurred with the permission of the authorities; this now seems "criminal" only in retrospect.

Before *perestroika*, official sources in Central and Eastern Europe either disputed the existence of organized crime in their countries or used the term to refer to *ad hoc* affiliations among a few offenders for the purpose of committing offenses together. Organized crime (*à la* the Mafia) was assumed to exist only in the decadent West.

It did, however, have a fertile soil in which to grow. What is now recognized as organized crime took root in corruption and the "shadow economy." The official economy rarely operated effectively, and was notoriously poor in the area of consumer goods. A barter economy developed, where each consumer relied on a network of friends and relatives to secure necessities. In such an atmosphere, it was difficult to distinguish between gifts and bribes. A shop clerk would be bribed to set aside a few oranges from the next shipment, or a hospital clerk would be bribed to take in a patient requiring treatment, past the long waiting line.

This petty corruption became endemic. When 4,500 respondents were polled nationwide in the (former) USSR on what they considered the main reasons for the country's "current difficulties," 57% cited corruption and drunkenness (Smith, p.90). Not even the criminal justice system itself was immune: for example, *Newsweek* (1992) reported estimates that 70% of the police in St. Petersburg were corrupt.

This corruption was supplemented by the shadow economy, which sought to supply whatever the rigid and moralistic legal market could not produce and distribute in sufficient quantities and/or of adequate quality—which often seemed to be just about anything and everything. This led, among others, to employee theft, theft of state property, and currency violations. It also led, by definition, to profiteering and speculation; essentially, unauthorized free enterprise. Government sources estimate that the annual amount of money involved in the shadow economy in the (former) USSR in 1990 was about 150 billion rubles, and the material losses from the activity of known criminal groups to have exceeded 8 billion rubles (USSR, 1991).

The shadow economy consists of two sectors. The black market was and is entirely illegal, and deals with for example smuggled goods, foreign currency, pornography and drug. The gray market provides goods and services in competition with the state-controlled market, but at free-market prices. The gray market often serves as a channel for goods embezzled from the state, and/or it provides services on "company" time. For example, many state factories have siphoned off part of their raw materials to be used in the "illegal" production of high-quality goods, and have then shared the profits among the employees involved.

The state was unable to stamp this out, primarily due to the lack of resources and the unwillingness of the public to cooperate with the authorities on this issue. The state was also, to a large extent, unwilling to intervene, since the shadow economy worked after a fashion, thus cutting down on public discontent. Finally, the state did not intervene in many cases because often, the responsible officials were raking off bribes.

The shadow economy was lucrative for many, but the opening of the markets and the gradual onslaught of foreigners (businessmen and tourists) with their wallets full of hard currency raised the stakes. Fraud, theft, embezzlement, assault and robbery against locals was supplemented by currency violations and prostitution, with foreigners willing participants. The new international connections brought in the weapons trade, a thriving trade in contraband (in particular, icons and other valuable *objets d'art*), gambling and economic crimes.

These crimes continue to be committed by enterprising individuals acting on their own. However, they have also become a growth area for organized crime, which is entering the petty crime area and using its organization and resources to produce greater profits. At a United Nations expert meeting organized by the Ministry of the Interior of the (former) USSR in late 1991, the host country reported that there were between 3,500 and 4,000 stable, hierarchically organized criminal groups in Russia created for the systematic commission of profit-oriented crime, with the number of members ranging from a few dozen to several hundred (USSR,

1991). These groups had divided the country geographically and, in part, according to specialization. They were usually named after the name or nickname of their leader, according to the territory they control (e.g. Solontsevo and Lyubertsy in Moscow), or according to the ethnic background of the members of the group (e.g., Chechen, Assyrian; see United Nations, 1991; Ward, 1991).

One very likely growth area is drug trafficking. In Central and Eastern Europe, the drugs most commonly used (aside from alcohol) are heroin and hashish. The primary source is the Central Asian republics, although low-grade heroin is also made from home-grown poppies in other areas. Some indication of the size of the market is given by official statistics, according to which the (former) USSR had some 120,000 drug addicts in 1989, or 42 per 100,000 in population; the true number is undoubtedly higher (Gilinskiy, 1992). Poland is estimated to have between 20,000 and 40,000 drug addicts, or 50-100 per 100,000 in population (Moskalewicz and Swiatkiewicz, 1992).

Currently, home-grown heroin is the drug of choice in Poland and some of the Baltic republics. Government sources estimate, for example, that this accounts for 90% of the drugs used in Lithuania (Maertens et al., 1992). This is very much a private enterprise, with no discernable links to organized crime. Following Dorn et al. (1992), it could be said that the drug market in these countries is still at the early stages of development, where drugs are traded more for an ideological motive or friendship than for profit.

This is not the case with Central Asia, where the drug business is alleged to be controlled by a "narco-Mafia," with connections across the borders to drug-growing areas in the "golden crescent" of the Near East. The scale of the production and wholesale distribution of heroin and hashish, and the recent aggressive expansion, can be seen in the size of seizures. Two recent cases involved attempts to deliver hashish via Latvia to the Netherlands. The first case (in 1989) involved 1.2 tons and the second (1990) 3 tons (Maertens et al., 1992).

The interest of organized crime is explained by the considerable potential profits from shipping drugs abroad. The average outlay of a heroin user in Lithuania, for example, is said to be $1 (currently, 600 roubles) per day (Maertens et al., 1992); across the Baltic in the Nordic countries, the same amount of low-grade heroin could fetch $50 or more. At the same time, selling drugs abroad provides an opportunity to obtain hard currency and highly prized Western goods, which can be traded in the shadow economy for a tidy profit.

The interest in drugs is not entirely limited to export. At the end of February, 1993 an attempt to import 1,000 kilograms of cocaine by ship from Colombia was uncovered by the customs in Viborg, near St. Petersburg. This amount of cocaine would scarcely find a ready market within the Russian Federation, and most of it was presumably intended for re-export to Western Europe (Ilta-Sanomat, 1993).

Other growth areas for organized crime include theft. The amount of art theft has been estimated to have increased by three to six times over the past two years (International Workshop, 1992). Officials in the Russian Federation claim that emigré communities in Austria, Germany, Israel and other countries are used by organized crime to establish contacts for international car theft, as well as, for example, for arms and drug trafficking (USSR, 1991).

One direct result of the dismantling of the Soviet army has been a burgeoning illegal domestic and international trade in firearms. Because of the sharply reduced size of the army, there is a great number of surplus weapons. Since large units are being shifted from Central Europe and the former constituent parts of the USSR back to the Russian Federation, and the allegiance of many units has been transferred to newly independent republics, the records kept on firearms and other supplies are in disarray.

At the same time, military personnel are suffering from a considerably lowered standard of living, poor morale, and sheer boredom. The temptation to sell firearms to supplement the poor pay has proven irresistible to many; anything from handguns, rifles and machine guns to tanks are on the market. Internationally, arms have gone, for example, to war-torn areas in former Yugoslavia, in the Caucasus, and in the Carpathians.

It has thus not been surprising that Russian officials have noted a rapid increase in the use of firearms in the commission of offenses, both by individual offenders (in, for example, burglaries and robberies) and in organized crime (in extortion and in settling rivalries between different groups). The number of homicides per 100,000 in population has increased rapidly in the Russian Federation and in many other former constituent republics of the USSR, with the increase largely to be found among stranger-to-stranger homicides, often connected with organized crime. Across the USSR, the number of homicides and attempted homicides increased from 5.3 to 8.6 per 100,000 in population in the five years from 1986 to 1990. More recent data from some of the republics show a continuous increase since then. For example, according to the forthcoming Fourth United Nations Survey (European Institute for Crime Prevention and Control, 1995), the rate in Estonia rose from 4.9 in 1986 to 8.8 in 1990, but then jumped to 15.2 in 1992. The corresponding rates in Latvia were 4.0, 6.2 and 11.0; in war-torn Georgia, 4.9, 7.3 and 17.3; in Russia, 6.6, 10.5 and 15.7.

POST-PERESTROIKA GROWTH

According to one dominant explanation for changes in the structure and level of crime, the routine activity approach, crime is affected by three factors: the number of suitable targets for crime, the number of likely and motivated offenders, and the absence of capable guardians to prevent would-be offenders from committing crime (Cohen and Felson, 1979). In all three respects, the potential for organized crime has grown in Central and Eastern Europe along with the changes brought about by *perestroika*.

Growth in the number of suitable targets for crime. The change from a state economy to a market economy has increased the amount of consumer goods available. Radios, televisions, video recorders, compact disk players, brand-name clothing, cosmetics and other goods are now being produced in greater numbers domestically.

Also the opening of the borders has greatly expanded the number of potential targets for organized crime. Residents returning from the West and tourists or businessmen coming from the West bring in a variety of goods both legally and illegally. Western tourists and businessmen themselves, who are clearly identifiable as foreigners and carry foreign currency or expensive status items, often find themselves the victims of crime. They also provide a ready market for organized prostitution.

Growth in the number of likely and motivated offenders. A large portion of the public has been willing or unwilling participants in what has been called the "shadow economy." The attempts to instill a socialist mentality never succeeded in erasing the capitalist urge for personal profit: the shadow market grew out of the iron laws of supply and demand.

The borderline between the semi-legal gray market and the illegal black market is often impossible to draw, and many people received their indoctrination into organized crime in this way. With the rapid drop in the standard of living, the spread of unemployment and the rising rate of inflation, more and more persons are turning to the black market and to crime as a means of supplementing their income. The reality (and perception) of increased crime has contributed to the readiness to commit crime; the prevailing attitude in Central and Eastern Europe is said to be one of *naglost*, brazen insolence (*International Herald Tribune*, 1992a).

The pool of likely and motivated offenders is also being expanded by the prison system. The prison population in those Central and Eastern European countries for which data are available is far higher than in any Western European country. Conditions in the prisons appear to be very poor by Western standards, and they can thus do little to rehabilitate the offenders. On the contrary, the time spent in prison can provide the prisoners with information on new crime techniques and suitable targets, as well as supply them with willing partners in crime. Prisons have proven to be one of the main recruiting pools for organized crime.

Finally, as a result of the relaxation of restrictions on travel, offenders are far more mobile than before. Previously, international travel was possible only under certain conditions, and even internal travel was subject to regulations and restrictions. For example citizens of the USSR could generally travel only as diplomats or members of an official delegation. Today, a passport and the necessary visas can be obtained readily, either legally or illegally. At the same time, border controls have become very relaxed. It has become almost impossible for the police of one country to investigate offences, since more and more often the traces end at the border.

Absence of capable guardians. The current resources and approach of the criminal justice systems in Central and Eastern Europe cannot provide an effective response to the increase in organized crime. There are shortages in personnel, facilities and equipment. Training and the level of knowledge among practitioners in many cases is woefully inadequate.

Personnel. The criminal justice professions in general have not been held in high esteem in many Central and Eastern European countries; for example, a judge does not have the same high status as in Western Europe. Salaries have always remained relatively low. With the recent economic changes, the relative salary level of criminal justice professionals has gone down even further, making it difficult to recruit and retain competent individuals. To take one example, the average monthly salary of a police officer in Moscow, when converted to hard currency at the black-market rate, is $10.

Special personnel and resource problems exist in the newly independent countries formed from the USSR (and, to a lesser degree, in the former constituent parts of Yugoslavia), which must often build their criminal justice infrastructure from scratch. Many of the criminal justice personnel were Russian, and left soon after independence. The new countries have had to take over responsibility for policing, the courts and the prisons with minimal staff. For example, at the beginning of 1992, Latvia had only 150 customs officers, of whom only 50 had received any formal training in the field—a pitifully inadequate number to halt the burgeoning smuggling of drugs, firearms and other contraband (Maertens et al., 1992).

Facilities and equipment. There is a sharp contrast between the growing crime problem (both real and imagined) and the lack of facilities and equipment in Central and Eastern Europe. A recent international seminar elicited the pained reaction from one Eastern European participant that, to them, everything being said by Western European participants were "fairy tales" with nothing to do with reality. It is difficult for participants from Central and Eastern Europe to understand how Western European criminal justice practitioners can debate the finer points of the development of crime prevention and control when, for those coming from the East, even the basic tools of the trade (police cars, telecommunications equipment, equipment for drug analysis, even law books) seem to be out of reach.

Training and skills. Responding to organized crime requires not only resources, but also tactical and theoretical skills. In some countries (in particular Hungary and Slovenia, and to a lesser degree the Czech Republic, Poland, Russia and Slovakia), the standard of basic training has been good, and follow-up seminars, international contacts and general discussions keep practitioners up to date to some extent. However, elsewhere (in particular in Albania and Romania), the poor status of criminal justice practitioners can be seen in the lack of resources devoted to training.

In addition to the formal agencies of criminal justice, the *informal social control* agencies in Central and Eastern European countries may today be less able to intervene to prevent or control organized crime. The dissolution of the Soviet model has taken away the ideological base for much organized social control activities. The growing fear of crime may make members of the participants less willing to intervene, for fear that they themselves may be injured or otherwise harmed. The perception that crime has become prevalent (whether or not true) may also lead to a *laissez faire* attitude: why intervene, if everyone is doing it?

CONCLUSIONS

There is a clear potential for growth in organized crime in Central and Eastern Europe. The criminal justice system in most countries in the region is undergoing a crisis in morale, resources and direction, sapping its possibility to respond effectively.

One of the fears in Western Europe is that organized crime will begin to cross the borders from the East. So far, this appears to have occurred only on a small scale, primarily in connection with organized theft, drug trafficking and the illegal sale of firearms. The slowness of the development may be due to the lack of suitable international contacts, and to the fact that sufficient profits appear to be available in the domestic market. Furthermore, operating in the West has drawbacks and dangers: it is more expensive, there may be competition from local organized crime, and the police may be more efficient.

The danger posed by organized crime in Central and Eastern Europe nonetheless remains, both to the countries themselves and to the West. This has already been recognized, as shown by the growing network of bilateral and multilateral agreements, as well as the strengthening infor- mal contacts among the police. Many Western European countries are providing technical assistance to Central and Eastern Europe in the form of training, consultation and the exchange of information. Sadly, organ- ized crime control even in the West has lagged behind organized crime; both East and West have a long way to go.

REFERENCES

Cohen, L. and M. Felson (1979). "Social Changes and Crime Rate Trends: A Routine Activity Approach." *Criminology*, 25:933-947.

Dorn, N., K. Murji and N. South (1992). *Traffickers: Drug Markets and Law Enforcement*. London and New York: Routledge.

European Institute for Crime Prevention and Control (1995). "Report on the European and North American Results of the Fourth United Nations Survey on Crime Trends and Operation of Criminal Justice Systems." Helsinki.

Gilinskiy, Yakov (1992). "Alcohol, Social Problems and Deviant Behaviour in St. Petersburg." In: Jussi Simpura and Christoffer Tigerstedt eds.,

Social Problems Around the Baltic Sea. Nordic Council for Alcohol and Drug Research publication no. 21, Helsinki, pp.69-84.

International Herald Tribune (1992a). 31 August, pp.1 and 7.

International Herald Tribune (1992b). 2 October, pp.1 and 7.

Ilta-Sanomat (1993). 8 March 1993, Helsinki.

International Workshop (1992). Oral presentation by the representative of the Italian Arma dei Carabinieri at the International Workshop on the Protection of Cultural and Artistic Property, Courmayeur, Aosta Valley, Italy, 25-27 June 1992.

Maertens, F., J. Sailas and M. Joutsen (1992). "Report on a Joint UNDCP / WHO Mission to Latvia, 1-3 June 1992." Unpublished paper. Vienna.

Moskalewicz, J. and G. Swiatkiewicz (1992). Social Problems in the Polish Political Debate." In: Jussi Simpura and Christoffer Tigerstedt eds., *Social Problems Around the Baltic Sea*. Nordic Council for Alcohol and Drug Research publication no. 21, Helsinki, pp.85-108.

Newsweek (1992). "The New Chicago on the Neva." 5 October, pp.14-19.

New York Times (1992). October 4, p.5.

Royce, K. (1989). "Drug Supply — Money Laundering Linked to Bulgaria. *International Drug Report*, International Narcotic Enforcement Officers Association, New York, May, pp.2. and 12.

Smith, H. (1991). *The New Russians*. New York: Random House.

United Nations (1991). "Preliminary Results of the Organized Crime Seminar Survey, UN/USSR Organized Crime Seminar, October 21-25, 1991, Suzdal USSR." Unpublished.

Union of Soviet Socialist Republics (1991). Information supplied by the Ministry of the Interior during the organization of the International Seminar on Organized Crime, Moscow.

Ward, R. (1991). "Organized Crime, Corruption Add to the Law Enforcement Problems." *CJ International*, 7(1):1, 8-9